Best Wish

Anne

My Life on

a Cliff Edge

Anne aged 21 (sent to The Lady magazine for possible inclusion)

My Life on a Cliff Edge

Anne Beer

Published by Blue Poppy Publishing – Ilfracombe, Devon.
Edited by Sarah Dawes

Hardcover: ISBN: 978-1-911438-51-9

To Winden Wood

Additional Thanks

We could not have produced this book without the backing of the many who pledged on Kickstarter. We thank all of them but in particular the gold and silver patrons as follows.

Gold Patrons

David G Tubby
Robert Lövgren, Sweden

Silver Patrons

Peter & Joy Molony
Cara
Andrius Davidenas
Louise Rowe

Finally, thanks to the Ilfracombe Writing Group who kept on at me to do it, to Olli Tooley for the encouragement to carry it out, and to Sarah Dawes, for transcribing over 300 pages of my old-fashioned writing, all written 'on the fly', into computer speak.

Foreword by Oliver Tooley

I first met Anne when she came to a writing group that I set up in Ilfracombe. She had asked if it would be alright for her dog to come with her because she was nervous around large groups of people. I, of course, said it would be no problem and she duly arrived with Ellie, whom you will meet eventually in this book.

At the time Anne seemed very introverted and had been going through some tough times. She would introduce herself at the start of meetings with, "I'm…not important."

Since then she has become more settled again and we have seen the devilish, fun side of her character.

Her stories each month are written on the fly and seldom edited, yet they have charm, wit, and insight aplenty. Some of her stories were autobiographical and some of them shone a light onto some very dark places.

This book does not seek to be a contender for the 'most harrowing story of a person's life' award, although Anne has had several experiences I would certainly never wish to endure. Neither is Anne a famous person about whom millions will wish to know every last detail.

It does however chronicle the life of one ordinary lady from birth to nearly eighty, through ups and downs, heartaches and triumphs, from 1940 to 2020, in an easily accessible style. An ordinary lady, although one who has an extraordinary memory, and a natural gift for drawing, painting, and writing, which she has nurtured through good times and bad. A story of rejection, of abuse, of escape, and of true love.

Anne has had art exhibitions and sold many paintings over the years. Her writing has occasionally been picked up by anthologies, including *Seaglass*[1], but Anne has also held an ambition to get a book published and, when I was able to bring her copies of *Inspiration*[2] earlier this year, her face lit up. Seeing the kind and enthusiastic reviews for her collection of short stories, and encouraged to finish her autobiography, the change in Anne's demeanour was palpable. Her confidence returned along with the spring in her step. Being in a home where she felt safe and away from constant noise was also a major factor, but I don't want to give too much away.

I hope you enjoy reading *My Life on a Cliff Edge* as much as I enjoyed preparing it for publication.

Oliver Tooley

---

[1] *Seaglass*, Lulu ISBN: 978-1326229016 various authors. Edited by Rebecca Alexander and Ruth Downie

[2] *Inspiration*, Blue Poppy Publishing, ISBN: 978-1911438694 Anne Beer

Chapter 1 : Early Years

I was born on Saturday, 30 November 1940, in the blue room at Broomfield Park Nursing Home, 116 Aldermans Hill in Palmers Green, North London. It was a leafy suburb that had been frequented by the well-to-do until the Second World War started in 1939. I came into the world during the worst air raid of the war and I weighed in at 6lb 15oz. After the statutory fortnight in the nursing home, I was duly ensconced in the house in which I was to spend the first thirteen and a half years of my life.

This newly built house at Silverdale, Enfield in Middlesex was on an up-market estate beside a beautiful lake and, at that time, had mostly countryside surrounding it. There were many gaps in this estate, due to the war, as building had stopped. However, our road was complete: a small cul-de-sac with lakeside views and roadside shrubs. My earliest memory is of lying in my pram in the back garden, looking up at the blue sky with fast-scudding puffs of white clouds moving across it, and wondering why the chimney was moving as well. Of course it was an optical illusion, as it was the sky and clouds that were in motion, not the chimney.

My second memory closely followed. I was awakened by my parents from a dreadful nightmare in which I was in a dead-end cave with lions about to break out of their cages on either side of me. There was no escape as fire blocked the entrance and I felt extremely hot and terrified. The lions were roaring at me. In reality an air raid was in progress, fire was all around, plus the roar of falling bombs. My parents snatched me out of bed and I was roughly bundled to the shelter built in the garden. I must have been about two and a half years old. I have always had a photographic memory and often surprised my parents, later in life, with recall of events.

*Where I spent most nights; prior to being snatched up during an
air raid to go into the shelter. The floor was bitterly cold.*

My first four and a half years were war battered ones, with the air raids and night-times spent either under the kitchen sink, for a hasty exit to the shelter in the garden, or under the stairs amongst the mouldy shoes and electricity meter, or in an indoor cage-like shelter that had my farmyard on top. This was supposed to be used in the direst emergency when there was no time to get outside to the proper shelter and was supposed to protect us from flying glass from the windows, even though they were criss-crossed with tape to prevent this. I still bear the scars from flying glass today, at aged 80, on my left wrist and above my left eye, which I nearly lost. It was a close call as it nearly severed my artery.

It happened like this. A sunny day, standing at the back door of the kitchen and looking up into the sky, I saw something different from the usual aeroplanes. It wasn't making a noise and I shouted, "Mummy! Mummy! What's that?" She took one look and quickly bundled me into the indoor shelter. Moments later we were lifted up and then crashed down with a roaring sound and a bang, glass splintered all around. All I could see was red, the warm blood blinding me and glass stuck in my wrist. The farmyard toys had leapt off the top of the shelter as well. A rocket had fallen, the sort that was launched from across the English Channel and, when the fuel ran out, so did its noise and then it death-dropped without warning and destroyed many homes in one go.

The expression on my face in this photograph is indicative of how I felt about my parents and home life for most of my childhood.

I lived in a beautiful house built by Laing in 1939. It had a large garden with a gate in the fence at the far end that led to many allotments, tended by the well-off residents on the Laing Estate. They may have been well off, but shortage of food levelled everyone out and the allotment produce was sacred, until one night a bomb destroyed all that hard work. People were really devastated. I had a pet rabbit – or so I thought, as it kept disappearing and returning at intervals. Sometimes it reappeared a slightly different colour or a bit smaller than before. I used to get upset because it 'escaped' so much. I found out years later that it wasn't my pet at all: it was food.

Mummy made lovely rabbit pie, which I was led to believe was chicken. The rabbit droppings were collected into a piece of sacking, tied onto a stick and suspended into the water butt to create liquid manure for the garden. Oh, the pong on hot days! But it didn't stop me being fascinated by the mosquito larvae that used to zig-zag up and down in the water. I was told, "Get away from there as you will catch something nasty." Same with crouching over drain hole covers. "You'll catch diphtheria." But I still liked investigating the dirty depths and I loved the musty smell from the air bricks of our house below the windows. I could see through the holes in them from one side of the building to the other under the floor level.

Daddy made a cool place for perishable foods – no fridges then – under the shade of the lilac tree. He dug a deep hole lined with newspaper and sand. Into this he sank a square biscuit tin that had previously held 7lb of biscuits, which I don't remember ever eating or seeing. A thick wooden lid, covered in tarpaulin, was made to fit followed by several bricks. In this coffin was stashed milk, and margarine, which never went 'off'. The other perishables were kept indoors in the bottom of the larder on a marble slab and the zinc-meshed window kept it cool and airy and stopped the flies coming in. Two items, one of horror, the other delight, resided on the marble slab: cod liver oil and orange juice, of which I had one teaspoonful each per day. The kitchen was very modern for its day. It was well thought out and 'fitted'. The ironing table came down from a hinge in a cupboard; the brass electric iron blew up eventually in a multicoloured explosion. The black-and-white tiled kitchen table also came down from the wall and behind it were drawers. No chairs were needed as seating also came down in the same manner, with an alcove behind on which my carry cot, made from an old drawer, was placed in my early days. Yes, all the kitchen furniture would up and away into the walls: magic!

Above all these things were beautiful cupboards with pretty glass patterns. On top of these, near the ceiling, resided stone jars containing 'prunes' from the Victoria plum tree in the garden. Here, they would overwinter into 'wrinkled old men', sometimes with a hairy beard, if it got too steamy or damp with the cooking.

How I loved the Ideal boiler in the corner. Mummy would melt the marg and syrup together over it in a huge bowl to make cakes, adding dried egg and flour and, if I kept shut up, I could lick the bowl out. There was never much left though as every scrape counted with stuff being on ration. There was the latest Belling electric cooker in a recess. Above this recess was the landing part of the stairs. I used to delight in leaping, missing the five stairs down to the landing – bang! Unfortunately creating havoc if cooking was in progress and bits of plaster floated down like dandruff from the ceiling into whatever was boiling on the stove. I can clearly recall sitting in my high chair at the table, dipping soldiers into my boiled egg. The drop-down seating arrangement had a secret recess into which Mummy stashed her £5 a month housekeeping money in a Rowntree's cocoa tin.

A travelling grocer called Mr Johnson came once a week in his maroon and cream van. Oh, to climb on board and see and smell all the wares! He wore a massive apron and a pencil behind his ear and always came into the kitchen and lingered for a much longer time when Daddy wasn't there. Sometimes for so long a neighbour would knock at the front door and ask how much longer before he would be coming to them, further down the road. He got quite hot and sweaty and would rub his finger round his neck collar on departure and I always had a treat from Mr Johnson. One unforgettable day it was a whole packet of real, shiny dates in a wooden box which I eventually kept my pencils in. He kept on thanking Mummy, whose face was pink.

I think that my running prowess later in life began with racing against the other children in the road when the horse-drawn milk float was heard: clip-clops warning of plip-plops to be collected with a heavy metal shovel and bucket. I was off like greased lightning, as fast as my four-year-old legs could carry me, to collect that weirdly-shaped shit called 'manure' by the polite society. I would get a whole penny for the effort but only if I didn't soil my clothes, white socks, or Clarks sandals or, in winter, my Start-Rite shoes. Yuck! I longed for brown sandals or shoes but, before I even wore a new pair, Daddy would dye them black. They would stink the place out overnight, drying on the kitchen table, smelling like the disinfectant that covered sick on the floor in Sunday school. Apparently black didn't show my tomboy tendencies to scuffs and boggy muck. How my fashion-plated, lipsticked mother despaired of me. Beautifully smocked dresses, embroidered hankies, ladylike knickers, all ended up tripped, slipped and ripped on my unladylike excursions into the nearest mud bath or wet cement where, on one occasion, my footprints lay embedded for years to come on the front path.

Daddy was missing much of the time; he was serving in the war effort in the Royal Navy. I never, ever remember either of my parents giving me a cuddle and they never called me dear or darling and didn't say those things to each other, either. Neither did they kiss me or each other. Then again, I never heard them swear or even say, "Shut up." The, "Shut up," came later, when I was older, years down the line. The nearest my mother came to swearing was, "Bother, bust, blow it!" and Father's was, "Well blind old Pete!" and I don't know where that originated from.

In August 1943 it was decided that, as the air raids were likely to wipe us all out and Daddy had been away from home a long time, 'it' could no longer wait. The 'it' I discovered was to be christened. I was two-and-three-quarter years old and it was very memorable to me. I wore a lovely posh white dress. It was a boiling hot day. My godmother lived next-door-but-one and I loved her. She shared stews and news down the shelter with us and was always knitting. Her soft, cuddly bosom enveloped my woes. She cuddled when others didn't. Dear, lovely, 'not-your-real-Auntie' Ethel. My godfather, no thanks. Not around for much of the time, bristly chin, and bicycle with a painful crossbar that I was forced to sit on, on that fateful day as he wheeled his bike to the church, as it was too far for me to walk. His hand kept yanking between my legs under my dress. It hurt so much.

At the church it was lovely and cool inside, with the fragrance of incense and polish and the coloured windows reflected on the floor. I wanted to catch the colours as they spun around on my white dress when I moved. I so clearly remember being by the font. Even at that young age, I sensed the occasion and the pretty scallop shell that was used to dip into the holy water and the kindly face of the old priest. A big hush, a moment in time; I felt special. No music, hymns or singing, just a quiet, private service in a cool interior on a hot summer day. It was as if I had an adult mind in a small child's body. I wanted to walk home and not sit on 'Uncle' Bert's crossbar, so it took ages to return home and I insisted upon walking along the 'curd' as I called it. I couldn't say 'kerb'.

Auntie Ethel had made a white cake by saving up her sugar rations and I had condensed milk spread on bread. She also made lemonade with Epsom salts, which made me want to wee-wee. Every year on my christening anniversary she would give me a box of Black Magic chocolates and a five-shilling postal order.

The smell of that box was really magic as I ripped it open, but I was banned from keeping it in my room. The postal order went into a post office account, a book that was stamped each time a deposit or withdrawal was made. I used to have sixpenny National Savings Stamps collected in a book and when a page was filled up it was put into the Post Office as well.

Daddy made a swing for me when I was three and I really made it go! Up, up, and up until suddenly I was sailing out into space over the rockery, landing painfully in the aubretia. Although I was howling in agony, no one took any notice of my injuries. All they were concerned about was the hole in the wrecked aubretia plant. We had a Ford Eight car that was put on blocks in the garage for the war's duration, as Daddy was away most of the time and petrol was severely rationed. To own a car was a rarity and we had a telephone as well. We even had a stained-glass window, which cost £5 to replace when it was shattered in a hit-and-run air raid. I had the job of walking two miles with a note to the glazier. A raid could have happened at any time but here I was at just over three years old, going on an errand because my mummy's rheumatism was playing up. The doctor said it was because we lived beside a damp lake.

That lake was my escape hatch in years to come. I loved looking out of my bedroom window each morning, across to the island. The swans would nest each year on a massive pile of reeds. They never hissed or attacked me as I gave them bread and scraps most days. Their take-off, flapping along the water, timing it to rise up just before running out of lake, was amazing. Then the return, feet out in front, skidding and braking on landing. I loved the wait to see how many cygnets would hatch and the preening and fluffing, the changing of ugly into beautiful. For the next ten years, my love and study of nature would be learnt around that swan lake. I was to be an only and lonely child. My love was to come from the animals, birds, and trees around me.

Looking back on it now, I am sure that I was created to stop my mother from having to do war work in some factory: if a child was under five the mother could stay at home. She had never gone out to work in her life; she was a lady. I was from thenceforth always referred to as 'the ugly duckling' and 'Kipper Feet', so I always had an affinity with the ducks and swans. Little wonder, eh?

When I found dead beetles and butterflies I felt sorrowful and would beg a matchbox to bury them in, beneath the Bramley apple tree in the corner of the garden, beside the pongy compost heap. This heap was a source of delight as I loved delving into its smelly depths to release all sorts of little creatures. I wondered why it was so smelly and was told it was because of the horse manure and rabbit droppings, which were good for the garden, so I followed suit and went to the toilet on top of the heap! Unfortunately, in the middle of all this, I fell off the heap with my knickers round my feet. I was severely punished for doing something which I thought everyone would be pleased about: helping the garden to grow. The only growing that came about was the growing despair of my parents as I went from one tomboy disaster to the next. The more my fashion-plated, clever-with-a-needle mother dressed me up, the more my beautifully created clothes quickly wore out.

One dress I hated had puffed sleeves and was pink with white pigs all over it. I got jeered at and called 'Piggy'. I was a lonely child being moulded into an adult, being made to wear posh stuff before my time. As despair set in, I was dressed in clothes of an opposite nature. My mother made me some ghastly grey flannel shorts, which flapped around my knees, held up by braces; grey socks instead of white; those awful smelly dyed black shoes, and a cut-down re-modelled shirt of Father's. I had just started school and was a laughing stock, especially as I wore navy blue bloomers that had a pocket, in which I had three jelly cubes wrapped up to eat at playtime (sweets were on ration). When trying to dismantle the braces in the girls' toilet, the jelly cubes shot out and into the lavatory pan, along with an apple. I felt so sorry for the apple I tried to retrieve it as I was told that everything that disappeared down there was gobbled up by a monster and that was why I mustn't sit on there for too long, as a big hand would come out and grab me, too. No wonder I used to sit, terrified, being made to 'go' before setting off for school of a morning. It was, "Hurry up; you'll be late," and, "Have you been yet?" so I used to flush the pan if I hadn't been and pretend, just to get to school on time. But eventually even that didn't work as I was told there was no smell left behind!

My first day at infant school was when I was four years old. It was a mile away and I had to go all by myself; no one took me or fetched me home. So round the lake I went, though the woods, then an excursion down into and up the other side of various bomb craters on the way. I carried pongy egg sandwiches wrapped in paper inside a gas mask case. It was just inside the field gate entrance that I encountered the two bullies that were to be the bane of my life at that school: Jimmy White and Robert Pickering. One was fat and podgy with slitty eyes and his sidekick was thin with steel-rimmed glasses. The first thing they did was to hang onto my hair and take my sandwiches. I was left with an empty gas mask case, which was ridiculed. They said they would get me at playtime and if I told anyone they would take my knickers down.

On arrival in my classroom I was relieved by their absence; they were several classes above me. I crept into a corner and let the rest of the world pass me by as best I could. I was not used to mixing with other kids, having no brothers or sisters to gain experience with. I moved exclusively in an adult world on one hand and a solitary one in my bedroom or around the lake and woods, where the birds and other creatures were my companions.

At playtime I refused to go outside, for fear of meeting the bullies. Therefore, I wet myself in class and was punished by having to stand, with my hands behind my back, on a three-legged stool, which was very hard to balance on without falling off. I very much wanted to play with the sandpit, which was raised up on legs at chest height, but was not allowed. Then it should have been my turn to play in the Wendy house but I missed that too and, at lunchtime, I had no sandwiches to eat. My bottom was raw with wetting myself and I spent the rest of my first day in isolation at the back of the class. I did not want to go home, first because of the bullies waiting for me and secondly from the smacking I would receive for wetting myself.

At home time, I stayed as long as I could, until I was the last to go. When I got to the cloakroom the bullies were waiting for me with three other boys. They threw me to the hard floor and sat on me and whacked me and kicked me everywhere. I was terrified and screamed. After they had left I could barely stand up and my clothes were ripped. I was terrified to go home: I would be in more trouble.

My journey home was painfully slow. I could barely walk, my chest hurt and my mouth was bleeding. I was swelling up in various places and was expecting the bullies around every corner in the woods. I sat on our doorstep and cried, dreading the prospect of punishment. My tears and blood spread over the lovely red polished tiles of the steps. More trouble for spoiling them. Ooh, heck!

The next thing that happened surprised me. My mother got me onto the kitchen table and was kind towards me, bathing my wounds and sore places. She rang the doctor, who came and helped put me to bed, and I had warm bread and milk with sugar sprinkled on it; a luxury as sugar was rationed. But no one cuddled me. There was no school for me for some time. Maybe, I hoped, forever!

I hated that school, Merryhills. I withdrew more and more into myself. I found it hard to join in any games and sat alone in the playground. My only company was reading. I learnt to read quickly when I was confined with measles. I devoured books and wrote nature poems and illustrated them, drawing from nature. I was well beyond my years and stuff just rolled out of my head. The parents had a job to keep me supplied with paper, as there was a shortage, and I had to use both sides.

Just before and around this time I used to be dragged off to Devon, usually by train and always in the dead of night it seemed, to wake up when we got' there. Father used to wear his naval uniform when travelling and my mother wore the latest thing she could conjure up on a sewing machine. I was to be 'seen and not heard'. I took everything in and noted it all down in my head to be surfaced and thought about at a later date, when being banged up as punishment in my bedroom. I spent solitary hours on the sand dunes and around the rock pools. There was literally no one around and I tore my clothes on the barbed wire coiled up along the beach that, along with the sandbags, was a war defence. On one trip, I broke into a holiday chalet in the dunes and decided that it would be my secret new home and to decorate it accordingly with the brushes and tins of paint that I found inside. Just as I was enjoying this escapade we suddenly returned home and the following day we went to Kings Cross Station in London with my father in his uniform and kit bag over his shoulder. I felt the solemnity of the occasion. We were saying goodbye to him and I so remember asking where he was going and he was not supposed to say because 'walls have ears' but when he said, "Canada," I asked where it was and he replied that it was across the water. Well I couldn't see any water so he said it was at the end of the railway line and I couldn't see the end of that, either.

My mother had out-fashioned everyone else on that railway platform in her bright red costume and lipstick and Dick Whittington hat. As my father bent down to kiss me goodbye (a previously unknown event!) I could just about hear him, above all the noise and steam, saying in my ear, "Whatever you do, always remember your Daddy and be a good girl."

They didn't kiss; it wasn't the done thing in public, although everyone else seemed to be doing it. I never, ever saw them kiss but I do remember the sadness of my mother and the journey home on the tube as all the lights went out and we sat out an air raid, out in the above-ground section of the Piccadilly line between Southgate and Enfield West (now called Oakwood). It was a long one-mile walk, in the blackout, from Oakwood to our home.

My Cat

My godmother, 'Auntie' Ethel, gave me a very smart black and white cat called Dandy. I loved him so much and he used to listen to all my woes. I groomed him and made him a little ball from knitting scraps and was told by my mother that it was a waste of time as the cat would never play with it. Well, he did. I would throw it and he would bring it back to me, just like a dog. An outside shelter was made for Dandy as it was unthinkable to have a cat in the house-proud establishment I lived in. I felt upset when it was raining, and he used to paw at the window asking me to let him in. I loved him but was not allowed to show it. He was fed outside, too, although he so wanted to be with me. Auntie Ethel knitted him a blanket, which was better than the newspaper and straw that was his bedding. Dandy and I loved each other; he understood me and knew all about me being a school misfit. We had such a rapport. So it was with terrible grief and sadness that I received the news that he had run away from me and I would never see him again. Here was something living that actually loved me; how could he do it? I was reprimanded for crying my eyes out and told, "Stop moping; it's only a cat!"

I spent days looking out of my bedroom window towards the lake and wondering if he had drowned in it. I was inconsolable. Then Auntie Ethel told me the truth: Dandy was dead. He had been run over by a removal lorry, next door, when it reversed over him.

Although I was upset, at least the hope and waiting were now over, and I knew that I would never see him again. And I knew who to trust in the future to tell me the truth about things: my dear godmother, Auntie Ethel.

Neighbours

By what must be an extraordinary coincidence, both our neighbours either side of us had the surname Roberts and both neighbours had girls called Patricia! The snooty side always called their girl Patricia and kept well hidden behind a high fence, while the non-snooty side called their girl Patsy. Later, a brother, Andrew, came along for Patsy and I hated him. Always snot ridden and with his nappy dangling, he would stick his jammy fingers in his golden curly hair and get on my nerves, screaming his head off. I have a photo of him and myself together on VE Day. I was four and a half and he was about three years old. I had tried to get rid of him by getting him to eat deadly nightshade berries but he didn't like the taste and spat them out! Thank goodness he did! I didn't know what murder was; to me this was just a good way to not see him anymore and I knew about deadly nightshade because I had been shown the plant and warned against it.

Patsy's parents had an old Morris car with yellow celluloid windows. This vehicle used to take ages to start up and on a cold and frosty morning would belch out noxious fumes whilst the celluloid windows wobbled. Patsy and Andrew would be squashed in the back seats with Andrew's snot being spread across the window on his fingers, both looking decidedly liverish by the colour cast from the celluloid. The car would then pop-bang its way out of their driveway, leaving a dreadful smell in its wake. My parents used to view this with distaste as my father kept his car and garage in meticulous order and my mother used to comment on how the woman next door, whom she labelled 'the beige woman', had worn the same camel coat and brogues for seven years, never wore make-up and had her hair scragged back in a bun; she thought that was really awful. I didn't; I found that lady was particularly kind towards me and on the few occasions that I was allowed to go into her house I found it in deep contrast to my own. Hers had toys everywhere and smelt of cooking and newspapers. Mine had a place for everything and everything in its place, colour co-ordinated in green and cream and smelt of polish on the shiny parquet floors. Besides, we had one large room known as The Long Room and they had two separate smaller ones.

Dances were held in our Long Room, hence the shiny floor and latest radiogram that had far-off romantic names on the dial, such as Moscow and Helsinki. We also gave film shows in that room. The next house along contained a 'reserved occupation' civil servant and an upper crust wife and their three girls, who all won loads of rosettes riding horses in gymkhanas. I was friends with the youngest one. They were very posh: they had a coffee percolator – unheard of in most homes at that time – and also a refrigerator! I felt very awkward in their house and always managed to upset or spill something. I used to be invited to their birthday parties but always felt left out as I found it hard to join in. Besides, I could never invite anyone back to my house as my parents didn't want their place messed up. So everyone else had parties and went to tea with each other but it didn't happen for me.

Another house had two elderly sisters residing in it. They smelt of mothballs and wore frightening fox furs, which had beady eyes and real teeth, around their necks. They wore real diamonds and had felt hats with little veils going over part of their faces. My mother used to say they were out of date and looked like Queen Mary. They went everywhere by taxi, taking their two yappy Pekingese dogs with them. They also had a huge parrot in a cage, which escaped one day and sat on the roof laughing at them whilst they wrung their hands and sniffed their smelling salts, urging it to come down. I was delighted when it flew off, never to return, as I thought it was unkind to keep it in a cage.

In another house there was a couple whose boy was a boarder at a famous school. He wore blue breeches and stockings and a waistcoat as his school uniform. He was lucky to be living away from home most of the time, I thought. I wished that were me! My parents always used to threaten me with, "You'll be sent to boarding school!" after my latest misdemeanour and I used to say, "Oh, goodie!"

Some houses in our tiny cul-de-sac were either missing or badly damaged in the bombing. I loved playing in the ruins. The stairs always remained, as did the quarry tiles on the kitchen floors. It was difficult to avoid getting black on my clothes from the burnt out, charred wood. I wondered what the sign with UXB meant outside one of my favourite burnt out haunts. I went in there a lot, finding cutlery and broken china to play with. It was spooky and exciting, and I liked it because no one else would go in there, so I had it all to myself. Only later did I find out what UXB meant: Unexploded Bomb!

VE Day

My father was still at sea on Victory in Europe Day but, as he said in a letter home, the German U-boats were still sinking boats in the convoys he was sailing in. He was on MV *Adula*, in the Fleet Air Arm, serving in the Royal Navy as a petty officer on radio and decoding alongside merchant navy men. His ship was an oil tanker, with a flight deck carrying Fairey Swordfish planes, and the convoys travelled between Halifax in Canada, across the North Atlantic to Scotland and back.

So no Daddy on VE Day, but I was sent out all day to collect firewood from the burnt out ruins. Everyone was soppy, gone silly and drinking, except Mummy. She didn't touch alcohol but was in a good mood all the same. Lots of food in tins came out of previously so-called bare cupboards. I wondered what KLIM was on a label and was told it was 'milk' spelled back to front and thought perhaps I would be called Enna instead of Anne. There was a huge tin of apricot jam called KOO, which came from South Africa, and someone said '*koo*' was South African for jam.

All through the day, wood was heaped up along with rubbish to make a big bonfire on which an effigy of Hitler was placed. I remember one neighbour shut themselves out and couldn't get back into their house, so I was put through a tiny high-up window to go and open the door from the inside. I couldn't work out how to do it; I was standing on a chair and the adults were getting cross at my lack of intelligence. The neighbour whose house it was, was living alone as her husband was away in the war somewhere and she was in a terrible mood, shouting at me to hurry up. I got so frightened that I ran upstairs into her bedroom and was shocked to see loads of clothes and rumpled bedsheets everywhere. How untidy! I would have been in trouble if my bedroom had been left like that. Just as I was wondering what to do next, there was a groan and out stepped a naked man from the wardrobe! I ran downstairs and said through the window that everything was alright now as a man with no clothes on was coming down to open the door.

* * * * *

My clothes were getting blacker as the day wore on, but nobody cared. The more wood I found, the happier people were with me. Oh, if only life was like this all the time: everyone happy and laughing.

As darkness fell the bonfire was lit. It was so high, so big, and everyone danced around it with joined hands, singing, faces eerie and orange in the reflected light from the flames. Suddenly, that 'Uncle' Bert caught a hold of me, his boozy breath all over my face. He lifted me up and his hand was up my private bits again. I yelled at him to stop hurting me but he grabbed hold of me tighter and held me so near the fire that my hair got a funny smell to it. He said he was going to throw me in to burn. I was so frightened and scorching hot and he said I was going in on the count of three and with that he swung me, head first, bodily towards the flames.

"One!" In, then out.

"Two!" In, then out.

"Three!" And then, at almost the point of no return, I was saved from death by burning. Lots of people got him to the ground and rescued me. I don't remember any more of VE Day after that, only to be told that 'Uncle' Bert was socked out and taken away.

Chapter 2 : School Days

Things got worse for me at school. Around this time, when I was about five to six years old, my parents used to go to 'olde tyme dances' and I would get home from school at around 4:30pm and go straight to bed. At 6pm we would have dinner and then, twice a week, we would get ready to go to a dance. How hateful this was, as I was dressed up all posh, driven to the venue and expected to be on top behaviour until nearly 11 o'clock at night and then the drive home, usually perishing cold, and getting straight into a cold bed. This went on for a number of years. I got very tired and found it hard to concentrate at school. Although I learnt my times tables without any trouble I couldn't do sums and was sent along with a few others to the headmaster's study for correction by cane. I was labelled as 'backward'. We wore dunce's hats and were put to shame as arithmetic was unsuccessfully drummed into us. We were more 'backward' than ever as this was even more terrifying than just sitting in class being laughed at.

I was still wetting myself and the woman teacher at the time would not allow me, along with several others, to be excused when we put our hands up. We were known as 'the Wetties' and Wetties always sat at the back of the class.

We had sixty pupils in a class and three pupils to one desk. This was because the people in the East End of London, who had no homes after the Blitz, were being rehomed in prefabs where we lived. These ugly homes were built in the spaces beside the houses in our unfinished estate. They looked awful, those grey prefabs, beside the lovely red brick Laing houses. There was also a massive class divide, with cockneys and East Enders living beside middle- and

upper-class people. This class friction spilled over into the school playground. The East End kids were tough and old before their time and did the most outrageous things. Their language was dreadful, and some had to learn how to use a knife and fork when school dinners were eventually introduced.

Sitting in the dunce's 'backward' class, I nearly used to fall asleep. What no one could understand though was that I was top of the class in reading and writing, way ahead. So far in fact that at age seven I had finished all the text books up to age eleven and was left with nothing to do in class as I had done it all. I'd sit at the back in my own little world and write poetry and do composition, whilst the rest of the class buzzed on. How had I achieved this? Well, every time I was punished at home I was locked in my bedroom for hours on end, so I would read. And when I had read everything several times over I would invent my own stories. All I had to write and draw on was grey government issue sugar paper, supplied to my father from his office as he was now demobbed from active service and returned to his peacetime job in local government as the chief auditor.

At age eight I had another serious beating-up from the school bullies. They tore up my artwork and took my dinner money, along with my navy blue bloomers, which they stuck on top of a weather vane that my father had made for the school. I had no friends, so nobody stuck up for me and I was an utter laughing stock. The next day they held me down and took my sandals. The teachers took no action; I think they had too much on their hands with too many pupils to a class and, as I was still wetting myself, I was disregarded and shunned; there were several of us like it.

One day we filed into class and sat down. On the teacher's raised desk was a pile of exercise books to be given out. After they were given out, me and the other Wetties hadn't received ours. Looking more closely, the other pile on the desk was nappies. These weren't given out; we were made to go up and collect a nappy each, complete with safety pin, being thoroughly humiliated and sniggered at by the rest of the class. Our punishment couldn't have been better. We were sent to work in the school vegetable garden, which suited me down to the ground, literally. Everything I ever sowed or planted grew. I was in the great outdoors!

By the time I was nine, the wetting had nearly stopped but I was still fearful of walking past a cement mixer, and road drills I couldn't get near and had to pass by on the other side. I was terrified of balloons and Christmas crackers but worst of all were fireworks. My parents got some and I was so terrified that I shot indoors and was told I was stupid and a coward. Even the electric flashes on the tube train rails drove me into a panic.

Moving up into the next class at Merryhills School I thought would be something better. How wrong I was. It was a male teacher, with a mean face, called Mr Beat. Yes, beat by name and beat by nature as he kept a cane by his desk. He favoured all the boys in the class and always picked on the girls. The boys could do nothing wrong in his eyes. His subject was arithmetic, unfortunately for me.

No jewellery was allowed in class and some of the East End girls had pierced ears with little gold sleepers in, which he demanded be removed. There was a terrible row about this as some of their parents forcibly entered the classroom demanding his explanation! I hated this teacher.

One day I smuggled a garnet and diamond ring to school in a matchbox. It had recently been given to me by my grandma and I had begged my parents to let me wear it, but they said no. Well, you can guess what happened. I was looking at it inside the matchbox, under cover of the desk in class, when along came 'Beater' and said, "Matches are not allowed in school; let's be having them, then!" and he snatched the box and ring and put it in his desk, saying, "You can collect it at home time." Each day at home time he refused to return it to me and I didn't dare tell at home what had happened. I never got it back, even when I left that school, which to my joy was about to happen.

The Leaving of Merryhills

Because of overcrowding I was about to be sent to another school, along with some of the others. I was nine and would start at the new school in September, not long before my tenth birthday in November.

I had been going to the GLB, as it was known, the Girls' Life Brigade, attached to a Baptist church, since the age of seven. I loved going there, working for various badges, and being treated as someone of value. I was praised for working hard and never criticised or put down. I adored the uniform and marching and church parade each month. I was in the cadet section and in September would move up into the juniors, something to look forward to along with the new school.

The school holidays passed with me getting into more muddy scrapes as I pursued my mucky nature studies around the lake and beyond. I played in 'the mountains' amongst the huge hills of clay left by the builders of the prefabs and left a trail of dirt everywhere I went. I mixed with some of the prefab kids and, to the horror of my parents, started talking like a cockney. From then on I was forbidden to play with them and was sent to elocution lessons to repair the damage!

A New Start, A New School

The new school, called de Bohun, was miles away and I had to catch a school coach to get there. Gone was my old maroon uniform; now I was wearing a new navy blue one, complete with a beret. The Merryhills motto had been 'Manners Maketh Man', of which there was no sign on that unruly coach ride! The 'old hands' quickly whipped off my beret and chucked it out of the window. 'More home trouble later', I thought. Surely this new school couldn't be any worse than the last one. I hadn't had the opportunity to visit before my first day so it was with pleasure, when we drew up outside, that I saw it was built of red brick over two floors and had playing fields, complete with an old air raid shelter.

We filed in, had a fire drill, filed out, ran round the playing field and then into a new thing called Morning Assembly, complete with a headmaster on stage, in a black gown and mortar board, in front of a lectern. As his eyes roved over the whole school it felt as if those eyes had come to rest on me alone.

"Shut up!" he shouted, rather like, "Silence in court!" at a court hearing. His wife was the headmistress and dealt with the girls when they needed either a caning or first aid.

I was put in an A stream class but soon demoted to a B stream because of my arithmetic. There was proper art, in which I excelled, and music, which I loved. I was the first to be able to pick out a tune on the recorder; I didn't need the music to read. Whilst everyone else was struggling on three notes I was playing complete tunes, mostly old-time dance songs, by ear! Yes, I was still going to these tiring late-night dances twice a week and once a month to a ball.

I had a lovely teacher called Mr Bladd. He fired my imagination with *National Geographic* magazines, which I was allowed to take home. Books and magazines were still in short supply and textbooks had to be shared, one between three pupils.

My greatest achievement came when I was given the lead part in the annual school play. I could learn a part in next to no time. Where others took months, I was finished in three weeks. How proud I felt! Here at last I would be doing something that my parents could see I had worked hard at. I was full of confidence, word perfect... But they never turned up, just like other school events – sports days and prize giving – no parent present.

I got into a bit of trouble as I could perfectly mimic all the teachers, especially the one who took us for elocution. I was egged on, of course, and got caught and was caned for it. I was hated, because I always got 100 per cent for spelling tests, writing poetry and composition, always top in art and music and going up the ladder, so to speak, in sports.

I was not struck on country dancing as I was often partnered with a boy whose surname was Selnic, nicknamed Smellnicks. He had scabby hands and was cross-eyed.

All the rage at that time for girls was swapping beads, which would be brought to school in tobacco tins. Cut glass beads were highly desirable. Swapping beads was strictly a playground activity and my tin of beads was unfortunate enough to pop undone during school assembly, all over the floor. I was in massive trouble and not allowed to recover them, so it was goodbye to another of life's small pleasures. Of course, I was laughed at. I was still a loner, preferring to read a book or draw at playtimes. I found it hard to integrate. I was okay at doing solo things like that lead part in the play and the art competitions, or winning races. I think I was one of the only children to have no brothers or sisters, right through my school life. But I did make a friend called Janet. The one downfall in my parents' eyes was that she lived in one of the prefabs and, "No good will come of it; you'll see!"

Well, to me it was a perfect friendship. We travelled on the school coach together and I felt at last someone liked me, but even that didn't last. We played truant for two days and got found out, resulting in our being separated in school and my parents banning me from seeing her.

In the late 1940s and early '50s an old custom was still observed if you had a close family member that had died. If someone came to school wearing a black diamond-shaped piece of cloth sewn onto their left upper sleeve, or a black band, then everyone knew to be kind and not to ask any questions. Sometimes they had lost a parent, even at this late stage after the war, from war wounds, especially those POWs returning from Japanese prison camps. Most kids at school respected those that had a loss. Needless to say, there were some bereaved pupils who would milk the situation for even more sympathy and get out of schoolwork by laying their head on their arms across the desk, the normal position for when you felt unwell.

On the eve of my tenth birthday my grandfather had a heart attack and died as he was writing in the flyleaf of a book to be given to me as a birthday present. Upon learning that he had died, I wanted to wear one of those black diamonds, but my parents refused point blank and said that this was not the Victorian Age anymore and told me to just get off to school. Of course, I wanted to wear a 'mourning badge' so that everyone at school would feel sorry for me and share their sweets and be nice and cast me pitying looks. I would also have been allowed to stay in at playtime, which would have suited me fine as I hated playtime and the bullies, which I seemed to attract wherever I went.

At home, I was given no information, or love, or cuddles. This was my grandfather who had died, someone who actually seemed to love me, who put his arms around me and produced coins and sweets from his waistcoat pockets, where he also used to bring out a gold watch on a chain. He smelt of eucalyptus and snuff and always had khaki handkerchiefs. He was very proud of his grapevine, which he had nurtured for over thirty years in a very long greenhouse that stretched the length of his house. He was devoted to it. A week after he died, the grapevine died as well.

At school, I put on the sorrowful look and felt very important when my father came to collect me in school time to go to the funeral. Well, my father had a car; not many dads had one of those and I was treated as a novelty. Plus, I was going to a funeral! I soon found out that I wouldn't be going because, upon reaching my grandparents' house, I was to be left behind to watch over a huge cauldron of stew until everyone came back. I was stomping cross, as I had always wanted to go to a funeral to see if what they said was true, that you were put in a hole in the ground. I couldn't think of my poor grandaddy in a hole. My imagination ran riot and I couldn't bear to let anyone sit in his chair when the stew was dished up. Of course, I spilled some down my clothes and was sent upstairs to lie down on my grandaddy's bed, which still smelt of him, and there I wept. I had to part with my week's pocket money of sixpence (in old money) to buy a bunch of anemones to put on his coffin, which I never saw.

At a later date I was given half of his watch chain, made into a bracelet that had silver coins added to it as charms. The silver coins were ones that he had saved to put in the home-made Christmas puddings, something which my parents were set against me eating as I, "might swallow one and die." What they didn't know was that I had accidentally swallowed a threepenny bit coin whilst lying in bed and I was not dead (yet) but a bit worried!

Now, as 1950 was drawing to a close, I would soon be having to endure something else that would make me feel even more of a loner, set apart and ridiculed: dental work.

1952: One Missed Mark Decides My Fate

"So she's got a small mouth, has she? Well you'd never think so with all the noise that comes out of it!" So said my father after I was taken by my mother to the family dentist in a posh suburb. She was over smart in *that* red costume, whilst I endured wearing a kilt plus ridiculously large black patent leather shoes, stuffed with cotton wool where my toes should have been.

Of course, ours had to be no ordinary family dentist. He was the King's dentist, an orthodontist, and as we left after the examination I embarrassed my mother by falling down the grand flight of marble steps and ending up with my kilt over my head, exposing my navy-blue knickers. My over large shoes had shot off across the polished floor and mother had her thin-lipped look about her. No matter how it hurt, I was trounced along to the tube station feeling utterly miserable as I had been told I would have to have 'plates' in my mouth. Matters were made worse when my ten-year-old mind spoke up and said that I thought that plates were for eating from, not for actually putting in your mouth.

This was to be the year when I would miss a lot of schoolwork because of orthodontic visits, where I had special plates made in three parts to straighten my remaining teeth, several perfectly good ones having been extracted. I had no bad teeth, just too many in a small mouth. My plates were made with screws holding them together and these screws had to be turned, with a special key, one revolution twice a week. The plates were completely invisible in the top of my mouth. They were made of a clear material, very modern and upmarket. All the other kids with this condition wore ugly pink plastic ones with wires and elastic all showing.

My first attempts at speech came out all slurred as my plate covered the entire roof of my mouth. I was the laughing stock of the school, especially when I followed the specialist's instruction to rinse my plate and brush it after each meal. My journeys to the school washroom amongst the carbolic soap, jeering kids and then the indignity of brushing out the school dinner debris, made me feel sick. Boiled school greens, lettuce and hard-boiled egg were the worst offenders to get out of the plate's crevices. I used to heave as I watched them disappear down the washbasin plughole.

The orthodontic specialist, Mr Borgman, was such a lovely man. He was so kind to me as I endured the monthly casts made of my mouth and saw the plaster of Paris models of my teeth, upper and lower. He explained everything and showed me the x-rays, plus the workings of how my teeth should look, and promised me that he would give me a smile, "like Hollywood." It would be another seven years before I was finally signed off.

But even this got me into trouble as, one dinnertime, the bullies followed me into the school washroom, dragged me to the floor and tried to take my dental plate out of my mouth. I had been told to take great care with it; I had to sleep with it in as well. Oh, how tempting it was to remove it as it was far more comfy without it! But it was more difficult to replace the next day and it hurt. I was determined to keep slogging on. Five boys held me down. One was trying to pull my knickers off, whilst the biggest boy put his finger in my mouth. I was kicking and writhing as I knew that I would be in deep trouble at home if my plate was gone and how upset that kind Mr Borgman would be. So I bit that finger as hard as I could. Something went crunch and I tasted blood. Oh, what had I done? Suddenly, everyone had run off and left me there, in a pool of blood, and the top of a finger, on the floor. I was sick and sat there sobbing, but my plate was intact. I had bitten off more than I could chew: a finger top!

Big trouble. I must have fainted as the next thing I remember was waking up in the sick room with the school nurse beside me. I was on the bed and she was being kind and loving toward me. Big, deep trouble, I thought, as I was now shaking all over.

"The headmaster is writing a letter for you to take home," she soothed. That was the last thing I wanted, more trouble. As I returned to my classroom later and with the letter in my pocket, there was a deathly hush when I entered. I went to my desk and the teacher said I could take up the 'sick position' and be excused the rest of the day's lessons. So, head on arms on the desk lid, I dozed off as the class droned on.

I was in my final year at this school before taking the 11-plus exam. I missed two weeks twice that year as I had to go on holiday with my parents, plus odd days. Not many people went on holiday then, so I was yet again classed as different. The only holidays kids went on were what were known as The School Journey: an annual trip for a week to a special place by the sea, which was learnt about for the whole term before departure. It cost £5 but of course I was the only one not going. My parents said they couldn't afford it. I suppose they spent it on their own holidays, the ball gowns, dresses and dances, the car and telephone and buying the house. Well, even the poor kids managed to go on The School Journey. I was left behind, and the teachers didn't know what class to put me in for a week, so told me to go out nature studying, which suited me just fine!

When The School Journey came back to resume lessons, it was all taken up with what they did, and tests were taken and for two whole weeks I was classed as the duffer because I didn't know anything about it.

The next exciting thing to happen in that year was the formation of a school orchestra. As mentioned before, I could pick up any tune and play it by ear on the recorder. At home, I was sent up to the bathroom to play it as my parents hated the sound, or I would be sent down to the lake and the ducks would come up and listen, their heads going all ways at the sound. At school, we were introduced to reading music. Well, I thought, what's the point when I know it already. The music teacher played the tune on the piano and I could immediately play it by ear. So impressed was the music teacher at my so-called fabulous ability to read music that I was plonked straight away into the school orchestra! Oh, it was wonderful, and I was good on the percussion too.

We were going to do a Christmas concert. Perhaps my parents might come! I was firing on all cylinders with making music, that is until we had to play new pieces by sight from music sheets. This was stuff that I had not heard before, so I just pretended to play by moving my fingers up and down and appearing to be breathing in the right places. The players around me hadn't noticed until I was delegated to turning the page of music. I got away with it a few times but eventually we each had to demonstrate a certain line of music and I was found out. I had been mimicking it for half a term, so it was no surprise that I was thrown out. But I still played on, down by the lake, where I met a man who went there to practice his bagpipes. We made a howling duet!

I hated school playtimes. I just didn't fit in, even the skipping games and playing tag or hide and seek. I was hunted down by the bullies. I had a 'thing' in my mouth, I wore horrid dyed black lace-up shoes and ghastly clothes. I was gawky and had ugly-looking straggly hair. My knees were prone to boils, which my mother used to spend ages pricking to let the pus out and then applying boiling water followed by iodine. The school toilets harboured sadists and my old problems reappeared; I started to wet myself again as I was too afraid to go in there.

I was a loner. I spent playtimes either reading, in the winter, or in the summer on the school field, where I could go round the edges and study the creatures and plants or pick a daisy and look in wonder at its amazing white petals tinged with pink. I would draw them, marvelling at how easy it was to make an accurate likeness, which astounded the teachers and other grown-ups. To me it was simple, as natural as talking, and so I started a sketch book and a life-long hobby. I could draw and paint anything, sing well and make up good poetry. I thought a lot, whilst all the other kids were into film stars, cowboys and Indians. I was locked in aloneness and solitude, not only at school but in my bedroom at home, too.

The long school summer holidays came. Whilst other kids went around in gangs I spent the summer on my own, around the lake and in the woods. I became adept at tracking, following, and hiding and observed all sorts, including one awful Sunday, returning across a secluded area of scrubland after Sunday School, when I saw some of the bullies with a very young boy. He came from the prefabs and was about five or six years of age. He was sobbing as his trousers were missing; next the bullies took his pants down. I froze into the undergrowth; if they could do that to a boy they would do that to me, so I stayed as still and as hidden as possible. I was already terrified, but what came next was worse still and will haunt me for ever.

They had built a huge igloo type of camp from dried grass and bracken, which had just one hole as an entry and exit. It was very well made. The bullies were pinching the little boy in the privates and when he wouldn't stop crying they pushed him into the camp. I daren't move. Then they set fire to it with the little boy inside. The screams and smell have stayed with me to this day. The bullies were laughing. Frozen with horror, I wanted to run but didn't dare, for fear that I would end up the same way. If they knew I had seen what they had done, I am sure that they would have silenced me. The screams stopped. Silence, except for the sound of the fire's last crackles. The white-faced bullies ran away and so did I, in the opposite direction. Someone might say that I had done it if I had been found there. I wanted to tell someone and yet I knew it would have been futile. Children were not usually believed and my parents would never have backed me up. I dared not say anything as not only would nobody have believed me, but I would be told off for telling lies, not to mention the fact that I was playing out on a Sunday in a place I was not supposed to be.

That poor little boy was burned to death and no one knew how, only me. It haunted me badly and I withdrew even further; the only child with horrid clothes and hair, who felt unloved and unwanted and yet came from a 'good' home.

Sundays were sacrosanct. Although the parents were not religious I was sent to Sunday school, which I loved. The teachers were soft-hearted and kind, and I used to feel so sorry for them when other children used to play them up, so I would be extra nice and well behaved for those lovely teachers. I always remembered the Bible texts that were supposed to be learnt each week and could memorise long passages. I sat the Scripture Union exams each year and always passed with a first-class certificate. This was the same church where I used to attend the Girls' Life Brigade and that was a godsend, as I sailed through all the badges to be earned and became a leader.

There were no bullies here. Instead, there was a great love and encouragement, which touched me so deeply. One year I won the Proficiency Cup, no mean feat, but yet again, I had no parents at the prizegiving event, just a scornful, "Proficiency? That will be the day! They must have made a mistake." Well, I went on, with three other girls, to win a highly coveted award for our brigade. It was a great achievement, the International Friendship Shield. The four of us worked hard as a team and won this out of the whole world of Girls' Life Brigades. Yes, the whole planet! We were to be presented with this special shield at the Royal Albert Hall by the Queen. Everyone in our company, 1st Southgate, was thrilled at the news and our captain was beaming. New uniforms were allocated for free, which of course meant that I would have the unenviable task of removing my many badges and re-sewing them onto the new uniform.

Oh, how excited we were! What an honour! Oh, yeah? What a *flop*, as my parents said I couldn't go as they were going on holiday that day. Never had I hated going away so much, yet again to Devon, to the same old holiday camp where the parents did all their dancing, running the whole place and dressing up, which I also had to do and loathed it all... But that was a little bit ahead of the time I am now writing about; that was 1953 and I am still in 1952.

That fateful year on 6 February, the day the King died, was the day that would decide my whole future, the day I took my 11-plus exam. Going down to breakfast and hearing the mournful tolling of a bell on the 8am news on the radio, "What's that?" I asked.

"Oh, just a bell," replied my father. "Just eat up and get off to school." No good luck wishes, but one concession to this special exam day was no school uniform, so my mother made me wear the most horrible multicoloured striped twinset and a cut-down tweed skirt. I was immediately a laughing stock yet again at school.

As we sat before the unopened exam papers on our desks, the headmaster came in to make an important announcement.

"Before you open your papers, I have to inform you that the King is dead." And, with no further explanation, he left the room.

My mind was doing overtime. How? Why? When? What did he look like dead? Was he wearing his crown? I loved all the pictures I had collected, from newspapers and magazines, of the royal family. That lovely, lovely family, who all loved each other. That's where my thoughts were during that fate-deciding exam. I had been promised a bicycle if I passed, as were all the others who were quite well off in our road. But I digress, as that was in the future. The results came at the end of the summer term so parents would have all the school holidays to buy the new uniforms, depending on your exam results and which school you would be attending.

That ghastly February in 1952 changed me in ways that made me inwardly resolute and defiant. I realised that I could think up things about people without saying anything, write them down and then quite amazingly these things came true, so when I wished my parents were dead, because I was so fed up with what they wanted to do, I got really spooked up when my father suddenly became dangerously ill with pneumonia. I heard the words, "dangerously ill," and knew this was serious because sometimes, on the wireless before the news, would come an announcement: "Here is an SOS message. Would..., son of..., please contact... as their father / mother is dangerously ill." That meant they were dying. Oh heck! What *had* I done?

Of course, he recovered but that didn't stop me worrying about it endlessly.

11-Plus Exam Results

Each day I was dreading the moment of the 11-plus exam results until, sitting indoors on one fateful August day, the rain running down the window in rivulets, I saw the postman coming to deliver the tell-tale brown envelope. I had to wait all day until my father came home from work before the bombshell dropped: FAILED! Everyone else in our road had passed and spent the rest of the summer school holidays riding up and down past our house on new bicycles, ridiculing and making faces at me if I was at the window. My parents were so ashamed of me that they didn't go dancing for two weeks. They almost disowned me. They went to see my teacher; if only they had taken the trouble to go to the school when I was winning things and in the school plays.

The 11-plus winners in the road gleefully sported their new County Grammar School uniforms even before the school holidays had ended, showing off. The smart bottle green blazers were in contrast to the pukey green of that disgraceful institution, the secondary modern school. Only the prefab kids, the bombed out so-called dregs of society went there. My parents said I had brought disgrace on the whole family, my grandparents, the neighbours, and their dance club cronies. My dear teacher told me I had failed it by one mark. Whether this was true or not I don't know. This was transition time, the leaving of one school (hurray!) and the starting of another.

September 1952

So my father got me a bike, a third-hand bike, to go to school on. It was too big for me so he fixed wooden blocks to the pedals so that my feet would reach and I would, 'grow into it'. More ridicule and being laughed at. I set off in my pukey green uniform and cycled up steep hills to my new school, Oakwood Secondary Modern. Maybe things would be better here. It was in an area new to me, strange and unfamiliar. A satchel and shoe bag were compulsory items, as were pens, pencils, rubbers, and rulers as there were still shortages from the war.

After assembly in the main school we were decanted into prefab huts in the school grounds. These had a central coke stove in the classroom; the fumes made it hard not to fall asleep! My class teacher for the first year, Miss Long, was also the art teacher and English teacher, so we got along really well! In my first school report I came third out of forty-seven in our class. I would have been first if arithmetic had not let me down. I had first in English, composition, art, craft, literature, and French, plus music. Geography was top marks too, although in PE and sport I was classed as theoretically being top but couldn't as, "She must learn to be more a member of the team." It was so hard to join in with others and those bullies from way back were now in my class too.

We had needlework, where we had to make aprons and caps in green gingham for our domestic science (cookery) classes. These articles had to have our initials embroidered in chain stitch on them and we made a bag to keep them in. Those unable to afford the materials, or who didn't complete them by the end of term, were not allowed to do domestic science for the rest of the school year. Oh, how the parents, including mine, kicked up a fuss! People were still trying to rebuild their homes and make up for losses after the war.

The first domestic science lesson was to make sandwiches. We each had to take a carving knife to school. Yes, a sharp carving knife! Can you imagine that in today's society? My father made a sheath from wood for mine.

The school bullies got to hear about the knives and waylaid one of the girls and threatened her with her own knife. The following week we had to take a glass jelly mould to school to make a blancmange. A boy called Brian Pickering snatched my satchel at home time, swinging it in the air, and it smashed on the concrete path. I was in awful trouble at home because of this. It really upset me. Ensuing weeks were fraught with danger for us girls after cookery class days. Gangs of boys would try to steal whatever we had carefully made; it was frightening. That winter there was a dreadful smog and a number of pupils died. I couldn't see more than a yard ahead of me and it took several hours to get home. At least I didn't have to go to those dreaded dances during the smog.

And so it came round to spring and summer of 1953, which found me excelling at athletics, especially long jump, in which I broke the school record. I soon gave it up though as gangs of boys would gather at the end of the long jump pit to watch as the girls ran towards them to do their jump. They were interested in seeing the girls' breasts moving up and down; bras were not worn until you left school. Although I had no breasts as yet I was too embarrassed to continue.

I gave up the 100 yards race because a gun was fired at the start and the noise terrified me, so I did the 400 yards as a whistle was blown for that instead. I kept winning so went in for the mile. No first year had ever won it before, but I did! My parents were not interested and never came to the sports day or prizegiving. They said it would be time better spent doing arithmetic instead.

The coronation of Queen Elizabeth II took place on 2 June 1953 and our school put on a huge pageant with other schools. Whenever I hear *Greensleeves* it reminds me of that awful hot day, amongst a thousand bodies dressed up in Elizabethan dress, when I felt ill and was sick in the middle of the arena and the whole thing ground to a halt as I was unceremoniously hauled off to the St John sick bay. They were so kind to me; why couldn't everyone else in my life be kind and loving?

As the summer holidays approached and my maths (as they now called it) had gone from bad to worse, I was now moving down positions in class and dreading the end of term report. You see, in geometry I came first in the first term; it was all drawing, which I was good at. But I came bottom after that when the number work came in. And algebra, well, I was bottom with an exam result of nought out of a hundred! It was hateful. I was made to give up all that I excelled in and to concentrate on numbers. And so after the holidays, in September 1953, I moved up into the second year and one of the most miserable times of my life at that school.

Whacker Wilson, the maths teacher, was my form teacher for that year. He would whack me across the back of my hands with a ruler as I was writing. He was formidable in his black gown and he smelt of anger. Yes, I could smell it building up and one fateful day I 'saw', in my head, a boy unconscious on the classroom floor. This boy was what they called 'simple' and his name was Simon so, as I'm sure you can guess, Whacker called him Simple Simon. My vision came to pass shortly afterwards. Simon had done nothing wrong but Whacker, spittle flying, was shouting at him and bending his cane, ready for an onslaught. As the cane hit the desk, Simon fainted clean away. Whacker kicked him to make him get up. I, the laugh of the whole class, went to help him as I had passed my first aid at the Girls' Life Brigade. I was rewarded with a swipe on the face with the cane and I ran out of the class to the headmaster's office, which was very daring, to report that a pupil could be dead.

It was a blur after that as Simon was taken by ambulance to hospital and I was sent home in disgrace for 'breaking class'. My parents never forgave me, saying I should mind my own business.

A few weeks later, my nice first year form teacher, Miss Long, passed me an envelope and told me to promise her that I would open it in private, where no one could see me, as she knew what it contained. On my way home from school I hid away up a tree. I was absolutely stunned to find a £5 note (lots of money in those days) and a lovely letter from Simon's mother, thanking me for being brave and helping her son. She knew about Whacker and told me that Simon was now at a special school and that he was epileptic, but happy. Simon's mother was a film star and knew one of the girls in our class, the daughter of a member of a well-known singing group at that time, known as the Mike Sammes Singers, who appeared on TV every Sunday. She also knew of my parents' reaction to my deed as they used to dance for the Mike Sammes Singers. Hence the secrecy! I hid the £5 note, all folded up small, in an empty mustard tin, ready for when I eventually – hopefully – would run away from home.

Oh, that school! What misery; extra since my 'deed'. Whacker Wilson, constantly on my back, had me slipping down in class to 39th position and I grew more and more withdrawn at school. "She is very polite but must try harder," one teacher put on my report. Another said, "Capable of great things but seems unwilling to learn." Yet another, "Such a well-mannered girl but manners don't pass exams!" and so on. Was there any way out of this? How many aspirins does it take to kill you, I wondered?

The only saving grace in all this was the Girls' Life Brigade, where I pursued all my badges with gusto and was rewarded with praise. The theme that year was safety and I was to be made the central figure at the annual GLB display. I was the Safety Queen: how thrilled I was! With costumes, lines to be learnt and all the parents coming to this special annual event, at last here was something for them to be proud of. But would they turn up?

Cycling home from school one week before the event, going down a very steep hill at great speed, I hit a brick and went over the handlebars. I didn't know what had happened but thought I had broken my arm as I was in such pain. I then passed out. The next thing I knew, I was sitting in front of an electric fire in a strange house and our doctor was there, the formidable Dr Hill, a woman I hated. She more or less told me off and drove me home to my unsympathetic mother, to whom she handed the bill (the NHS hadn't quite kicked in yet).

"She needs two weeks in a darkened room if you don't want her to die..." I didn't realise then that the, "if you don't want her to die," bit was said in jest. I just thought how brilliant, what a relief to get to heaven, out of all this disappointment and horrid school life.

"Huh, Safety Queen! That's great coming from you," said my mother. "Look at you now. Trust you to mess it up."

I wasn't feeling great. I needed sympathy, not sarcasm. I had wrecked my school uniform too, which didn't go down too well. I was wearing a gaberdine raincoat, a blazer, jersey, blouse and vest and it was all ruined where my left hip had dragged along the road, with my arm (which wasn't broken, as it turned out) in tow.

My father came home later, carrying my bike. The front wheel spokes had been completely ripped out, every one of them. The police said that I had hit a brick, which dislodged my lamp, which was slotted onto a bracket down by the wheel. This had gone into the spokes and I had travelled on my front at least thirty yards down the steep hill. The brick had come from an adjacent building site and one of the workmen witnessed my accident. I could have been killed, he said.[3] I wished I had, the way I was feeling: shame, disappointment... The tears welled up as my headache got worse. My father came and was very subdued and didn't tell me off and said not to worry about the bike, which surprised me. I slept a lot and the doctor came at intervals to shine a light in my eyes.

And so 1953 merged into 1954 and still the loathed dressing up and dances went on. I took my sketch book to these dances as a way to get out of dancing with old men with clammy hands. One was an undertaker and I always wondered where his hands had been that day. I felt sure he was sizing me up for a coffin!

I produced some amazing artwork at school, which at least got me out of the pit of despair. So stunned was the headmaster that he sent a letter to my parents, suggesting I should go to art school in Hornsey. They turned down the idea so the headmaster put me through the entrance exam, which he knew I would pass, and then re-approached the idea. It was turned down. I had done an outstanding exam piece of half a cabbage and various other things in different mediums. It was easy for me; it was natural. I sailed through the exam but that only caused more trouble from my parents, whose response was, "How *could* you?"

That was the only redeeming aspect at that school, that the headmaster was interested in helping me get on, but alas his efforts failed.

---

[3] Publisher's note: The concept of suing the building site for damages was not even considered. If this happened today the contractor would, quite rightly, be held liable for significant damages.

Chapter 3 : Better Days

During the school holidays of 1954 and at the age of thirteen and a half, a bombshell hit my life. Happiness and sorrow: my parents said we were moving. Oh yippee! I thought we were going to live in Croyde, Devon, where they already had a property by the sea. But no, it was to be about seven miles from our current house, in the country, where they were having a bungalow built. This would mean a change of schools. Alleluia! Happiness! But such sorrow: I would have to leave the Girls' Life Brigade, where I had found a purpose in life, hope in my despair, comfort in my rejection. They understood, those GLB officers. I would be leaving my beloved lake, which many a time received my tears into its waters.

We drove out to see the half-built bungalow at Crews Hill. I stood in what was to be my bedroom and I didn't know what to think. I had no choice in its décor. I just stood rooted to the spot. My whole life, although not fantastic, would be uprooted. I should be excited but wasn't. With the Girls' Life Brigade gone, who could I go to? There was no one. I was on my own. The parents were wrapped up in their move – the furniture, carpets, garden – and I was in the way. I clung to the thought that I still had that £5 in the mustard tin!

School term started on 5 September, so I had to cycle to my new school from my old home until the move on 5 October. The school would be Chace Girls' School in Enfield. It can't be any worse than my old one, surely, I thought. At least the uniform was more pleasing: maroon and blue-grey.

And so, on 5 October 1954, a new and important chapter of my life unfolded. I cycled away from the home where I grew up and into my new school; by the end of the day I would be cycling several miles into a strange area and a different home.

The trepidation mounted on my very first day as I approached this new school. To be honest, my legs were shaking as I padlocked my bike into a reserved space, with my name on it, in the cycle shed. There were girls everywhere, not taking any notice of my arrival, but even so I felt self-conscious as I mounted the stairs to report to the headmistress in her office.

"Enter!" she called out. What a kindly-looking lady, I thought; how could a head look so friendly?

"You look really smart in your new uniform, Anne. Welcome to this school; I hope that you will be extremely happy here." And with that, she stood up, shook my hand, and gave me a brand-new briefcase! "That is for your books or whatever else you girls like to carry around with you. If you are at all worried whilst at this school, always come to me first and I will listen."

Wow! This was a good turn of events, a bit different from my other schools. But how long would it last? I was so used to things collapsing all around me.

My new form mistress, Miss Harris, was firm but kind. I received much encouragement and as I was introduced as a new girl to the class no one sniggered or smirked. Someone was designated to be my buddy and show me the ropes. I took a test and was put in the A stream. I was then shown around the whole school, a solid Victorian building, and into the overflow classrooms. There was a beautiful playing field. Every teacher shook my hand and wished me well.

My parents didn't even ask me how I had got on at my new school and I didn't bother to tell them how much I liked it; that would have been wrong, to actually be seen to enjoy something!

I got on very well in my lovely school, where seemingly no bullies existed, and we pupils, instead of being downed, criticised, and shouted at, were encouraged with kindness and drawn out at what we were good at. The emphasis was on what you *could* do, not on what you couldn't grasp. I settled quickly into my first term at that school and ended the year with an excellent report.

"There must be something wrong; this report is too good," was the parental comment!

My fourteenth birthday came and went, and I cycled my way into 1955. I no longer felt so alone as I made two friends at that school. They were 'only child' girls like me. One was to introduce me to a church choir, which I sang in for seven years, and the other was later to be my bridesmaid. The school had so much love to give me.

I was in the netball team and also played hockey for the school. At Chace, we actually had hockey boots that came in pairs! My last school had a box of assorted single boots and if you were lucky you might end up with a proper pair. If not, the session was spent limping up and down the pitch, freezing in navy blue knickers and blouses, whilst the teacher was muffled up in coat and scarf. The teacher at my new school wore the proper gear and suffered with us in all weather and was respected for it.

I was eventually picked to play for the county. I was so proud, but my parents weren't interested, especially when they learnt that they would eventually have to pay for an official county hockey stick and all the appropriate gear. So, another disappointment. I thought they would have been proud of me.

Back home, I was demoted to my bedroom whilst my parents watched television. Not many families had one in those days. Then there was still that dancing three times a week. How I hated it!

Disturbing things entered my now reasonably happy life. My father always took breakfast to my mother in bed, every morning, before he went to work. She used to have an infra-red heat lamp each day to help ease her rheumatism.

Father would then come into my bedroom, shouting, "Wakey wakey, rise and shine, the morning's fine! Lash up and stow, wakey wakey!" which is what he used to do as a petty officer in the navy to get everyone out of their hammocks. If I didn't immediately leap out of bed he would rip the bed clothes off. But that wasn't the worst thing.

Sometimes he would slip into the bedroom and sit on the bed and put his hand down between my legs. He would say it was our secret, our special secret, and to tell no one and that if I lay still I would like what he was doing. He said it was part of every girl's education for a father to be doing this, so that she would know what it was like when she got married and that it made you feel nice 'down there'. He said I was to let him know when I started to 'feel nice'.

If I managed to get up and dressed before he came in my bedroom, then at breakfast he would try a different tack and eat his cornflakes standing up by my chair and tell me to watch the lump rise beneath his trousers and then to touch this bulge.

Although I was fourteen, I had no knowledge of the workings of the human body. I hadn't even got any breasts and I hadn't got my periods; I didn't know what they were. All I had was a vague idea, because my mother gave me a brown sealed-up paper package to take to school in case I had an accident and started bleeding. I was on no account to open it until that time! Well that time never happened when I was at school, although there used to be some mysterious goings-on in whispered huddles amongst a few girls in the outside toilets, which were situated in the playground. These girls had breasts and were soppy about film stars and fashion. I wasn't interested; all I wanted to do was work hard and claim the reward of praise from my wonderful, caring teachers.

A weekday, spent at school, was the great escape from home. School was where I was appreciated for working hard. I was made a prefect and proudly wore my prefect's badge on my blazer. I was a monitor and enjoyed some early morning escapes from breakfast to arrive before school to fill all the paper towel machines, fill the inkwells on our desks and then have the prefect's privilege of joining the teaching staff in the staff room for coffee. I then cleared up after, saving the tea leaves and coffee grounds for the caretaker to use at the end of the day to 'lay the dust' when sweeping the assembly hall.

My end of term report had the remark, "Anne is a kind and courteous girl who can be relied upon to do her best." When my parents read this they sarcastically said it was the first they knew of this and that I should try doing it at home.

By now I was going to the church choir practice twice a week and services on Sundays, weddings and also ringing the bells. This got me out of some of the dance dreads but I was never allowed to have a house key, so I would sit and shiver outside until the parents came back. It was worth it though! I loved singing and had a fab music teacher at school who rewarded me and another pupil by taking us to the Royal School of Music, next to the Royal Albert Hall, in London where she sang in the Royal Choral Society. Here, we sat on the stage a few feet away from Sir Malcolm Sargent, who was the choir's director and conductor. What a privilege, to meet this great man. He chatted away to us and handed us the baton to have a go! I was in seventh heaven, hearing all this beautiful music in a fine building.

What a difference! A teacher who cared, no money asked for to finance the trip and she took us to a Lyons Corner House for a meal. In years to come, I was to meet Sir Malcolm again and he remembered me. I would also meet Harry Davidson and Victor Silvester and Diana Dors, but that's another story.

Chace School also encouraged me to take up cross-country running, in which I excelled and was privileged to run with a guest athlete named Mary Peters, famous in those days. Little did I know that I would meet her again sixty years later when she was the guest VIP who came to a national competition run by McCarthy & Stone, at Lantern Court in Ilfracombe, Devon.

My running career started at that school and I ran the 440 yards at the White City in London. My first javelin throw went over the school fence and into the road, narrowly missing an old lady, who dropped her shopping in surprise! I did not pursue javelin any further.

Domestic science was sheer bliss at this school, with a whole day set aside for what was to stand me in good stead in years to come. Our teacher was patient and kind and this kindness came to my rescue one day, when we took a letter home to our parents asking for five shillings (a lot of money then) to pay for an educational trip to London, to visit Cadby Hall, the headquarters of Lyons, the cake company. I was the only pupil not provided with the money for the trip and this kind teacher somehow paid for me to go. The trip was wonderful! We watched in the factory as Swiss rolls were made at a one-hundred-yard-long piece at a time before ladies, listening to the radio programme *Music While You Work,* spooned jam onto this great long piece of sponge and then a machine rolled and gobbled it all up, cut it into pieces and wrapped it. Fascinating! We were also shown a six-foot-high iced birthday cake being decorated for the Queen Mother's birthday. So big, so opulent; however would they transport it? In a carriage apparently, drawn by white horses to match the cake.

We had a lunch in the factory canteen, and everyone had a large box, filled with goodies, to take away. Our domestic science teacher was Miss Fugle and had been nicknamed Bugle by everyone but after this trip we reverted to her real name. She had opened up an interesting new world for us and was so kind.

As Easter 1955 came I was completely immersed in church. I was the equivalent of an altar boy and helped the vicar and also the organist, whom I felt sorry for as that kindly old man was getting frail and not playing so well. He got me a new cassock and choir outfit and thanked me for looking after his music sheets. You see, my parents, although showing off to their dance cronies, "Our daughter sings in the church choir," wouldn't put any money towards a new cassock for my forthcoming confirmation of choristers. They never went to church and they didn't come to my confirmation either. It was so meaningful to me, so moving, on a beautiful Easter Day.

There was a lovely innocent friendship between us choristers, with no mickey-taking and no bullies. It was like having a proper family around, with the vicar our father and the organist our granddad! The Bishop of Willesden came to confirm us and gave us all a Bible and a five-shilling piece (a crown). There was a lovely celebratory lunch to which all parents and friends were invited. Yes, you've guessed it: mine didn't come.

I cycled back home with my school friend June, who had originally introduced me to the choir. She lived a few doors away but, as her father worked on the railway and so was working class and her mother – horror of horrors – also worked, it wasn't deemed fit that I should mix with her. I was trapped yet again. I could have her as my friend at school but not as a neighbour. But her mother worked at the local plant nursery. You see, we lived where there were quite a few market gardeners and greenhouses and June worked in one on a Saturday morning to earn some pocket money. She said she could get me a job. "Come and have a look," she told me, so I did and fell in love with a glasshouse full of carnations. I was captivated by the smell, the peace, just everything about it and I stored it away in my mind for future reference.

N.A.L.G.O., CROYDE BAY.

The school year came to a close with another glowing report but what wasn't so glowing was yet another visit for those so-called holidays at the camp in North Devon. Ever since 1947 we had been going there several times a year. It was set up for local government officers (NALGO) and their families as a holiday camp. For me it was a place of mental torture as my parents took over and ran dances and prances and dressed to impress. Father was chairman and vice manager, giving out notices over the mic at breakfast, running all the tournaments for billiards, snooker (he was runner-up at Carnegie Hall for Amateur Snooker UK) and table tennis and arranging sports day as well as concerts. He was the dance leader, putting on the programmes and records. My parents were completely wrapped up in it and would meet with another couple there year after year to run all this, unpaid. It was one big ego trip.

They had a son, this other couple. I will call him 'T'. We grew up at this camp, seeing each other several times a year, every year, from the age of seven. We would go off in our childhood innocence, exploring sand dunes, cliffs, caves, sharing ice creams like some Enid Blyton children. So long as we turned up at meal times and entered the obligatory fancy dress competitions and dances we were left to our own devices. We had a great carefree friendship. We were seldom apart and had very similar home situations. We loved one another with a brother-sisterly love, and we were both lonely, only children. So long as we were seen and not heard we were allowed to do our own things.

Well, that summer, in the school holidays at that wretched holiday camp, I arrived with pert little pointed breasts, as my mother had purchased a bra and stuffed it with cotton wool to make me look bigger than I really was. I was tarted up for the dances and 'T' was made to wear a dinner jacket and bow tie. We were fourteen years old and made to take to the dance floor. What the parents didn't know was that we had, in protest to all that Olde Tyme Dancing, been practising a modern quickstep during our days on the dunes. We had gone to a holiday venue across the bay and hooked up with some like-minded kids with modern parents who had a private, specially made, dance floor in their huge house. Here, we danced to Victor Silvester music, learning all the fancy moves, and they lent us the record. Yes, we danced all right when asked by the parents to, "Lead the floor"! 'T' put on the record and how we did go!

As one, we tripped around doing all the fancy stuff, fast and smooth. Soon everyone was standing there open mouthed and clapping in time to the music when it suddenly stopped. One moment I was floating on air and the next moment came mentally tumbling down as the record was halted. The parents, both sets, didn't want us to be better than they were, that was the truth of it. We were growing up and they hated it.

At fourteen, I still had to share a chalet with my parents. In the mornings, my mother would go to the main assembly point to collect hot water while my father made the beds and fiddled with 'our secret' before she returned. I hated this deceit but couldn't tell anyone. It was so awful. This well-thought-of, upstanding (literally!) member of society, vice mayor, president of NALGO, MC, pillar of the local government community; who would believe me anyway? Certainly not my mother. I had to act as if nothing was going on and I could feel myself getting hot and flushed in the face. Difficult times. I wanted to confide in 'T' but couldn't for fear of losing his friendship. Besides, I was so embarrassed. My mother had no idea and I thought this was some kind of special bond daughters had with fathers, but I felt very uneasy and lonely. He kept saying, "Are you there yet?" and, "Hurry up." Where was I supposed to be going if I wasn't 'there' yet?

To make matters worse, both 'T' and I squirmed when it was announced that we were voted as Mr and Miss NALGO and had to dress up, wearing ghastly ballroom gear and big sashes. Mine said, "Miss NALGO" and all the cameras were clicking for posterity as we were crowned. Oh yes, the parents oohed and aahed and gloated, puffed up, and 'T's mother broke into song and delivered an operatic aria into the mic. She was an opera singer after all, but 'T' said under his breath that he had brought some cotton wool along. Sure enough, he had, which I thought was hilarious. No one knew what we were laughing at, but we couldn't stop; it was a release valve.

"See you in September," 'T' said, as bookings had been made to secure a return stay at the camp. We would both miss yet more time off school. In my case, the parents said it wouldn't matter as I would be leaving at Christmas anyway, as I was to be fifteen in November, the school leaving age at that time.

Shoehorning back into a new school year and resuming the choir gave some structure to my life. The headmistress was thrilled to award me the senior art prize, the athletics trophy, and the prize for earning the most house points – the award of merit – thus my name went up 'for all time' on the special board on the hall wall. Again, no parents turned up.

Then, in November, I had to think about finding a job. My mother took me to a posh dress shop in Wood Green, run by two lovely Jewish sisters. I definitely didn't want to work in a dress shop!

"Help! Get me out of here, please God," I prayed. "Make me fail the interview." My mother was wearing her latest creation and I cringed at this blot on the lipsticked landscape. The two sisters eyed her up and down and I wished the floor would swallow me up, ankle socks and all.

"We would like to speak to your daughter alone," they said. I went into their little office at the back and they petted and cooed over me and gave me a chocolate. I was fearing the worst: they wanted me! Oh heck, what a ghastly life.

"You poor darling," they wailed, wringing their hands. "You don't really want to work in a dress shop, do you? Besides, we couldn't possibly employ the daughter of a mother who wears such a monstrous outfit!" And then, "But don't say we said so!"

Back at school, the headmistress laughed, and tears rolled down her face when, at my finding-a-job interview the next day, I relayed what had happened. She came up with two job possibilities, on the basis of my artistic flair. One was in a big store in Oxford Street, London, to learn window dressing. The other was a sort of apprenticeship in a drawing office. I did *not* want to work in London! I hated stores and shops and tube trains, smoke, and crowds. So I decided on the drawing office. I didn't really want to work indoors at all, but I supposed drawing would be the lesser of two evils. This meant going for an interview at Ferguson Radio and Television, a big factory and offices on the Great Cambridge Road on the other side of Enfield. It was overwhelming: so big with so much to take in. However, I was taken on to start the week after I left school, just before Christmas.

My tears rolled down at the final school assembly as we sang, "Lord behold us with thy blessing, once again assembled here," for I had been truly happy in this place. I did *not* want to leave. I wanted to learn more. I felt I could go on to greater things if only I could stay. As I shook hands with all the teachers, they each gave me words of encouragement. The sports and PE teacher said that one day my name would be up there on a winning streak. The English teacher said that I had a book in me and I laughingly quipped, "I haven't swallowed one!" The domestic science teacher thought I would make a good wife one day. Even the maths teacher said I had made a vast improvement! If only my auditor father could hear that.

Then finally, at the exit door, that dear headmistress took my tearful face into her bosom and said, "You never did come to me, did you, to tell me of that awful problem you had?" Did she know? Did she guess? Could she see right through me? She told me, "If you keep our school motto in your mind, then through life you can overcome anything. Hold onto that which is good." Then she said she was sorry I was going and that it had been an honour to have me as a pupil. And so I walked out of my beloved school, into the next part of my life.

Chapter 4 : From Ankle Socks to Stockings in One Week

Within one week I was thrust into an alien world. My fashion-plated mother got me stockings and roll-ons, a horrid tight girdle that had suspenders that dug into the top of my thighs. Then court shoes, something I had never worn before, plus a ghastly bra that stuck out, pointing to the world. Mother gleefully propelled me round to show me off to a neighbour who was a model and who gave me a handbag, which I was forever losing in the weeks to come.

My first day at work saw me tottering along the cinder path to the station on my high heels. My pencil skirt restricted my stride and I had a stupid Peter Pan collar with a tie. Last week I was at school, this week I was about to board a train, then a bus, and go to work.

It was like being in a swarm of ants: hundreds of people outside the huge factory all cramming to get inside to clock in on time. Trying to find the card with my name and number on was hard and someone showed me how to put the card in the machine and pull down the handle, which then printed the time of my arrival to start work. One minute late, and fifteen minutes' pay was docked from your wages. So many people were crammed into the corridors, pushing and shoving, trying to get to their assembly lines in the factory.

I finally located the RDDO, the Radio Design Drawing Office. It was quiet in here. Draughtsmen, perched on high stools, nodded as I went into the inner sanctum of the boss's glass box office. I felt very shy and my face had gone hot and red with nerves. My skirt slid up above my knees as I sat down, my tits stuck out a mile, aided by my cotton wool padding, and my handbag clattered to the floor. I was a nervous wreck!

It was one week before Christmas 1955. The boss, Mr S, was nice; his evil sidekick – his secretary – was less so. It was to her that I was assigned, to do every job that she put in my path. I became the office runner, sometimes covering miles each day carrying memos and heavy bits of machinery to all parts of the factory. I would pass rows of women soldering television parts together. Wearing overalls, they would snigger at me as I passed in my stupid office outfit and men would wolf whistle and make rude comments and signs.

One part of this factory had giant machines that crashed down, cutting out metal parts. The ground shook as I passed, and it was deafening. I had to deliver all my items to various offices dotted around the factory. Each item I would have to write the name on and one day, to save time, I just wrote the surname and nearly got the sack because I had not put 'Mr' in front of them! Some offices could only be reached by an open wooden staircase far above the factory floor and the men would be waiting underneath to get a view up my skirt. I was barely fifteen years old and was excruciatingly embarrassed. I was supposed to become a tracer, doing circuit diagrams, but instead I was the office dogsbody and only found solace in the ladies' toilet, where no one could find me.

One day a nice lady came to work in the office and showed me how to do work developing the films of the drawings in the dark room. This I quite enjoyed, away from the boss's secretary. I got quite good at it, fascinated at how the images appeared in the trays of chemical solution and then pegging them up to dry by the red light. The finished product I then took to the print room, which stank of ammonia. The images would grow into huge diagrams at least a metre across. I would have to take these, thirty-six at a time, back to the office then fold, name, and deliver them to the thirty-six offices dotted around the vast factory. They were still warm from the print room as I folded them with the aid of a ruler to press down on the creases and I cut my fingers many times on that thick paper. Thirty-six pieces, plus the memos, were very heavy to cart around but the load lightened as the pile diminished on my deliveries. Some office bosses wouldn't even glance up as I placed them on a desk. Others had hoity-toity secretaries who looked down their noses at me and never said thank you. A few older bosses were kind and one always had a box of sweets, which were dispensed to anyone entering his domain.

We had to purchase a number of tickets off a roll for food to last the week: sixpence for a lunch in the factory canteen and tuppence halfpenny for a cheese roll and cup of tea for elevenses, which would come around mid-morning on a trolley, pushed by a jolly, elderly lady. I often missed this as the boss's secretary would deliberately send me out delivering drawings at that time.

The next trial was queuing up amongst hundreds of noisy, coarse factory workers, the language of which I had never heard before, to collect my lunch. "It's dinner, lovey. We don't call it *lunch*; that's for the poshies," I was told. The noise and oily machinery smell were overpowering but the food was good! By now, my feet were killing me in their unaccustomed high heels, so I filched my school plimsolls from home and wore them at work and no one seemed to notice.

Although the dinners were good, one day I got a griping bellyache and a bad headache, which I presumed was down to the different food and a noisy environment. It wasn't! I went to the sick bay when I had a dreadful shock discovering blood in my underwear. The kindly nurse explained that I had started my periods and fixed me up accordingly. The boss's secretary smirked and pointed at me through her glass office window, in between making eyes at the boss. I couldn't look at the draughtsmen in case they had been told. The lady from the dark room found me lots to do in there, although there was barely anything that really needed attention, and gave me a cup of tea and sympathy and let me sit in there for the rest of the day. My first week at work ended on Christmas Eve. I had become a woman.

Embarrassment and Shame

Christmas Day 1955 found me being treated as an outcast at home because I had 'become a woman'. I could hardly look at my father as we drove to my Nanna's house for the big annual lunch and get-together of relations. As it was clear I was not feeling too well, and a bit sick when presented with Christmas lunch, an auntie said, "What's up with Anne? Doesn't she feel well?"

With that my mother, who normally wouldn't dream of mentioning anything to do with bodily functions because it was 'not ladylike', came out with, "Oh, she's got her first period!"

There was a sudden hush, then shockwaves as everyone stopped eating; a moment suspended for what seemed like hours in time as I felt the flame of shame creep over my face. I ran upstairs and cried on Nanna's bed. It was awful. I couldn't go down and enjoy all the fun and games that we usually had in Nanna's house. No Christmas tea either. I just lay there until it got dark, no longer a girl, wishing I wasn't a bleeding woman!

* * * * *

Then it was 1956, a new year. I was getting worn out with so much travelling by train and bus to work and back, gulping my meal down at home and then having to wash and change into that

58

blasted ballroom gear and be propelled onto whichever dance floor my parents were going to that evening. It was okay for me to 'escape' to go to choir practice, so I decided to also join a local choral society, just to avoid one of these dances each week. It was a three-mile cycle ride away, mostly in the dark as we lived out in the rural area, minus street lights.

I enjoyed the singing. I was a natural alto and the first piece we did was Haydn's *Creation*. It was a bit heavy going but worth the effort to escape. One huge drawback was still not being allowed to have a house key, so I would shiver in the back garden until 11pm and the return of my parents. I was in an in-between world: old enough to work yet having no money, as I had to give it to my mother for housekeeping. I had hardly any possessions as my things would 'make the place look untidy'. I was not allowed to choose my own clothes or what to eat. I had a bedroom but it wasn't a sanctuary; the airing cupboard and immersion heater were by my bed and my mother would barge in after I'd gone to sleep and switch the light on full glare to put some ironing into the airing cupboard. My father would use getting some clean underwear from the cupboard as an excuse to come in for a 'fiddle'. The immersion would keep me awake, boiling away at night, and I was in an exclusion zone. I was an appendage that didn't go away. All I had was my sketch books and I was told I could keep these so long as I went out and drew the local wildlife. In other words, if I got out of the way!

By the end of March 1956, I had done my preliminary groundwork in Ferguson's office, seen colour TV for the first time in the laboratories and was about to be promoted. Hooray! I would no longer be working in the huge complex. I was sent to a small establishment about a mile away, sandwiched between two factories: Gor-Ray skirts on one side and Smiths Clocks on the other. A nice 1930s' building with spacious windows greeted me. It was quiet inside and I was led up a nicely designed stairway, which curved in a pleasing way and led into a sunny office with a good view. There were five tracers seated at their draughtsman's drawing boards and one place by the window was assigned for me. I had a set of special tracing tools and was put to practising for one month.

I had a natural aptitude because I was used to handling drawing materials. It wasn't easy, as I had to fill strange pens, which had screws that I had to adjust to the exact width of the lines I was tracing. The tracing was done on slippery blue linen over a complete circuit diagram of a TV set's innards. One mistake and two weeks' work would be ruined because it could not be rubbed out; sometimes you could scratch it out with a blade, but it showed. Rulers, compasses, pens, oh, I was in my element! The only thing missing was that, because it was so exacting, I couldn't do my own artistic thing. There was no room for error. I put my heart and soul into the work, but there always seems to be one office overseer who puts a spanner in the works. Or, in this case, accidentally-on-purpose spills a bottle of ink all over my drawing board. The other ladies were okay; they didn't say much all of the time I was there and when the weather was nice we would eat our lunchtime sandwiches sitting out on the flat roof. I made no friends. I was just an oddball concentrating on doing my work well and not saying much.

As spring turned into summer I hum-drummed my way into passing my tracer's exam up in London and returned to the tracing office minus any congratulations there or at home. I spent my evenings as far as possible from ballrooms, pursuing my singing and spending lots of time in the woods, painting and studying nature. Whitewebbs Park was a favourite haunt, where I would watch the water rats. Here, I found peace: a loner yet again.

I didn't really like working in an office, or with other women, but I excelled at what I had learnt and had become proficient to the point of perfection. There was an unannounced visit into the drawing office one day. It was a German professor. For some weeks now we had all been detailed to work on a different diagram, not a television circuit. We had the same piece of work to trace but no one knew what it was. I thought it might be a radio of some sort as it had the kind of valves that I had seen when my father built one.

The professor asked us to leave our work and stand against the wall and I jokingly said, "Is this a firing squad?" which didn't go down too well, with him being German and WWII still a recent memory. He wore a monocle and inspected everyone's work. Round and round he went. Finally, he turned to the person in charge, the office overseer, and walked over to my drawing board saying, "Zeese one!"

Gosh, what had I done? I was taken into another room and learnt that my work had been chosen as being the best. And so I spent two weeks at the Hawker Siddeley Aircraft factory in Hatfield, locked in a room doing secret work, tracing, for this lovely German, who was an absolute gentleman, consigning my thoughts about Germans being horrible to my mental dustbin![4]

I was driven there every day in a chauffeured car and had to get the parents' permission as I was under the age of twenty-one. The people I met at Hawker Siddeley were so nice. At the end of my time there the professor was so pleased with my work that he asked my father's permission to take me to dine out at the Savoy in London as a thank you. I had such a wonderful time; it was all gold and glittering and as we stopped on the way back home after such an amazing experience I thought he was going to do something. But, oh no, it wasn't like that at all! He thanked me for work well done and handed me an envelope to be opened later on the condition that I promised to tell no one of the contents. Intrigued, I promised. As we drew up outside my home

---

[4] Publishers note: It took people a very long time to overcome years of propaganda telling them that Germans were evil. I know of one Methodist lady who had two German pastors at her church, one after the other, before finally, sometime in the 1970s, she realised and stopped hating Germans.

all the neighbours' curtains were twitching, and I was walking on air.

That envelope, which contained three £50 notes, never left the inside of my vest for weeks. I only earned £2 a week and didn't tell anyone of my windfall. It became a problem concealing it but to open another post office or bank account whilst under twenty-one needed a parent or guardian's signature.

Returning to the drawing office after my two weeks' absence I was met with a hostile reception. The least experienced person had been chosen for that special job. The office overseer made my life hell because she hadn't been chosen. It seemed everyone had ganged up on me and 'sent me to Coventry'. Shunned, dejected, I decided it was time to move on, out of the confines of an office, the exacting work with no artistic leeway, and the restriction of heels, handbags, and haute couture.

"Our child! Our daughter! Daughter of a white-collar worker! How could you, without asking our permission?"

Oh yes, I only went and got a job five minutes' walk away in the local market garden and nursery, where my friend, June, from the choir worked on Saturday mornings.

"Working on the land! Have you taken leave of your senses? Not that you had any, anyway. There's no future in that."

Well there was, for a while anyway. I really loved the things I did at the nursery. The smell of the greenhouses full of carnations, where I learnt to take cuttings and watched them grow under my care. Every Friday would be spent cutting, packing, and labelling the carnations into large wooden boxes lined with tissue paper. I graded the flowers, becoming expert at the job, and wheeled the finished boxes of carnations on a barrow to the railway station to be sent to Spitalfields Market by train.

I was tanned, fit, in shorts and shirt and hardly able to conceal a smirk as my other choir friends got onto the train all poshed up to work in the city. They cast some jealous glances at me, with my laid-back lifestyle. At work, we were always singing; it echoed beautifully in the greenhouses. I was disbudding, watering, cutting. I was being trusted to work on my own initiative and felt proud of my achievements. The work was varied and interesting. Out in the fields, I was cutting dahlias and chrysanths or, when the weather was bad, there were tomatoes and cucumbers and geraniums to see to in the smaller low greenhouses.

Tea break was a welcome relief. The boss and his 'woman friend' provided all the food and drink in a dark but cosy shack where we would have a good laugh. There was a very old gardener who had a permanent drip on the end of his nose, which used to seep down into his tweed jacket. He even wore a tie!

The banter between this old man and the young Boy was highly amusing but the Boy was more than a little bit creepy. He was the son of a local stud owner, and he took it upon himself to show me what happened at his father's stud as we sat outside the far end of a very hot greenhouse to get some air. With his jeans undone he fiddled about for some time and then all this white stuff came out. I didn't understand what I was seeing but I thought it was very rude and revolting. I kept out of his way after that. I had been really enjoying my new job until he came along.

As summer rolled into autumn my boss sent me on a floristry diploma course as my artistic flair with flowers had bloomed, literally. I was doing a 48-hour working week and had to take a change of clothes to get into after leaving work, get on the train and gobble down some sandwiches whilst travelling, get a bus, then another train to get to Tottenham Technical College by 7pm. Two hours were spent learning horticulture. The following evening was learning the actual floristry: how to make buttonholes, wreaths and bouquets and which wires to use. We had to pull apart seven roses and then wire each petal on the thinnest of wires, then wire all the petals together to form one complete rose. The same method was used with hyacinths, picking off all the individual flowers. I loved it and those evenings kept me away from the blasted ballrooms but still I had no house key and had to wait for the parents to come home at around 11:30pm. I started work at 7:30am and had a job to wake up in time before my father pulled all the bedclothes off me and tried to perform his jiggling act. I was still an innocent; I didn't know what this 'thing' was for, but it revolted me, and I knew that it was rude.

My mother wasn't keen on my coming home for a midday snack. My overalls and boots were the complete opposite of her fancy ballgowns and dance shoes. I had to go into the garage and remove my work gear, standing on newspaper so as not to soil the garage floor, then hose myself down in the courtyard before entering the home. But I had a plan to get her to quite like me coming home in my lunch hour. The boss at work put out seconds for us to take home. There would be misshapen tomatoes, cucumbers, vegetables and crooked bedding plants but most of all lots of 'shorts', that is carnations that had weak or damaged stems. So, I would bring these things home, all above board, and she liked all this extra stuff which eked out the housekeeping. She made lovely arrangements with the flowers, as we were also given dahlias and chrysanths.

As the autumn of 1956 progressed, there being no lighting at work, I had to leave work as it got dark, However, the boss didn't deduct any wages for shorter hours. He was a good man, with a wicked Irish sense of humour, who one day had us in fits of laughter telling us about a glazier that had fallen through a greenhouse roof and had landed on his backside. He had to be carted off in an ambulance lying face down because his buttocks were full of glass splinters; I don't suppose there was much laughter at the time.

My sixteenth birthday, on 30 November that year, had passed without comment at home but, upon arriving at the nursery, the boss and his lady friend took me into our lunch shack and there was a beautiful birthday cake she had made. They lit the candles at tea break and made me feel so special and wanted. I was valued not only for my work but for me as a person. Here, I was not put down or ridiculed. A parcel on the table revealed a complete new set of work clothes and boots. It didn't matter that they were ex-War Department from the Women's Land Army. They said that in future I could leave my shirt and overalls with them every Saturday to be laundered now that I had a spare set. They knew of the difficulties I faced at home, where my clothes were handled with distaste, and the reluctance of my mother to wash them. She wouldn't send them to the laundry either and didn't want the neighbours to see working class gear on the washing line.

The old gardener gave me a special horticultural penknife, saying in his taciturn way, "Well I think you could do with one as you *do* work, sometimes!"

There was an envelope beside my birthday cake and the boss said to be careful in opening it in case I fainted away with shock and that I had better sit down. It was two weeks' wages and a notice to say that as I had reached sixteen I had been given a rise. I now earned the princely sum of two pounds, seven shillings and sixpence a week! The trouble was, though, I had to hand my wage packet over to my parents, unopened, every week. I had no say in clothes or shoes and had to ask for money for my fares to the floristry course and for the collection plate at church on Sundays. From that day, when I became sixteen, the boss and his lady would give me five shillings a week extra, in cash, on a Saturday morning. Saturdays were great; the boss gave me the special job of cutting the finest red carnations every week for a local florist. They had to be extra special and three dozen were always selected. I think this is where my five shillings came from as I was told not to mention the extra cash at home. What a kind boss I had. He worked hard with fun and vigour, with his lady friend looking after our tea breaks and his meals. He was thoughtful and generous, squat, with bowed legs and outsized wellingtons. He had unruly curly hair, a permanent red face, which always bore a grin, and mischievous twinkly Irish eyes. He made us all laugh and it was a pleasure to work for him.

We worked very hard sometimes, especially in that winter of 1956, including heavy digging, washing clay pots and cleaning the greenhouse glass. Sterilising the soil was also a heavy task, as was stoking the boilers with coke. I learnt to use the rotavator inside the greenhouse. Stones would fly up and hit the glass, making me jump. I used to light nicotine cones to burn overnight to fumigate all the bugs in the greenhouse. Turning the manure heap was another winter job. Oh, how it steamed in the cold air! One morning, I arrived to find that, overnight, mice had eaten five thousand carnation flowers. That was three years' work lost in one fell swoop. The worst aspect of this job was going to the loo. It was in a solitary hut, so everyone knew where you were going. There was no flush; it was a chemical bin that you couldn't sit down on because the Boy was supposed to empty it every week and didn't get round to it. Consequently, all the poo piled up in a mound. It was very difficult when wearing bib and brace overalls and one day the brace bit fell down into the muck and I was stuck ponging until home time.

Yes, Saturdays were special as the boss would drive off into town with his lady in their open-topped green Riley and return with a week's shopping and a special treat for us at break time: delicious crusty cheese rolls and fruit cake, plus our wages and a bunch of flowers each. I'd never met with such kindness and I was very happy at work.

The winter of 1956-57 was bad and work was hard, especially keeping up the stoking. I would sit on the hot water pipes in the greenhouse and occasionally I had to pull out a wooden peg in the pipes if they got too near boiling point, to let off pressure. Water would come out, useful for warming hands on a cold day, but on one occasion I lost the wooden peg as it shot away into the soil. It was a job to find it and the water was dribbling away. I found a twig as a temporary measure and told the boss what I had done. He wasn't cross; we just all searched the area together until we found the wooden peg and put it back.

Spring of 1957 was spent sowing seeds and pricking out seedlings. I was still going on the floristry course and I was put onto making wreaths at work for the florist who came on a Saturday for his red carnations. He was so pleased with my work that he offered me a job at much higher wages, which I refused as I was so happy where I was.

Then came the summer of 1957. Firstly, I caught German measles, which was going around the choir at church. Being older, it made me very ill. My boss visited me with some flowers and didn't get a good reception. "I wonder what he is after," was the unkind remark from the parents. I never even had the flowers in my bedroom. Then, during the heat of that summer, I got sunstroke, despite wearing a hat all day out in the field. I collapsed in the packing shed, hit my head on a carnation bucket and woke up in the boss's car being driven home. Oh, I felt so ill and sick and I was a great inconvenience, not to him but to my mother, who had to look after me. I had upset her routine. Feeling isolated and unwanted, I was left alone in the bedroom just as I had been in my younger days. The warning bells started ringing. I just knew my lovely job was too good to last. The doctor said I was to rest in bed for a week on light food, egg custard and barley water.

Mother wore a permanent frown as she thrust a tray of sustenance at me. She then departed and I could hear the sewing machine going most of the day, creating yet another ballroom masterpiece. With nothing in my bedroom but a Bible, poetry book, and pencils and paper, I had nothing to do except draw and write, but I was too tired and nauseated and dead worried in case I had lost my job.

I missed being at work with the plants and people I truly loved. They cared about me. Where was the boss? He came to see me last time; why didn't he ring up as he had before?

At last the doctor signed me off as fit to return to work but I never did. I was devastated.

"If that's what working on the land does to you, you are not going back there. You will find something more suited to the daughter of a white-collar worker, especially as your father will be the next mayor."

It was like descending in a lift: my stomach sank. My life was in pieces.

"There's no going back!" Well she was wrong there: I secretly visited the boss and his lady. They told me they had both come to see me whilst I was ill, and they had phoned to see how I was. I was told none of this by my parents. The boss said they did want me back but, as I was under twenty-one, he and I had no say in the matter and I had to do as my parents dictated.

So I was left minus a job. The big snag for me was that to continue my floristry course I had to be employed in horticulture or in a florist's shop. I had to be quick to find a solution that didn't land me up in an office job, considered more suitable for me by the parents. I loved working outdoors and in the greenhouse, loved the miracle of watching things growing. The course had already been financed by the boss and he wanted me to complete it, even though I wasn't in his employment anymore. How gracious of him.

I quickly found a job seven miles away, at a florist's shop on a busy street, and had to cycle there and back in all weathers. I was promised all sorts of money and promotions, but it quickly became clear that I was less than a junior, I was a general dogsbody, making coffee for the woman in charge. She had hers made with all milk; the rest of us had it made with hot water. One day I let the milk boil over and it stank the shop out.

This woman made me cycle into work at 6:30am to haul in sacks of frozen sphagnum moss, which I had to prise apart with my bare hands to make it workable, for wreath bases. She was so ingratiating to the customers, simpering and grovelling, catering to their every whim. She didn't want me to serve or even be seen by them. The other staff members were under her thumb and not nice to me either.

I was supposed to be gaining work experience for my diploma and had to take a wreath or sheath to college that I had made in the shop to my own design. I did make one and it was fantastic, in purple and yellow spring flowers – iris, tulips and daffodils – and it was on the cool floor of the shop having been sprayed prior to my taking it to the college after work. A customer came in, saw it, and bought it. That awful woman let the customer think she had made it, not me. She even charged me for the flowers I had used, and I was left with no permission or time to make another one. She accidentally-on-purpose knocked over a bucket of water and then handed me a mop. My tears dropped down into the water as I mopped it up.

One day, as she wasn't there, the staff let me make some more wreaths, which turned out well. I also wrote the messages to be wired onto the wreaths. Then, as a final touch, I was told to spray them. The cruel staff fell about laughing as all the ink ran on the messages. It was a deliberate ploy, as they obviously knew that the boss would be returning at that point and would go mad at what I had done.

Cycling in all weathers to the shop was a challenge as trousers were forbidden in those days and I would get wet and sore between my legs from the rain, the hard saddle and soaked skirt. One day I went to a local workmen's café for lunch. Steak and kidney pudding and veg was a shilling and sixpence and a pudding was just another sixpence. It was so cosy and warm in there and I didn't want to go back to the shop. I sat there for ages and pondered my fate. My finals for my diploma were imminent but I couldn't stick the job any longer. But what else could I do?

Suddenly, amongst all those workmen in the café, I broke down and cried. The café became a fuzzy buzz and the workmen gathered round. The café owner gave me a drink and one kind workman got out of me what had happened. He said he would sort it out and to go with him back to the shop. He sorted it all right; he told the woman off and I got instant dismissal. She wouldn't let me collect my bike, which was out the back, and I didn't get my wages. The workman gave me a lift to the college in his van and gave me some money to be going on with. I never saw him again. I had to tell college what had happened. Fortunately, I didn't lose my place; I took my finals a week before Christmas 1957.

I was now seventeen and minus a bike, which I told the parents had been stolen, and also minus a job, which I told them had ended because I had taken my final exam and was no longer needed at the shop because of this.

Christmas at home was the usual squeaky-clean, sterile, loveless, 'mustn't mess the place up with decorations' affair. No Christmas dinner, as it creates too much mess, so they went out to lunch with their dance cronies instead. I did get a present from them. It was a book on The Facts of Life, containing weird drawings and shocking descriptions. Did they really do that? No wonder I felt a misfit and not wanted! How disgusting. Would my father now start leaping into bed with me after all of his weird antics? Is this what it was all leading up to? I shuddered at the thought. So that was what the Boy at the nursery was up to that day out the back, showing me what happened at his father's horse stud.

I had a lovely Christmas with the church choir. We all clambered on the back of an open-topped lorry in our maroon cassocks and white surplices with the processional cross and went singing around the neighbourhood. The pubs were generous and fed us with hot roast potatoes. The climax was singing in the hospital wards as we went around with lanterns. Then we had the choir party. Oh, how happy I was, in a world that my parents never entered. I rang the carillon bells to bring in the new year of 1958 and we had a beautiful service. I loved the church and singing; at least it was one constant running through my life.

My friend June and I earned ourselves some extra money during the new year celebrations; a choir member got married and had their wedding reception in the church hall and they wanted two washer-uppers. It went on all afternoon and into the evening and we collected all the plates and glasses, some of which still had champagne or wine in them. We had never had this forbidden thing before, so we decided to give it a try. We were well and truly pickled by the time everything was cleared away. We felt so happy, it seemed a shame we had to go home! I kept a scarf round my face and mouth when I got home and said I'd worked so hard I had a headache and needed to go to bed.

"Not before you've had your cocoa!" Oh yuck. Down it quick and make my escape!

The following week, my exam results arrived. Typically, I was not allowed to open the envelope despite it being addressed to me. I had passed with distinction. I had crammed three years' study into just over one year and I was now a fully qualified florist.

But my life took a different turn, away from the flowers and plants that I loved, as my parents found me a job which I had to take. It was at a private veterinary practice in a well-to-do area. This was better than an office and I soon got into the swing of things by burning the veterinary swabs and instruments on top of the gas stove; I was supposed to be sterilising them but forgot to put the water in! The smell was awful as it went through the surgery and upstairs into the bedrooms. The kitchen was a black disaster area with bits of charred lint drifting in the air and settling into cups of coffee. I wondered how many people got sacked on their first day in a job; I surely must be one of them! To my surprise, the vet gave me a white coat and said I was to assist at an operation. He said assistants usually passed out the first time and not to be surprised if I found myself on the floor. Wow!

But I didn't pass out, it was too interesting, and I passed him the correct instruments, which were lined up in order. I was fascinated. He was spaying a cat. I cleared up afterwards and nursed the cat while it recovered. I learnt how to give the anaesthetic in next to no time and seemed to have a special gift for helping the animals but I was very nervous answering the phone and dealing with the appointments book and also some of the hoity-toity clients who would look down their noses at me. The surgery was in the front room of a large private house and Jaguars and Rolls Royce cars were the normal means of transport for the clients.

Despite the kindness of the vet and his wife, and the enjoyment I found in this interesting job, my mind was hankering after my time at the nursery. I missed my old job and the happy times there but, as was said before, there was no going back and I just had to get on with my veterinary assistant job.

Of course, my parents notched this job up in front of their ballroom cronies. I had to sit there and listen as they gloated about my top professional job and the wealthy clients. Yes, I had to go back to those dreaded dances of a night as my diploma course had come to an end and I couldn't escape to the college of an evening. Eventually I invented fake choir practices and would sit in the church porch with my friend June to pass the time away.

Chapter 5 : A Brief Stint for Queen and Country

A month after starting at the vets I happened to mention to my father that an assessor had been at my place of work with an independent stock take. Being a chief auditor for local government he said it sounded bad and it was. Next day I had a week's notice as the vet practice was closing down. There was no money to pay my wages and I had to pay my parents, but with what?

Hearing rumours of the council where Father worked wanting office clerks, I got hold of the veterinary magazine and found a job in the ads section that would keep me out of a dreaded office career. But no, the parents had different ideas. I was to join the WRNS, the Women's Royal Naval Service, affectionately known as the Wrens.

Unwanted, I was bundled off to the London headquarters for a medical and an assessment as to what branch of the service I would be suitable in for training. I passed the medical and would be learning cinematography and deciphering reconnaissance photos. But not yet: I had to return home and await a call to join up.

During this wait, one of my church choir friends was having a twenty-first birthday party and, as she was our neighbour, we were all invited. My mother gave me some of my money back to buy a dress. It was lovely and really suited me; cream with pink and red roses all over it. Such a good fit and style. I felt happy in it and showed my mother. On the day of the party we got ready and imagine my shock when my mother appeared in an identical dress! She'd seen how good it looked on me and went out to get one for herself, telling me to wear something else. I refused and we drove to the church hall for the party. I felt so embarrassed as we left our coats in the ladies' cloakroom and people were eyeing us up and down. I told my mother I would catch up with her in the hall as I wanted to use the loo first.

I didn't catch up at all. I escaped out into the freezing dark night and walked three miles to the cinema. I sat watching I don't know what, but I was seething inside. I had been reckless in running off; I had no plan and I couldn't and didn't want to go back home. I got some fish and chips after the show, but they choked me up.

It was cold, almost midnight, as I sat by the war memorial in Enfield in a thin dress and a stole, clutching my handbag. The street lights went out and it was a long walk home in high heels through the country lanes. What would be my reception when I got back? Behind the fridge, Father still kept a cane, which was used on my bottom even though I was seventeen. It was now becoming foggy as well as cold and damp. Then headlights appeared, slowly, through the gloom. It was my father out looking for me.

"Come on, jump in, we're going home. How are you?"

"Got a headache," I replied.

We drove home in silence and at 1am he made me a cup of cocoa and gave me some aspirin and said, "Don't worry about what your mother will say; I've fixed it."

I never heard a word from her about what had happened, and we carried on as normal. Inside, though, I was seething and had to explain to my friend why I had missed her party.

Things went from bad to worse and, as I would be leaving home to join the Wrens, all sorts of sarcastic comments came my way, with the 'Kipper Feet' remark rearing its head again.

"I hope you take those awful shoes; we're fed up with seeing them, Kipper Feet," and, "Marching will soon cure your sloppy walk," and, "You'll have to toe the line or be up on a charge!"

The parents made it obvious they would be glad to see the back of me and get on with their ballroom balls-ups and mayoral duties.

How did I feel about leaving to venture into the unknown? Mixed emotions, really. I would miss the church choir, which had supported me through bad times. I would miss the vicar, who loved us all, and the organist. And I would miss the spiritual comfort and doing the altar flowers every week.

The day finally came for me to leave and no one saw me off at the station. I had a small cardboard suitcase containing a few essentials and had to find my own way when I got to Kings Cross. I had to find Paddington Station and I had never gone across London on the tube alone. I had a travel warrant, which helped as once that was seen I was pointed in the right direction. I was on my way to HMS Dauntless, the training establishment for Wrens. It was at Burghfield, near Reading, and was known as a Stone Frigate. There were several nervous-looking girls on the train, and I guessed where they were going! At Reading station we were met by Wren officers and told to jump up into the back of a lorry and that it would be the first and last time that an officer would ever be carrying a case for us! The cases were dumped in a trailer. The blind was rolled down on the back of the lorry and we could not see where we were going. We sat on hard benches on either side of the small vehicle.

Upon arrival at the camp, known by residents simply as 'the ship', we were taken into the mess for a meal, given instructions and assigned to various huts with our newly issued kit. Black stockings – ugh! And 'blackouts', long-legged navy bloomers.

When the gussets wore out, we were told, you cut a big hole, put your head through and used the knicker legs as sleeves so you then had a sweater! We had navy blue overalls, we probationer Wrens, for six weeks before passing out. That first night lots of girls were sobbing after 10:30 lights out. I wasn't. I just didn't know what to think. I felt cast off, abandoned. I had to make the best of a bad job. I was not used to being with a lot of girls and once again the past caught up with me in my head. Me, a loner, an only child, an individualist doing my own thing, liking the quiet and peaceful life, how would I cope?

I awoke to the 6:30am reveille when a bugle call, known as the 'bugger call', roused us to stand, bleary eyed, to attention as the third officer made sure that all were on their feet. Thirty minutes for bathroom ablutions and getting into our naval kit, then off to the cookhouse for a massive breakfast, which I ate with gusto, although some girls were looking wan and sick. It didn't last long as we were soon learning drill and marching to some rousing music. Oh, how I loved that! The Girls' Life Brigade stood me in good stead now as I knew exactly what to do. There was a white ensign on a pole and a painted line in a large area around the base known as the quarter deck. We had to salute the quarter deck each time we crossed the painted line, even if we were on our own on the way to somewhere. An officer would pounce out of nowhere if one failed!

I really got stuck into the marching and excelled on the running track. Every weekend, people got letters from home. I didn't. I was out of sight and out of mind. One evening I took 'shore leave' and left the camp on a naval bike, black with number 13 painted in white on the mudguard. I had to be back 'on board' at 9pm. I happily rode around the countryside, enjoying my freedom, when I suddenly got punctures in both tyres. I walked back, was put on a charge for being late and the following day had to do fatigues, cleaning the officers' toilets, as a punishment. We had done a fire drill the previous day and were told to drop whatever we were doing if it went off and to muster at various points. I was applying thick polish to the wooden toilet seats when the alarm went off and, as instructed, I left everything. Later, I was hauled up to the officers' mess and told off because an officer had sat down on the toilet and had promptly slid off onto the floor with a bottom full of polish. Oh, how I laughed to myself!

We had exercise books to keep vital notes in and over the weeks these got dog-eared and creased. There was a cure for this in the laundry room: we passed the books through the mangle and flattened them out. The food at the camp was good, we were fit and our division (Victory Division) lived up to its name and won the Probationers' Cup. All the parents and families came to our passing out parade, except mine of course, and we looked and felt proud.

I flew to the base in Malta, my first posting, where my job was to take reconnaissance photos. It was solitary, working in the dark room, which suited me. I also put films together, splicing and joining them as I had learnt from watching my father, a prize-winning amateur cinematographer. I put together film shows for a few admirals, gathered in the dark musty rooms, shows of various ships' parts and past arenas of war and divers planting limpet mines on ships' hulls. I found the work absorbing and intriguing and time flew by.

I was doing well but finding it hard to join in with the other girls when back in our huts. My bed and cabinet were always the best turned out on daily inspection. Our bedspreads had an anchor design in blue weave and woe betide if it was found to be the wrong way up. There was a small NAAFI bar on site but, as I didn't drink or smoke, I didn't use it, preferring to read alone on my bed. I found the chapel to be a place of refuge, especially when I realised I had been dumped minus any letters from home. At least I was out of that situation but here I was in another controlled situation and I just had to think of it as being the lesser of the two evils.

Once a week we had to do physical training. Although I enjoyed the athletics and cross-country running, I never enjoyed the rope climbing, parallel bars or the vaulting horse.

The worst piece of equipment for me was the buck. It had no handle; you just ran up at speed and leap-frogged over it. An officer was supposed to stand either side of the landing mat, just in case you misjudged the jump. Well I did misjudge it, just as the officers had turned away, and I landed on my back in a heap of agony. I was carted off to sick bay and then off to the Royal Naval Hospital at Chatham, where I was put through painful tests. Meanwhile I was given work to do in the dark room and gave film shows in the mess, but it was very painful. Eventually, after x-rays revealed a cracked vertebra I was given a letter. I was invalided out, and on my way home.

It rained all the way, my tears joined the weather and my cardboard suitcase became a soggy mess. Worse, my parents had been sent a telegram to say I was returning on a particular train, but they did not even meet me at the station. They had been glad to get rid of me, while the navy had welcomed me with open arms. But now I was injured, they got shot of me without any thanks and here I was, returning to my so-called home a dismal failure and no one to greet me.

Ringing the front door bell I was met with, "Oh it's you. I suppose you expect us to put you up for the night!"

My back was hurting, and I just wanted to lie down but my bedroom had been turned into a sewing room. I spent the night on a camp bed in the living room.

Things were grim. With nowhere else to go, I kept my painful hospital appointments every week, doing physio. At last, a few months later, I was signed off. The parents were so ashamed of me, saying they were hoping to see a smart Wren in naval uniform coming home on leave (for all the neighbours to see) and I had let them down.

An Exciting New Job

Undeterred, I looked through the *Veterinary Record* and went for a job working for the PDSA. I travelled by train and trolley bus to North Finchley and worked in the clinic in the High Road. It was demanding work, with long irregular hours and low pay, but I loved it.

Being a charity meant that the very poor could only pay by donation and sometimes not at all. There was no finesse in this clinic. It was in vast contrast to the private posh vets I worked in previously. There wasn't much money to buy up-to-date equipment. Animals were put to sleep in a box which had a rag dipped in chloroform hanging inside it. It was heart rending, watching a mother cat and her new-born kittens running and pawing on the spot until she finally collapsed inside that box. Instruments and sutures were boiled in a dish on a tiny gas ring. The bodies of animals were put in dustbins out the back and collected twice a week by a man with a huge sense of humour. He had to be like that, the job he was doing.

Through all this tragedy, love shone through. The ex-army vet who worked wonders with what little the charity provided was so dedicated and to see the joy on a child's face when his pet budgie had pulled through an operation against all the odds was ample reward.

We had no sophisticated machines or resuscitation drugs. It was manual, bringing back a cat or dog from the brink of death, swinging them through an arc in the air! We did have some laughs though. We were so busy that sometimes the queues went right round the waiting room and outside, down the street, as we worked a 12-hour day. We could only get a tea break by pinning a notice on the surgery door saying, "Operation in Progress", as we drank our tea, loudly rattling instruments into kidney dishes and swishing the taps on and off for effect. When finished, my vet, in white coat and deadpan face, would open the door and carry out a bundle covered in a white sheet and disappear into another room. There would be a deathly hush from all the people in the waiting room.

Sometimes we would have a locum visit from another clinic and one of them was a real joker. One day we fell victim to one of his outrageous hoax calls. He told us, in a voice we couldn't recognise, that a delivery had been left outside the clinic but that 'they' couldn't get in as the door was stuck. Of course, it was him messing about. So when someone rang up to say their cat had been run over by a steam roller and what should they do, my vet said, thinking it was the same joker, "Oh, hang it on the line to dry and when it's stiff, put it in a stout envelope and post it to us."

Five minutes later we had a call from head office about a complaint from someone who said they had been given some not very nice advice about their cat. It turned out that only the tip of its tail had been flattened!

There were many poor people and their pets, and it was rewarding to see folk so genuinely grateful. I had a great vet to work with; he had a wicked sense of humour and whilst travelling home together on the train, amongst the bowler hat, brolly and pinstripe trouser brigade, he would open up a veterinary magazine and pretend to study it, sitting opposite these city gents with their *Financial Times*, but with a picture of a gory operation on an opened-up cow or horse. I would sit there trying not to laugh, my stomach in stitches to see the men from the city looking like they were going to puke up! One day, in front of all the passengers on the trolley bus, he got out his stethoscope and placed it up and down my back, apparently listening intently. I just didn't know what he would get up to next.

Once a week I would have to take all the donations, which were in a locked PDSA box, to the bank to be opened by a clerk behind the counter. This was half a mile up the busy road, thronging with people. As a safety precaution against a mugging, my vet said to wear my PDSA uniform and to put the box inside a cat basket. Well, sometimes if we'd had an extra busy week it was mighty heavy and one passer-by on the street said to me, "Gosh missus, what kind of cat you got in there?" because I was struggling and leaning over to one side. Quick as a flash, I replied that it was heavily pregnant! Customers queuing at the bank would gawp in amazement to see a cat basket being handed over the counter.

It was my turn to gawp in amazement when I got home. I received £5 a week in wages, of which I handed over four pounds and ten shillings to my mother. I had to find my fares and food with what was left. I had to tell my mother that my fares had gone up and ask if she could take less off me, so that I could still get to work. The answer was no. What was I to do? I had found a rewarding job, working alongside a vet who performed miracles out of practically nothing, had a wicked sense of humour and was a travelling companion on the commute. That vet helped me for a while, brought sandwiches to work to save me buying a lunch and would get me a pork pie from the shop next door.

As Christmas approached, the bad weather came and my shoes leaked. I was getting the 'pity it's not your kipper feet shoes' jibe again. I took refuge in the church choir as we repeated our performance of previous years, out and about carolling. The parents were dancing and prancing and doing a demonstration of quadrilles at a nautical ball on Boxing Day and I was left at home to go to a party across the road at a neighbour's house. This was something I would live to regret for the next twenty-six years.

Chapter 6 : Out of the Frying Pan...

The party had dim lighting, lots of smooching and pop music, which I was never allowed to listen to at home. I was taken aback at what went on, right opposite where I lived. The parents would have a fit if they knew! As the evening wore on the cigarette smoke became a haze and the wine flowed. It was not my scene. A charming, well-dressed man came to my rescue and suggested we go outside for some air. We ended up walking around in the moonlight. We were both like fish out of water at the party. As I shivered in the frosty night air, he removed his jacket and placed it around my shoulders, and we chatted about our likes for classical music, art, books, and nature. As we stopped walking, he looked at me in that moonlight and cupped my face in his hands. I thought he was going to kiss me but instead he said I looked magical, like an elfin. As we strolled back he said he would phone me and arrange to meet again. I asked him to call on a certain evening as my parents didn't allow me to receive phone calls and I wasn't allowed to use the phone anyway.

I was moonstruck; someone actually liked me! On the pre-arranged night we spoke for ages on the phone but when the parents returned, they spotted that the handset had been placed down right-handed instead of left. My secret was out. They wanted to meet him before I was allowed to go out with him, so one Sunday teatime he was vetted and interviewed by the parents.

He was dressed to impress in an immaculate suit, white shirt and conservative tie, plus he worked in local government and was well spoken and good looking. He had my parents' approval.

They still dragged me away to the holiday camp at Croyde, where I met up with my dear friend 'T', the boy I hoped to marry someday. We had known each other since we were children and, now teenagers, we were serious about settling down in a couple of years. However, the idea was quashed by both sets of parents. Now I had a real boyfriend! He was suave and sophisticated, handsome and charming. He wined and dined me in expensive restaurants. We went to the ballet and theatre. I was swept off my feet. He never kissed me or tried to do anything wrong. He was an absolute gentleman, a cut above the rest and the fact that he worked in the town planning department suited the parents very well.

I was still working for the PDSA. My handsome boyfriend would meet me from work and whisk me away up to the West End to see a show and have a meal. I had to be home by 10pm so we used to miss the end of some shows, because I had to get an early train back. He gave me money for my fares so that I could keep my job. This was the life.

"What sort of engagement ring would you like?" he queried, only six months after we met. Was that a proposal of marriage? Yes! So Ken got my parents' consent, as I knew he would, because it would get me off their hands, and I now had an exit route out of all my misery at home. Ken's parents came to tea to meet my parents. They came by train, not owning a car. Black mark number one. They were clean but shabbily dressed minus fashion sense. Black mark number two. His father was a mere civil servant and his mother 'looked like a washerwoman', my mother thought. It was a stilted meeting, and the very worst thing was that they lived in a street of back-to-back terraced houses. "Just like Coronation Street on the telly," said the parents in disgust when we toured the area by car to show them where Ken lived.

Desperate to leave home, we set the wedding date for 2 January 1960, one year after our first meeting. My mother went soppy, taking me to Pearsons department store to get a veil and headdress and material for my dress, which she was going to make. It was a full six months before the wedding! I had no say in the choice of material or design of dress. She picked out a cheap basket weave cotton and chose a shirt-waister design pattern with a high collar. It was crap, but it was a means to an end. An old schoolfriend was to be my bridesmaid, much to the chagrin of my future sister-in-law, whom I didn't like. She was Ken's kid sister and very jealous. She caused me much grief.

I had no say in the details of the wedding reception, choice of cake, or guests. Not one of my friends was to be invited; it would all be ballroom cronies. I was nineteen on 30 November 1959 and my wedding day was only four weeks away.

No excitement, no build-up, not even a bath on my wedding day. I was never allowed one the whole of the six years I had lived in that house as I, "might make a mess." The only choice I had in my wedding was the flowers. I made a bouquet of fragrant mixed freesias and arranged pink carnations on the church altar the evening before.

The rain poured down all day. I felt and looked stupid in my mother's creation. My father embarrassed me on the drive to church in the big chauffeur-driven car by saying, "You'll be alright tonight, eh?" The sliding glass window that divided us from the chauffeur was open and I know that his ears twitched. I was completely down-dressed and my parents were stunningly turned out. It was as if they wanted to show me up in the worst way possible. I had no jewellery, no make-up, and horrid schoolgirl hair as I was never allowed to visit a stylist.

We progressed up the aisle and I felt a right twerp as people turned and saw me and I recognised the look of disappointment on their faces. Worse was when my fellow choristers saw me. We had all witnessed our singing friends getting married and having lovely weddings but smirks on some faces said it all.

The old organist kept making errors, my dear vicar was not looking his usual happy self and Ken kept making mistakes during the vows. My bridesmaid never turned up. She refused to be given a lift in my father's car. I wonder why… Job done and into the vestry, where Ken was heard to say, "Thank God that's over," in front of the vicar.

Next, the group photos in the pouring rain. My in-laws wore old gaberdine raincoats and plastic hats. My sister-in-law was messing about with a school friend she'd invited and making snide remarks like, "Who would want to be a bridesmaid anyway, with *this* lot!"

The reception in the church hall was a disaster. My new husband disappeared into the pub, the catering people forgot the soup and rolls and the wedding cake was half eaten when the photographer finally put in an appearance at the so-called happy couple cutting into it. He, also, had been in the pub. The hall was perishing cold and the fold-up chairs kept collapsing. The ballroom cronies were not impressed. When Ken and I finally left, the parents had tied my favourite shoes to the back of the getaway car, ridiculing me with shouts of, "Good riddance, Kipper Feet!"

We drove to see my grandparents in our wedding gear. Grandma was crippled but Grandpop stood outside his house in full wedding kit, complete with buttonhole, to welcome us indoors. He had a glass of champagne for us all and we had a toast. That night, in my new home, I took off my wedding clothes and removed my engagement ring – or so I thought. I had accidentally removed my wedding ring and it is considered unlucky ever to take it off once placed on your finger. Oh, how true a portent this turned out to be.

I gave up my job with the PDSA for two reasons: it was too costly and too far away. It was not the normal thing for a wife to go out to work, especially if her husband had a local government position. The husband had sole control of the purse strings and in my case I had to ask for housekeeping money. I had none of my own. For the first few months I was the dutiful wife. I cooked well, polished the floor on hands and knees and budgeted the housekeeping for food and sundries. I did everything correctly apart from one day when I ironed a new shirt with a too-hot iron. The shirt was made of this fanciful new material called nylon, something I just wasn't used to. I placed the iron on the lower front portion of the shirt, that tucks right over the crucial place in a man's anatomy. When I lifted the iron I was greeted with a complete iron-shaped hole and a stinking mass of melted nylon on the iron. I was in trouble, especially as the shirt was beyond repair and the hole kept getting caught up on that certain piece of anatomy. I couldn't help laughing though!

We had moved into a back-to-back house in the next road to my in-laws, having secured a mortgage. I had nothing to do with the financial side of things, so it came as a shock one day, when I was three months pregnant, to see my father-in-law on the doorstep asking me where the 'payment book' was. I knew nothing about this, or the fact that Ken had borrowed £500 from his father for the deposit on the house and not paid anything back at the supposed monthly terms into said payment book. So, six months in residence and no payments, but lots of wining and dining as the wife of a new Freemason, to be on his arm at the Mason's ladies' night and other functions that I did not enjoy. I didn't dare tackle him about it and kept the newly acquired knowledge to myself. My parents would have been horrified.

Ken stopped me from writing thank you letters to his relations which, as a new bride, was the correct thing to do when receiving wedding gifts. I soon found out that the bedroom suite, dining and kitchen furniture which he said were presents from his aunts, were in fact on hire purchase from a local store. And I wondered why they had given me dirty looks as I passed by – Ken had not made any repayments. The local corner shop also was a victim of his 'on tick' activities. I was trapped before I had even flown. Out of the frying pan, into the fire, as they say. My sister-in-law, that outrageous teenager, was so wicked; she pushed me down the stairs and I had a miscarriage and ended up in hospital.

I soldiered on, doing my duty as a wife around the house and in the bedroom. A few months later I was pregnant again. I gave birth to a boy, Philip. At last I had someone to really love, and who loved me back, I could tell. But in the meantime the bills were piling up and the shock of no mortgage repayments and Ken's County Court appearances lost him his job and killed my darling baby with pneumonia, as there was no money to keep the place warm or heat a bottle. We were given notice to quit by the building society and had to find somewhere fast at a cheap rent, out of the area so that no one would know who he was and what he owed. My in-laws paid for Philip's funeral and then distanced themselves from us.

From Bush Hill Park in Enfield we moved to a second floor flat in Luton, overlooking Richmond Park. I soon found out why the flat was so cheap: when winter came it was full of mould. The landlord wouldn't rectify it because of, yes, you've guessed it, unpaid rent. How I missed the open-air days of working outdoors at the nursery. So much had happened since then. Would life ever get mended?

Ken had got another job bringing in more money, but it meant that he had to commute to Westminster in London, from Luton. Still in local government, he had another job in town planning at Westminster City Council. By now the debts had mounted ever further and we were in danger of losing the flat. Yet again, a local corner shop had been duped by Ken as he had fags on tick on the way to the station and booze on tick on the way home. Seeing no other way out of this, he relented when I said I was going out to work again, because this time there was a rent-free cottage with the job. Plus, it had a large garden for growing vegetables.

So another move, this time to an idyllic spot on a country estate. I was responsible for looking after some large greenhouses containing tomato and cucumber plants, along with some smaller ones with cut flowers and carnations. In addition I had to wash about 300 eggs a day, but I was allowed to keep any cracked ones. I had free firewood and milk from the farm, if I remembered to put my milk container in the dairy on the way to work. I was so happy there as the estate owner, let's call him Sir X, was also a concert pianist who every year hired the Royal Albert Hall and gave his own concert the week after the last night of the Proms. It was my job to grow the flowers and arrange them at the hall for this prestigious event. All the estate staff were invited and for the weeks leading up to this I would hear Sir X practising on his piano as he lived opposite me and had all his windows open on those summer mornings. The music, the fragrance of cottage garden flowers and newly cut grass floated across the air.

I did my work well; dug the garden, fed the fire, harvested my own veg, helped on the home farm. Life was good. The winter of 1963 saw us frozen in for three months without water, so I carried some from the spring borehole at the farm and used a sledge to reach the shops a mile away. By now, Ken had got the sack for continued lateness and had got another job, working for an insurance company as a door-to-door collector. He had to have a drawstring purse to carry the collected cash! The insurance company obviously didn't know his background...

Having settled comfortably into the cottage and the job it was with astonishment that I received a letter of notice to quit. The cottage was needed for a farm labourer with a family. All the garden work, the decorating and pride I had in making this my forever home, gone. I never had any help from Ken to achieve this. In between work and homemaking I picked berries and made jam, along with chutney from the garden's harvest. Now I was to leave it all for the next person and move into a dreadful annexe at the home farm. Downstairs was uninhabitable as it had three-foot fungi growing out of the walls. The Rayburn was broken, as were the windows. Stairs were partly missing. Upstairs, the beams had dry rot and it was missing many floorboards too. What else could I do but move into this slum, if I wanted to keep my job. So all our stuff was moved on the tractor and we went to bed that night with rats and mice for company, running in and out of the spaces created by missing floorboards.

Determined not to let it get me down, I began painting and decorating upstairs, but the paper wouldn't hold as the walls were damp. I really tried to make a go of it but things came to a head one Sunday morning as I awoke to a loud bang, bang, bang on the front door, followed by a gruff voice shouting, "Police! Open up!"

Ken sat up in bed, instantly sweating and pale faced. "Pretend I'm not here," he said. Whatever could this be about? I went down the stairs, remembering to miss the rotten ones. There was the branch manager of the insurance company, alongside the police. As they came in, past the fungi sticking out of the walls, my suspicions were confirmed. Ken had stolen the money he had collected and, worse, the finger was also pointed at me. I honestly knew nothing, but I couldn't convince them. The money would have to be returned within 48 hours or it would be prison. This time, I was not going to help. Aid a thief? No way! Ken was visibly shaken and looked worse as the day went on.

The following morning I went to work as usual but returned within a few minutes. I had been given the sack and ordered to move out within a week. Ken had lost our home, my job, my pride and good character reference. He was by now looking so ill and in terrible pain, doubled up in bed, pale and sweaty. I got the farmer to have a look at him and shortly afterwards an ambulance took Ken away with a burst appendix. I was left to pick up the pieces and find somewhere to live.

I approached the vicar of the church I attended. He got me a flat over a shop in Hastings Street in the middle of Luton, on the proviso that I promised him we would not get into rent arrears as the landlord was his friend and this was a big favour. He also got some members of the congregation to help move our furniture. Just imagine my shame and horror as, when Ken's wardrobe door fell off, loads of used condoms spilled out onto the floor. I was never allowed to go into his wardrobe, it was kept locked, and I had no idea. I was mortified. I wished the floor would swallow me up and that the helpers had never witnessed this or the dreadful place I lived in. How could I ever go to church again?

I soon found another job with Luton Parks Department. It was brilliant, so varied and interesting. I would be planting bulbs on a roundabout one day or cutting a 400-yard hedge and doing topiary on another. I grew the flowers for the county cricket match and decorated the pavilion and tables as well as the mayor's parlour and banqueting room. Then I would be off in a lorry with a gang of workmen tending bedding plants around the borough. We would call into a workman's café for 'bread and drip' and a pint mug of tea. I was the only female and treated with respect. My clocking-on number was 99 and I had equal pay, very unusual in 1964.

I spent two weeks looking after the boating lake in Wardown Park and it was here that I became proficient at rowing and feathering the oars, and this led me to take up rowing on the river at Bedford.

I got promoted and put in charge of the floristry and design and created the town crest in flowers in the park. I loved the tool shed with its store, the smell, and oiling up all the garden implements and stacking them neatly away.

Ken was in hospital for seven weeks. I visited him each day whilst holding down my new job in the parks and redecorating the flat. I paid off all our debts. Life was ready to start all over again, new, the slate wiped clean.

Chapter 7: A New Beginning and a Dreadful End

The council offered its employees a 99 per cent mortgage. I hated the dark flat above the ever-noisy shop in the middle of Luton. Every time a customer went in or out of the shop a loud buzzer sounded, right up through our floor and then the door would bang. So, with hope in my heart and a secure job which I loved, it was decided to take advantage of the council's offer.

We got a house in Sundon Park on the then outskirts of Luton. Ken got a job at SKEFKO ball bearing company in the organisation and methods department. He couldn't even organise the proverbial piss-up in a brewery, let alone an office job! Still it was a start, a new venture. He started coming home later and later from work to dried-up dinners. "Just helped out behind the social club's bar," he would say. This got to become a daily habit and he often came home sloshed, but still able to push me around and demand his rights. The result was no protection and I was pregnant. That meant I would have to give up work. I carried on for as long as possible without telling anyone, but with the end of my employment there, our special mortgage privileges became defunct. Bills came in: rates, electricity, water, et cetera, and they went unpaid. Ken was arrested at work and taken to Bedford Jail for non-payment of rates. His father bailed him out and immediately had a heart attack and died.

When Ken came back, he went out one day ostensibly to find a job and was brought back in a police van, drunk. He'd lost his job at SKEFKO and no one would employ him without a reference.

My baby, Peter, was born at home on 9 June 1965, a perfect being. He seldom cried and was a good and lovely joy to have around. Perhaps things would get better now that we had a baby? Ken finally got a job selling encyclopaedias door-to-door. There was an area manager whom Ken had to pay £50 to start off as a deposit for the books. I didn't like the look of this oily character, who used to leer at me.

One afternoon Ken was out doing door-to-door. I was feeding the baby, splayed out on the couch, when in burst the area manager, brandishing a .410 shotgun. He pressed the end of it into my naked chest, demanding 'the money'.

"What money?" I quavered. It turned out he had lent Ken £2000 and he obviously thought that I knew about it. Well I thought my life was up and to protect my baby I put a cushion over him.

The safety catch was off and I wondered who was going to look after Peter when I was gone. Just then a vehicle drew up out in the road and the oily man left with the .410 hidden under a raincoat. Phew! That could have dried up my milk for weeks. But worse was to come. I didn't think that was possible, but apparently it was.

When Peter was three months old the electricity and water were cut off for non-payment. I had no advance warning that this would be happening, had seen no 'red' reminders. The man from the electricity company was so sorry. He kept apologising and looking at Peter and when the job was done he went away with a sorrowful heart, shaking his head.

Next day, the water board man came to cut off the water. He, too, was sad and told me to fill my bath and anything else and he would come back in half an hour. He wanted me to have at least some water to be going on with. I had a tank of goldfish and he helped me replenish some of the water there as well.

This was all a dreadful worry for me but worse was to come, oh yes.

At twelve noon the following day there came a loud banging on the front door. Imagine my horror: it was the bailiff! I was told to leave in one hour. I had seen this happening to people in television dramas, people being marched out of their homes with just their clothes, and now it was happening to me in real life. One suitcase is all I had, to pack the baby's requirements and my own. Where was Ken? We had no telephones or mobiles in those days. The bailiff changed the locks. He was more concerned about the goldfish in my tank and calling the RSPCA than what was to happen to me. The police came to witness the eviction and curtains twitched up and down this otherwise respectable neighbourhood.

I sat down on the wall outside what had been my home, where I had brought Peter into the world. I looked down at his sweet little face, fast asleep, oblivious to it all, and I wondered where it would all go from here. As the twitched curtains dropped back into place I saw Ken walking up the road.

A Bus to Nowhere

"What are we going to do, Ken?"

He said he didn't know but, as it started raining, we got on a bus to gain shelter.

"Where are we going?" I asked.

"Nowhere," he replied. "We'll just have to think of something."

We had a long time to think: the bus route terminated in St Albans. He left me in a park shelter near the abbey to go and find us somewhere to stay for the night. I was hungry and cold as it was now dark. I fed Peter and waited and waited into the night. Where was Ken?

As dawn rose behind the abbey I was thirsty as well as hungry. Peter had another feed but needed changing. It was getting urgent. Then Ken appeared, looking the worse for wear. He'd found a hotel for us to stay in. I wondered where he got the money from but kept quiet. Of course it *had* to be a posh hotel. Wine with dinner and "Yes, Sir, Madam…" at the white starched cloth dinner table. Even Peter had a special, created by the chef, of suitable food for one so tiny.

Next day I spent wandering round the abbey, which I knew well from previous visits with the church choir to sing at evensong there. Its coolness and balm comforted me as I wandered or sat, wondering and waiting for Ken to return with a solution to our housing crisis, hoping that he wouldn't return drunk. He had left me minus money all day so when he eventually returned I was ravenous and eagerly accepted the idea of returning to the hotel for a meal. I was fortunate that Peter was always so good throughout this difficult time and people cooed over him, telling us what a lovely couple we were. Little did they know the truth, as Ken then offered to buy a round of drinks and, when they had been consumed, it was, "Have another, old boy," and the cigars would light up and the evening drag on and the brandy go down.

There was nowhere I could go to escape this mess, definitely not back to my parents. You didn't just leave someone then; you made a vow before God in church for better or worse. Ken had gone to the Masons (I was always told off for not using their full title, Freemasons) and they helped. A job with a house was found in Leagrave Road, Luton. The job was in a huge factory office opposite the house. Oh, how my heart sank when I saw the terraced house fronting straight onto a busy main road. The factory smell, combined with the gasworks and coal yard was awful, and on top of that we had a 'greasy Joe's' café next door. The mainline railway rattled along behind all this and our house backed onto a timber yard that was sawing up wood all day.

It was a very dark house and even darker when the electricity was cut off. I used to wait all evening for closing time and Ken returning home. My only comfort was a starving stray cat who adopted me and whom I brought back to health, only to open the front door one morning to find him dead on my doorstep from a traffic accident. I was heartbroken.

I managed to grow some sweet peas and runner beans in the overgrown sooty patch at the rear of the house. Oh, what a delight! The fragrance was a change from all that mucky air. There was a kindly neighbour next door who wanted to chat, but I couldn't get involved with anyone or our truth would come out. She did pass a comment about the number of times she had seen candles in the evening so she might have guessed we were in dire straits. To avoid any prying I would scoot in and out at speed to put washing on the line. Even that got covered in soot.

Peter, unaware of all the mounting tensions, was now standing up in his box (we had no cot) and chuckling and laughing. When Ken said, "He needs a brother or sister to keep him company," I flatly refused. This urged him on as I resisted and he became highly excited. I had begun to hate that side of married life a long time ago; his boozy and fag-laden breath all over my face as he pumped away, purely for his own gratification. Where had the charming, handsome boyfriend gone? He waited until our wedding night and was tender and loving in those first few months. He was sunk in the squalor of the pub's alcoholic grip, where he made the landlords happy as, perched on his stool, they engaged in crass conversation across the bar.

Now here I was, on 12 September 1966, at knifepoint, enduring his unprotected advances. I remember the date because we had been to a wedding. That's when Matthew was conceived. I knitted baby clothes by candlelight and wondered, yet again, where do we go from here.

I spent the winter in the dark, minus heating, and the only water we had was caught off the outhouse roof in a bucket, or from the washbasin in the public toilet. Ken had the warmth of the pub; I felt fear and trepidation as my bump grew and Peter was trying to walk around by clinging onto various boxes and the few bits of furniture we had left. I remember listening to the news about the Aberfan disaster and how awful it was for those poor dead children in that school in Wales, and how I would have felt if one of them were mine. I loved Peter so much; I just couldn't imagine the horror of it.

I had no friends and didn't dare attend the maternity clinic for fear of all our 'truth' coming out, so it was a great worry when, at five months, I had bad pains and a show of blood. I couldn't go to bed much because I had Peter and there was no one I could call on for help. I was hoping that I wouldn't miscarry all alone, which I'm sure I nearly did when Ken came home and said he'd lost his job and the house with it. This time it was for taking booze to work and drinking on the job. I was staggered when he actually owned up to the real reason and he said I would have known soon enough as our neighbour's husband was his supervisor! She never told me that. So, she knew all along what was happening but always spoke kindly to me. Now I was too embarrassed to put my washing on the line and come face to face with her.

Here We Go Again

Another move, another town and a brand-new three-bedroomed 'house with the job' in Stevenage new town.

Too ashamed to register my records with a clinic, my waters broke and an ambulance took me to Lister Hospital in Hitchin where, on 21 April 1967, Matthew was born whilst a snowstorm raged outside. My mother-in-law looked after Peter, who by now was starting to talk and who was returned to me sporting a definite cockney accent, prefixing everything with, "Cor blimey!" Yes, my mother-in-law had thawed, now that she had a new grandkid. She had barely seen Peter growing as she had no car and lived far away. My dreaded sister-in-law now had one though and we went to stay at my mother-in-law's for a few days.

It was during this visit that I had a great shock. Ken and I shared a bed whilst Matthew and Peter slept in my mother-in-law's room. My sister-in-law had a bedroom all to herself. I left Ken in bed one morning when I went downstairs to get some baby clothes and prepare some food. As I had forgotten something I returned to the bedroom to find Ken and his sister 'at it' in the bed I had just left. They didn't see me, but I could even smell what they were doing and found the soiled men's handkerchief under the bed later. I kept this new-found knowledge to myself. No wonder she hated me if she was in love with Ken, her own brother!

They went out for a drink later in her flashy new sports car; she had only just passed her test! Her backcombed bouffant hair style didn't last long, her false eyelashes blew off in the wind and her transistor radio playing Elvis Presley woke the whole street that Saturday morning. I was left laughing and crying at the thought of having to make the best of a bad job, caring for and protecting my babies as becomes a devoted mum.

New Start in a New Town

The house was so new that the cement floor in the garage was still wet. Houses were going up all around us. We lived in Jessop Road, about two or three miles from the town centre. It was modern, concrete, and soulless. The shopping centre and church had not yet been built and I had a big second-hand pram that I used to get to the shops and laundrette in another district, four miles away.

It was hard work but that summer I built a garden in the tiny rubble-filled space at the back of our modern terraced house. The countryside was just about within walking distance. Peter went to playschool but Matthew was too young for that, so I used to carry him in a sling whilst cycling to the allotment I had managed to secure. Here, I turned a wilderness into a productive plot, single-handed. Some of the old codgers looked on in amazement as they leant on their forks to see a woman grafting with success. I sold lots of produce, as well as home-made jam and marmalade, to the mums at the playgroup. My winter sprouts were champion and my fingers froze as I picked them to sell at the Christmas Fair.

Ken was working at Taylor Instruments.

I joined a choral society and cross-country running club. The performance of Mozart's Mass in C was outstanding, being recorded in St George's church in Stevenage for the BBC and I won the seniors' cross-country annual event. I went to evening classes and gained O levels, because Ken said I was no good at anything academic and he had seven. He scoffed and said I'd never pass; well I did! But although I was doing all these things I never had a friend. I was a loner, happiest on the allotment. But of course these good things didn't last. As a ploy to make me drop my enjoyment of an evening, Ken got home later and later so I had no one to be with my little ones. I couldn't afford a babysitter so had to give up my new-found activities.

Handcuffs to Hell

The drinking escalated and Ken was sacked, yet again. I put up a fight as he tried to get me to have sex with him. I screamed and kicked. He then went into the little ones' bedrooms as they were sleeping and beat them up in a rage. He went out the next morning as if nothing had happened. He was always smartly dressed and courteous to everyone and no one would ever have believed what went on behind closed doors.

Standing there, bathing my children's wounds and bruises, I knew I needed help. But where to go? I would be in dreadful trouble if I revealed this to the outside world. My children were too tiny to report or even understand what had happened to them. I had no money to escape this trap so I would have to hold my head up and yet again use my inner strength as my life drifted from one crisis to another. But even worse than what had passed already was yet to come.

An ambulance and police car suddenly appeared and two women I had never seen before, both holding clipboards, entered my home. Ken had reported that *I* had beaten the children up and that I was of an unsound mind and these things he had relayed to the social workers who were here now, right before me. Of course, they were crying now, Peter and Matthew, their wounds glistening under the balm I had applied, a black eye swelling up and only halfway dressed. It looked bad. Then the social workers and police looked in the bedrooms and saw that all was dishevelled from the night before. They took my Peter and Matthew away, handcuffed me and I was led into the waiting ambulance – but not before I kneed one of the white coats so hard in the groin that he couldn't drive the vehicle! So his mate did the driving and the other did the cursing. Where was I going? Where was Ken in all this? Probably toasting his victory in the nearest boozer.

The journey seemed to last a lifetime. No one would tell me where I was going. Through the black windows of the ambulance I could just about make out that we were travelling north, away from Stevenage.

Why was I wearing *plastic* handcuffs? Ambulance men at that time wore navy blue or black uniforms and these had white coats. I started shivering as the journey ground on. I could just make out Letchworth Garden City in monochrome through the weird dark window, then out into countryside. Miles and miles of it, far beyond my explorations. My breasts ached. It was time for Matthew's feed. Where were they, Peter and Matthew? We pulled up.

"Where are we?" I asked.

"At the looney bin," they replied.

Even through all of this, my sense of humour prevailed and I couldn't suppress a giggle as I saw one of the white coats walking doubled up and clutching his balls. "She's dangerous," he stated to an orderly.

The Naked Truth

I had arrived at the Three Counties Hospital, a mental establishment. I was marched into a long, low hut and then into a side room. Two huge macho warders stripped me naked and forced me onto a hard examining couch, strapping my hands and feet so I could not move. The harsh light glared down on my leaking breasts and I was shivering with anxiety. They prodded me and put their fingers in places they shouldn't. They mocked me, leered and spoke right into my face so that I could smell their breath and sweat. They took my measurements.

"Shall we suck your titties, then?" and, "Don't bother to report us; no one will believe you, 'cause you're mental."

Handcuffed again, I was told I was going to have a nice bath before going to bed. Bed? It was only about 11am. The bath was a freezing cold shower. Oh, how they laughed as I danced around. Then the toilet, going whilst handcuffed, no door, no chain (in case you hanged yourself with it, I was later informed). I was propelled to a bed in a mixed sex ward full of people in other beds groaning, wailing, crying. I was put in one and given an injection I didn't want. The more I protested my innocence, the worse things became. Then blackness.

Awaking to the call of nature I felt strange but needed to go. As I stood up from the bed I promptly passed out. Then I was manhandled and thrown onto my bed again and told to stay there. I attempted yet again, and the same thing happened. I learnt from the other patients that we were injected with Largactil to lower our blood pressure, to make us faint, so that it would keep us in bed and save the staff a lot of work trying to contain us.

As I lay there I wondered what would happen to my kids, my lovely little garden and the allotment. They all needed me to tend to them. I wondered about my life, where had I gone wrong, where was I going. No one believed me... But I stopped myself worrying about it all just for the moment and told myself to be strong, no matter what, just take one step at a time, the here and now, deal with it, in the present. Surely my strength will carry me through. I've experienced so many setbacks; these must stand me in good stead. Yes, one step, one problem at a time. I shouldn't be here, but I will have to make the best of a bad job. I told myself this is the lowest point I can reach; somehow now the only way is up.

Next day we all queued up for breakfast, filing past a staff member holding a huge plastic bin from which we were allowed one jam sandwich. That was breakfast, lunch and tea; it never varied. The diet was appalling and so were our insides. Then the medication, queuing up again. We had to take what was given, force down some water and then open wide to make sure we had swallowed and not hidden the pills under our tongue. We were roughly handled, our heads being pulled back by our hair during this procedure.

At 10am I was marched as a 'newbie' to witness fellow patients having ECT, Electro Convulsive Therapy. This was shocking (excuse the pun). Electrodes were placed on the strapped-down patient's head, then the current was switched on, which sent them into convulsions, wetting and messing themselves. It was barbaric treatment, a torture chamber that was supposed to make you forget recent bad things. "This is what will happen to you soon, especially if you don't toe the line." Later these patients were walking, blank-faced zombies. What kind of hell was this, in 1967? I had to get out of here but how? Every door was locked. If I had not been mad coming in here I would be soon.

I was offered the chance to do occupational therapy. Knitting and sewing were not allowed because of the needles being prospective weapons. I got stuck in and made a mosaic table lamp and tray to match. I made a seagrass stool. Basketry drove me nuts, as did weaving, so I did painting instead, and astounded everyone with the landscapes and marine paintings finished in next to no time. The OT's report said that I was balanced, quiet and courteous and that in her opinion I was in the wrong place as I was able to apply my mind to the job in hand.

I was now segregated into a female hut, F11. My second week found me with no news of the outside world, and none given when I asked. It seemed I had been abandoned here. One morning we were lined up in pairs, handcuffed together and taken outside. There were other huts like ours dotted around the grounds of a huge Victorian mansion, the whole country estate being surrounded by a 12-foot wall that had broken glass and barbed wire embedded in the top. The warders marched us to a church beside the mansion, where we were told to get praying. Oh, how I prayed and thought of my choir days in what seemed like another world, so long ago. Even the ever-pervading damp smell in there was the same and I'm sure one of the saints in the stained-glass windows smiled at me. My hands felt the smooth wood of the pew in front and the girl I was shackled to shed a tear. We comforted one another in silent commiseration.

Emerging into the daylight again we were marched across to that grim-looking Victorian mansion. As the massive door opened a vile stench came out. We went in to witness very old people chained together, shuffling round and round in an anticlockwise direction, heads down, mumbling, hair unkempt and wearing a sackcloth uniform. In the centre was a warder with a stick. I didn't see it used but these poor pathetic half-starved creatures were human beings treated like hamsters on a treadmill. Round and round aimlessly they went. Everything in there was grey, the stone walls, the slab floors, the uniforms, the hair. There were screams coming from a cubicle and side room. Heads were sticking out of boxes, those heads screaming because the boxes the people were in were steaming. I don't know why.

We were just told we had been brought here to see what happened if we didn't behave ourselves. This made me more determined than ever to do just that, to escape, and I hatched a cunning plan. Obtaining a sketch book from occupational therapy, I spent a lot of time drawing by the window nearest the exit. People got used to seeing me around with my book, but what I was really doing was calculating and observing the comings and goings of the outside area and how many paces it was to the large oak tree where the dustbins were situated underneath. A big branch overhung the wall and I aimed to get on top of the dustbins and crawl along the branch and drop down over the other side when the dustcart came round. It was then that the door was briefly unlocked, and the dustman had a chit signed and the warder's back was turned. I would get out when this happened and be covered by line of sight with the dustcart; I had already avoided taking the medication by sleight of hand, by putting the tablet into my sleeve cuff as I put my hand up to my mouth. I was still allowed to wear my own clothes, the biggest problem was I would be minus shoes, which we were not allowed to wear inside. I was still quite fit, but the diet and lack of exercise were starting to have an effect. It was now or never and pray for fine weather. I had also borrowed an extra set of clothes, which I was going to wear over my usual ones.

The day came and it was dead easy as I shinned up the tree trunk and out over the branch, only briefly touching the wall with my feet, avoiding the glass and barbed wire – just – but I made a very heavy landing. Only by taking deep breaths was I able to slow myself down and not panic. I crawled my way through bushes and scrub to the blue lagoon, an old quarry pit, very deep and filled with water, which was on the other side of the road from an old cement works. Several inmates had escaped in the past and drowned themselves in the lagoon. I took my extra set of clothing off and left it on the edge by the old wooden platform. This was the first place they would look for an escaped inmate and whilst they were searching the depths I would be elsewhere! I would have a head start.

My feet hurt already. I still had my socks. Entering the abandoned cement works I found various bits and pieces in the old bothy, including a workman's dusty old shoulder bag. Into this I stuffed old bits of cloth and string and cement bag paper. I tied some old plastic bags to my feet and set off along the dead straight road and then turned into the fields that ran parallel to it but hidden by the hedges. I had no plan except to reach home. There were very few cars, although the bus from Stotfold passed by. The expected police cars didn't materialise, but I still kept undercover.

By nightfall, and with sore feet, I had reached the outskirts of Letchworth. My hunger drove me to a chippie I knew and, being closing time, I had the free stuff that was unsold, as I had no money. I spent the night in a park shelter with my bits of old cloth and cement bag paper over me and the workman's bag for a pillow. At sun up I ate some saved chips and some blackberries from the hedge. I asked a passing milkman if he had any water and he gave me a bottle of orange juice and said, "You're from that place, aren't you?"

I said, "Yes, but please, you haven't seen me."

"No, I haven't," he replied with a conspiratorial wink.

Before Letchworth had woken up, I was out and through the other side. After reaching Hitchin, I thumbed a lift to Stevenage and trudged up the long hill to Jessop Road and home.

Retrieving the house key from its hiding place, I got in but, longing for a bath, found that there was no gas or electric. Even the water glugged to a stop. Where was Ken? I donned my trainers and jogged to a certain pub in Old Stevenage and there he was, perched on a stool, smoking a cigar, his solitaire ring glinting, entertaining a group of 'one for the road' old boys. When he saw me his mouth fell open and he spilt his drink down his old school tie. It was pathetically funny. His blazer sported his old school badge with its motto, which translated to 'As Much as I Am Able'. Well it was as much as he was able not to fall off his perch!

Pulling his sleeves down over his pure gold Masonic cufflinks, he then charmingly regained his composure for the benefit of those present and asked the landlord if he could make a phone call for a taxi to take us home as, "We've got things to sort out," as he put it. He went out the back of the bar, made a call, came back, and told me there would be some delay as the taxi was busy. As he said, "Would you like a drink darling, whilst we are waiting?" I could have socked him one. The landlord looked uncomfortable and kept glancing out of the window. There was a tension in the room, something was building up, I could feel it. Then it happened and my heart sank as the white coats burst in to take me away. Some taxi! It was an ambulance he had ordered. It seemed my escape had been in vain.

I was dragged off to see a psychiatrist. This was in fact the *first time* that anyone had thought to allow a proper psychiatrist to examine me. He could find nothing wrong with me. In fact, he admired my pluck and felt that it was my husband that needed to see him! Relief flooded over me. I was not out of the woods yet but at least I would not be sent back to that dreadful place. My children couldn't come home until all the utilities had been connected. I lived in a mixture of fear and turmoil, and the future seemed hopeless; my life on a cliff edge.

Eventually, I managed to get things back onto an even keel – that is to say, stable enough that the kids could return home. I caught up on the overgrown allotment, providing food single-handed. I kept a clean and tidy house, practised make do and mend until I could almost write a book about it and got back to some form of normality until one morning I awoke with a truly awful headache. I had never felt so ill. I had meningitis and was so poorly that, as the medics in the hospital were trying to restart my heart, my being detached itself from my body and I ascended into a peaceful and soothing blue space looking down on myself and on all those trying to save me. Oh, what a lovely place I was in! I never wanted to go back; but go back I did, because I had two little children who would miss me.

Being jolted back into my body wasn't nice. Now I had to get on with the pain and my weird unstable life after hospital.

With determination, I bounced back. My children were of a sunny nature and loved helping on the allotment. That's where I found peace, amongst the plants, with skylarks singing. Even in winter there was a bleak beauty about the place: earthy, frosty, our breath hanging on the air, the children chugging home pretending it was smoke and that they were steam engines.

To the outside world, I was a mother of two children who went to nursery school and playgroup. I was the dutiful wife, cooking, cleaning, doing all the normal things. I belonged to a choral society learning challenging oratorios whose musical threads ran through my brain like the friends I never had. I kept up my running in all weathers, pounding out my worries on the receptive pavements or woodland floor. I sewed. I wrote, knitted, laboured, cooked, and cobbled my so-called home together, whilst the pubs received my husband's wages, until one day, yet again, there were no more wages as another job went down the pan due to booze and lateness.

Yes, to the outside world I was a normal wife of a white-collar worker with a so-called respectable home. Little did they know!

The fruits of my allotment labour did much to carry us through, especially as the gas and electric were cut off yet again. I would make a game with the children of walking to the woods, where we would build a shelter and cook sausages over a campfire. Sometimes it would even be eggs and bacon! I also became adept at foraging, a great supplement to our gardening grub.

For five years we lived like this. I got no help, only the threat of social services removing my children if things didn't improve. By this time, Peter was at 'proper' school and was around six years old and being questioned about bruises on his body. I had acquired another allotment and sold the produce from this one. This enabled us to survive. As I thrust my fork into the ground it went some way, therapeutically, towards hitting out at the present and burying some of the past.

Every week I went to the church service held in a hall. The vicar had no church but he did have numerous children so I was able to give him some spare produce for his family. He was fully aware of my home situation and was able to speak up for me in court and to social services. He said I was a good mother under the most appalling circumstances as by now I was reduced to cooking an egg over a candle in a mini frying pan.

As we huddled together, minus heating, Ken was roasting his backside in the pub in front of the fire. I no longer had any fire, so it was with relief that I was given an oil heater. At least I could warm up some water on the top but not long after that there were no funds for the paraffin. Maybe the children would be better off in care after all. I'd done my best and with that in mind I wrote a farewell note, whilst I was completely sound, and went to a piece of rough ground with a bottle of water and thirty-five Mogadon tablets that Ken had to help him sleep. Here, I lay down and asked for God's forgiveness. As I started to swallow the tablets I could hear life all around me: distant traffic, bird song and children. Oh dear, some had come to play close by. I couldn't let them find a dead body, so I struggled to my feet and woozily staggered home to slump on the bed.

Through a misty haze I saw Ken looming over me. What was he doing home at this time of day? It was unheard of for him to be around. Whatever the reason, it was to save my life as the next thing I recall is being in hospital having my stomach pumped out. I was on the ward for the next three days, blind. I was in the same place where I was saved from meningitis. As the days went by my sight returned. Instead of being told off for what I had done I was met with sympathy, but Ken never visited me. The children were with his mum and that awful sister. I just had to get well and rescue them.

I resumed my training, always getting fit for some crisis ahead. I stormed home, winning the county cup for cross-country running plus competing at the White City in London. These things were easy for me; pounding out my troubles on the tarmac, mud or racetrack was never a problem. I took up swimming and shocked even myself at attaining near Olympic times for breaststroke in the local pool. Well, Father had swum the English Channel and there was a relative named Jack Lovelock who was a runner; maybe something rubbed off onto me! But no one was interested in my achievements and once again I became a nobody, useless, a failure, just like my first schooldays. Alone, with no one to confide in, it was just like being locked in my childhood bedroom with only a few basic things to hand and lots of time for thinking. So, I decided to get out of this hopeless situation with what little I had. I got my children back and hatched a careful plan that was to change my life path forever. I named it The Great Escape.

Chapter 8 : The Great Escape

My ever-conniving husband set up a fake burglary, a break-in to our own home. I knew nothing of this until I got home after being out all day at a school event and a children's party afterwards. The police were crawling all over the house and taking fingerprints, especially around the supposed point of entry, the window frame. Ken had to make a list of what was missing: not only his gold watch and chain, gold Masonic cufflinks and other things but also my personal jewellery, engagement ring and other items left to me by my grandma. His idea was to claim on a house insurance. That was a new one on me: I didn't even know we had one! Recently, he had hinted that I could sell my jewellery to pay off some debts but I was one step ahead of the game and had hidden my items in a tin, which I buried on my allotment under the compost heap, inside several flower pots.

The day after the 'burglary', I put my plan for The Great Escape into action. Retrieving my buried treasure, I sold it at a jewellery second-hand shop and gained my passport to freedom, making enough money to buy two small tents, a large holdall, two little bags-come-satchels and three coach tickets from Hitchin to Barnstaple, leaving in a week's time. I just hoped it wouldn't rain in the meantime as I had to pack and hide these items on the allotment inside plastic bags, under corrugated iron and old crates. That week, I had to keep my excitement and secret under control, hidden. I did much cooking: stuff that would travel well such as energy bars, flapjacks, and biscuits, plus sandwiches for the start. The equipment was heavy, and clothes were a major problem, especially as Matthew was still bedwetting at age five.

On 20 July 1972 I collected my boys from a party, but we never went home again. I told them that we were going on an exciting holiday! The long school summer holidays started the following day and I had deliberately chosen this time so as to blend in and not stand out amongst everyone else making trips at that time. We retrieved our belongings from the allotment. I had included two of their favourite small toys. Their eyes were shining, wide with excitement.

"Will Daddy be coming?"

"No, not this time."

"Oh good, we can have a great time then," was the reply.

From Stevenage we took a bus to a bed and breakfast place in Hitchin that had a swimming pool where we spent a lovely evening splashing and playing around. I spread plastic bags on the beds in case of accidents and we retired early, happy, and tired out. The landlady refused to give us an early breakfast. Our coach left at 7:30am and she wouldn't even give us some sandwiches or a drink, but she still charged in full.

As we struggled to the coach station it felt very hot, even at that time of day. The heat had been brewing all week and we had a 12-hour journey ahead of us in a hot tin box. I had filled our bottles from the sink in the B&B, a bit chancy but there were no tea-making facilities in the rooms in those days. As we boarded the coach, the driver gave us an odd look. Well, we were on 'the run' and my heart beat faster. There was no toilet or air conditioning on board at that time, either, and I had to hope that we could hold out until the allotted stops en-route. Great excitement for the boys as we began our big exodus, The Great Escape.

THE GREAT ESCAPE

We reached Salisbury by lunchtime and had a one-hour stop. It was so hot, but we went into the cathedral and cooled down. The boys stared in awe inside that beautiful building. Then we had a little picnic of my previously prepared food in the shade of some trees on the banks of a river and watched the trout in the shallows resting up under the floating weed. A quick washdown in the toilets and we were back on board the coach with a change of driver.

As the afternoon wore on it got hotter and ever more stifling in the coach. One passenger fainted and another was sick but fortunately the boys slept through it all until we reached Taunton at 5pm.

"Are we there yet?" as we clambered out for another hour's break and sat by yet another river and ate rather warm sandwiches and nearly boiled water. There was a long, long queue for the toilets and as we finally re-emerged I saw the coach pulling out. It was leaving with all our stuff on board. I shouted at the boys to stand still until Mummy stopped the coach. My running prowess paid off as I stood in the road some way off and stopped it, then signalled to the boys to come to me.

"You stupid bitch! You could have got yourself killed!" It was a different driver.

My eldest piped up, "You sound just like my daddy."

A fellow passenger came to my defence, they shouted at the driver "You departed five minutes before time; and that's a lady you are being rude to."

The rest of the journey got hotter and more tiring. We were snaking along familiar roads that I had traversed many times with my parents in the car, squashed between ballgowns on hangers on the way to that holiday camp in Croyde. They lived there now, right next to the camp, dictating all the dances, but I wasn't going to visit *them*. They moved away and disowned me many years ago.

"Watch out for the black cat, boys. It's at the bottom of a long, long hill amongst the trees. You will see a large sign of a cat silhouette; Black Cat is the name of a café."

They were tired, eyes drooping, heads nodding. Over the bridge, up another long hill, passing the old quarry on the left where we used to have the last stop for a cuppa from the Thermos flask before passing through South Molton and then the final push to Croyde, which seemed a lifetime ago. All my parents cared about then was whether the ballgowns and dinner jackets had travelled well; I was just an unwanted piece of luggage.

Now I had my own two pieces of precious luggage: Peter and Matthew. At our coach journey's end we stepped out into a nice cool breeze coming off the River Taw. With our bits and pieces and tents we had to wait for an hour for the bus to Croyde. We were tired, sweaty, and hungry. A VW van pulled in to pick up some surfers we'd been chatting to. They were going to Croyde as well and gave us a lift and told us of a quiet campsite, where they dropped us off. By now it was 8:45pm and I was weary as I erected the two little tents in all that heat. The boys fell asleep immediately as lightning streaked the sky over distant Lundy Island.

And then it came; the sultry bubble burst in torrents at 3am, running like a river through all the tents perched on the slope. Terrifying flashes and thunderclaps overhead woke everyone. The wind lifted awnings and snapped guy ropes on the bigger frame tents. A kind family man took us into his massive tent and we laid the boys on his family's beds, still asleep! It was a frightening night but in the morning our little tents had held secure and we lost nothing. We had a nice breakfast with the family but Matthew was dancing up and down, a sure sign that he needed a wee, so we had to use the public toilets off site and this is also where we washed and cleaned our teeth.

Peter and Matthew were loving the adventure and when I tried out the little camping stove they thought it was great fun.

"Look, Mummy, the kettle's laughing!" as it eventually came to the boil, its little lid dancing up and down.

Matthew had wet himself. Problem: I had to rinse his clothes in the public toilets which meant each time we left the tent I zipped it up and worried about the contents. Going off site to the toilet was not good. At lunchtime, the family man 'knocked' on our door.

"Can I have a word in private?" So the game was up, was it, before we'd even started?

"You're not on holiday, are you? You're running away from something. Whatever it is, I won't give you away, but I could help you."

Scenes flashed through my brain from the past. Oh no, not *that*, the jiggly thingy!

"I know just what you're thinking, but rest assured it won't happen with me." And he called his wife over to us. She explained that they were foster parents and that he was a chief children's welfare officer and could suss out a situation in seconds!

Confiding in them both was a relief. Peter and Matthew were happily playing with their 'foster family'. Their eldest went out and came back with fish and chips for everyone. I was beginning to feel quite happy. The family man and his wife drove us to an office in Barnstaple, for help, he said.

I was beginning to wonder if this was all a trick to trap us, but it wasn't. He got welfare vouchers for milk and orange juice, some clothes and sleeping bags. All very well but carting all that extra baggage would be a problem when we upped sticks.

This lovely cheerful family shared their meals with us, played guitars and sang of an evening and the boys were so happy, running in and out and no one minded. When the lovely family left we missed them, but now we could go down to the rockpools and play, spending all day on the beach. Oh, how well we all looked! Things were going fine. Soon I would look for a job with accommodation but we would enjoy the summer school holidays first. I had not been discovered. Maybe no one would be looking for us after all. Perhaps Ken was glad to be shot of us, with more to spend in the pub.

Awakening one morning and sitting up in my tent I yawned and stretched, undid the zip and looked out onto something that shot me wide awake. It was my father's face staring into mine. Oh God, now I was for it! How did he know where to find me? The campsite owner had recognised me and had just casually mentioned it to my parents, how nice it must be to see the grandchildren again. What a disaster. Well it couldn't last, could it? It all came tumbling down. We were rumbled. The police had been searching countrywide, issuing photos of us. Now they would be informed and would have to question us on where we had been. The children would definitely be removed.

After my father had gone I packed everything away – no mean feat – and got the Georgeham bus to Forda, a little hamlet with a campsite for only five tents, beside a stream. This was a farm and after two weeks there the owners asked us up to the farmhouse for the evening and said we could all have a bath and a supper, no charge. We had a lovely welcome and felt wonderful after our baths. There were clean fluffy towels, lots of farmhouse grub and dogs and puppies, which delighted the boys. They were always so well behaved. I was so blessed in that respect.

"You're not on holiday, are you?"

Here we go again; wouldn't anyone leave us alone? But these people were different: quiet and kindly as they listened to my story. They gave us milk and eggs from the farm. Their house was also a B&B.

"Come and see us early tomorrow morning; we can help you."

I couldn't sleep for wondering what would happen. The boys slept soundly, unperturbed. As dawn brought the mist up the valley I arose, burdened with curiosity.

An Unexpected Offer

I got the boys ready and we headed to the farmhouse. A huge cooked breakfast awaited us. Bed and breakfast guests were well looked after here. As we sat around the farmhouse table I sensed a feeling of love and care. Milk was set beside the Rayburn to turn into cream. The puppies lay content with their mother and I was proud of my boys, sitting with impeccable politeness at breakfast, so patiently waiting.

Afterwards, we were led out to the rear of the house and at the field edge stood a nearly new chicken shed, surrounded by nettles.

"Come back later today; this will be scrubbed out, the nettles gone, and it is yours to use, no charge, for as long as you wish. But in a couple of weeks you can have a temporary guest room in our B&B until the end of September. After that, we can offer you our chalet, which is a holiday let. You can use it until Easter in exchange for some housework, housesitting, milking our two house cows and anything else in between."

Wow! What fortune had dropped into my lap. I had all day to go away and think about it, but it was a bit too near to where my parents lived, just a couple of miles away. Soon I would have to think about schooling as the new term started in a few weeks.

After a day champing at the bit I returned and was shown a clean chicken shed. Inside were new blow-up beds, little chairs, boxes for tables, a new, larger stove, a crate of canned food and proper plates and cutlery. A bag of assorted adult and children's clothing and bedding had also been donated.

"See how you get on. Let us know if you'd like to stay, and it's free breakfast and dinner. If you would like it, that is? Oh, and use of the bath and shower room too."

What? Had I really fallen so perfectly on my feet? Where was the catch? This was the stability we needed. The endless golden days on the beach would come to an end soon anyway, as autumn edged in and summer moved out.

So my new life started, and we eventually moved into the little corrugated green iron holiday chalet. The window overlooked the steep valley, out towards the distant sea and dunes. Gales of autumn hail would push up through the valley and rattle against the iron walls. I was in my element, calling in the two cows, Buttercup and Ermintrude, to be milked. They would sway over the cold horizon and into the warmth of the barn, where I would hand-milk their velvet teats into a bucket. Buttercup, the Friesian, could get a bit temperamental but Ermintrude was a gentle Jersey with large, liquid brown eyes. I would then strain the milk and set the Jersey milk to make cream and the rest was for the general house use. The terriers followed me in the fields, rumps in the air, digging down into holes then catching me up as I moved nineteen frisky young heifers into fresh pasture. One day the heifers broke out onto the road and the quick thinking of a North Devon Farmers lorry driver saved the day. Being a narrow road at that time, he opened both doors of his vehicle to block the way and soon all cattle were regained.

Mucking out, hoovering, cleaning, I was Jill-of-all-trades, fit and well and enjoying life. The boys had started school a mile up the road and were enjoying their new existence. The hue-and-cry had not caught up with us here; at least not yet. I kept up my running and now had a bicycle. My swimming became much stronger in the sea. I could do anything. I accompanied the lovely couple who made all this possible to their chapel each Sunday as a sort of thank you. They certainly practised what they believed in, in a quiet and gentle way. My father appeared from time to time; the boys said, "Who's that man?"

One day I took them to my parents' home. It was an awkward meeting as we had to stay outside in the garden and weren't allowed indoors for fear of messing things up. Clearly we weren't welcome as my parents' routine would be put out of joint and we might create dust. I thought they would have been glad that I had made good, but all they could say was that they had moved away to Croyde to at last be shot of me and all my problems and, "Here you are once again". They were so well respected in the area, running charity balls, pantomimes, chairing some thing or another. I suppose we were a blot on their landscape.

I was still tucked away into my little chalet through that winter and into 1973. I had got a little white Jack Russell puppy, the runt of the litter, born into the palm of my hand, not breathing. I brought her back to life and carried her around in my milking apron pocket for several weeks. I called her Polar, as she looked like a polar bear when coming out of the water. What a lovely life we were all having on the farm. Hard work at times, but happy. But it never lasts. Easter was the deadline date to move out as the chalet holiday bookings would begin. As the date loomed nearer I was desperate to find somewhere but nothing, nothing prepared me for what happened next.

Shock! Disbelief! Upon answering my door, there stood Ken and my father. So, one had led the other to my hideout. Just seconds, that's all it took to destroy my new-found worth and confidence. My stomach plummeted.

"You two need to talk." With that my father left.

Ken had a small suitcase. It was obvious he expected to stay. As I made a pot of tea, he sat by the window that looked down the valley out to sea. Nothing was said about my disappearance. The boys came in and looked as they passed through to their bedroom.

"Oh, it's you," said Peter.

Matthew just said, "Hi," as they went to play.

I just busied myself getting the tea, not quite knowing what was to happen next, but pretty well guessing.

I had to suppress a giggle really, as the boys hadn't given Ken the rapturous welcome that he probably expected, so he just sat there tapping his fingers on his suitcase, waiting for my next move. I served up tea for everyone. It was quite early because I had the late afternoon milking to see to and the boys had their little jobs in the farmhouse, setting out tables for the B&B. Not wanting to leave Ken in the chalet, I said he would have to come with me if he wanted to talk.

His 'city' attire looked incongruous in the mucky farm setting and his nose positively wrinkled as I raked out old straw in the shippen and laid down new. The cows were waiting for me by the gate and made their measured gait into the barn to be milked.

They baulked a bit at seeing a stranger, until I soothed them. I wiped their teats, squirted the first drops of milk away from the bucket and then began to milk, deftly. Swiftly it came, as they munched the cattle cake I had put in their ancient, worn stone troughs. Their chains rattled on the wood, their sweet smell of hide and milk combined with fresh straw filled the small space below the low wood-planked ceiling. The oil lamp cast a warm glow in there, even in daytime.

Ken just had to follow me; I hadn't time for nattering. Next, strain the milk, set to cream, feed the heifers, lug the sacks around, open some bales, let the terriers into the barn for their daily rat kill, collect rats, dispose. Feed the hens, collect the eggs, shut the hens in for the night. The boys were scurrying around doing their jobs. Ken's mouth fell open when I jumped on the tractor and reversed it out of the yard. I think I nearly, accidentally-on-purpose, narrowly missed mowing him down as he was very pale!

Of course, he stayed. He had put all our furniture and belongings into storage back in Stevenage and had come looking for me and a job and forgiveness. He wanted to make a fresh start and was sorry. He was offered some temporary jobs around the farm but not being very practised he wasn't much good, so it was me that was blithely swinging the seven-pound lump hammer onto posts to set up a fence around a field. He was frightened of the tractor and the cattle. I just seemed to have a natural affinity for them and for the farm routine and the land. I loved it, but not the situation we were about to find ourselves in.

The week before Easter found us moving into an old caravan in the middle of a field of geese just a mile up the road. I could walk through the geese to the old wooden hut that housed a chemical toilet, no problem. As soon as Ken attempted it, he got nabbed in the crotch. The boys thought it hilarious, as the geese fed out of their hands!

The caravan was rent free until Ken found a job and accommodation for us. Meanwhile, I still did my work at the farm and Ken came along. He became very impressed with the lovely couple that had helped me. They were very nice towards him, despite everything. They got him to talk about himself, about his life and problems and where and why things had gone wrong. It was like a talking therapy and he became quiet, considerate, and thoughtful. He started coming to the chapel each Sunday. He even took up Bible study and it quite shocked me to know how knowledgeable he was. He gave up smoking and drinking – wow! Even the specialist at St Bart's Hospital in London couldn't persuade him to do that, despite warning him that if he didn't give up he would lose his ulcerated leg to Buerger's disease within ten years.

Meanwhile he nearly set the caravan on fire by putting too much wood into its tiny stove. The panelling was blistering and the moth-eaten curtains were scorched. The smell, combined with Matthew's bedwetting, the lack of facilities and the gradual sinking of the van to one side on a steep slope made it imperative that a move should be made soon.

A church minister had a farm, several miles out into the countryside from Barnstaple, upon which there was a farm labourer's cottage to rent. So, armed with a weekly rent book and with our belongings out of storage, we moved in on 5 October 1974.

Oh, what a place! I toiled in the massive garden and grew all our own veg and fruit. I rescued some battery hens, built a coop and pen, and watched them change from pale, terrified creatures into healthy egg-laying Rhode Island Reds. My little dog, Polar, had a wonderful life with many forays into the surrounding Forestry Commission woods. I had Muscovy ducks and built a little pond. I gathered wood for the Rayburn stove; we even had a spring that never dried up, not even in a severe drought, which provided pure, cool water. We were practically self-sufficient. A baker, butcher and grocery van called once a week, we were so isolated. An old coach would stop outside my gate for Friday market shopping, also once a week. What characters were on it! And as it usually rained on a Friday the return journey behind steamed-up windows would smell of pasties, chips, damp clothes and remnants of dung from farm boots, plus the odd drink or two.

We lived high up in the hills and the clouds would eventually clog down and slow the coach. We would narrowly miss a tractor, or a giant pothole, before finally arriving. Getting off the coach, the geese and ducks knew it was me and I could hear their welcome, combined with Polar's barks from inside the cottage.

This was a time of making jams, chutneys, and drinks from the produce of the garden and the surrounding countryside in the middle of nowhere. It was wonderful hard work, which I alone completed. Ken did nothing around the cottage or garden. He had found work and we slept apart, perfect!

We were driven to a chapel each Sunday, where he earnestly studied. I put up with it for the sake of keeping the peace. The boys came as well. I would nearly fall asleep during the long and dreary sermons but if this is what held the family together it was a small sacrifice to pay.

Ken seemed to have changed for the better and was baptised by full immersion into the strict ways of the chapel. However, this meant that I had to stop selling bunches of flowers, eggs, and other produce, on a Sunday outside my gate, because it was the Sabbath. This had been my boys' pocket money, as people driving back home from a day out on Exmoor loved to stop and make a purchase, look at the ducks and chickens and be served by two charming little boys. So strict were the chapel ways that the farmers in the congregation would rather spend the Sunday observances worshipping instead of harvesting fully ripened grain on a fine sunny day, and see it flattened by wind and rain on the following Monday. What a waste of money, time, and labour!

I had to be seen to be doing my bit in the chapel, so I chose the lesser of the evils and sang in the gospel choir. Much as I loved singing, I hated all the having to look smart and dressing up, wearing a hat – ugh! Bit by bit, I was beginning to feel trapped, just like the ballroom days in my past. In fact, I secretly resented it, sitting inside on a sunny day when I could be striding the hills or mucking out the animals. Then there was the 'visiting preacher' Sunday lunches to endure. By now, Ken was invited to preach at different chapels and the custom was to provide the visiting preacher and his family with lunch and sometimes tea.

These were creaky corset affairs, stiff white collars and ties and grace before meals. These graces could be so lengthy that the lovingly prepared dinner would be cold by the end of it all. I felt sorry for the lady who had cooked it.

It was during one of these graces, at a farm, when it got to the 'amen' bit, that my youngest let out the most almighty fart. Straightaway, the farmer looked under the table and said, "Get out, 'ort dog!" My sides were busting with trying not to laugh as there was no dog! Then there was the smell that followed the fart. As it travelled around the room the farmer's wife apologised because the stuffing she had put in the chicken smelt so strong. Oh dear, I was laughing so much I turned it into a cough into my starched table napkin and spluttered into a glass of water.

Monday was wash day. No machine, everything done by hand, but oh, the reward of billowing sheets and pillowcases blowing in the fresh air. Until, that is, the stench of dung spreading on the fields funnelled up the valley and made the clothes smell awful.

I was loving the life and was healthy and strong. The boys went to the village school. I ran cross-country clubs and did lots of training. I helped out at the swimming pool with the schools, passed the bronze medallion for life-saving and became a qualified swimming teacher. Life was full. I took up diving and became fascinated with underwater life. I went to evening classes and did my A levels, because Ken had always considered me only half-educated. I showed him!

I had the opportunity to go gliding at Chivenor airfield, for free, but being on a Sunday I wasn't allowed to take it up. I was in a trap, another controlled situation, but this time the trap was being sprung to propel me into an even worse situation, something I never thought would happen, ever again.

Chapter 9 : History Repeats Itself

"If you could perhaps have a word to your husband about it? It is now six months since the rent was paid," said the farmer's wife, a staunch chapel member.

Like a sudden drop in a lift, that's how my stomach felt, and I knew nothing. "The pub is opposite the chapel," she said. "We see what goes on and it's not right for one of our circuit preachers to be seen drinking, especially when they owe us money."

So that's why he was late home every night after doing his supposed overtime. I went to the pub one day at lunchtime and found out from the landlord that Ken and his co-worker in the office dropped in for a 'quick one' (or two, or three) on the way home from work. Ken got a lift to and from his job with this office mate, and the chapel opposite was perfectly positioned to witness these comings and goings during their weekly church business meetings. I suppose I always knew it was too good to last.

Word got around. We were still considered to be 'incomers' to the village, which was situated a couple of miles away. Suddenly, my help was no longer needed at the running club or the school swimming. The boys were taunted. Matthew was punished for nothing with a beating from the teacher. He ran away, too frightened to come home. The helicopter was out in the cold, frosty night searching for him. Peter was unhappy and now I had to send him to school with sandwiches: I had no money left for school dinner as it was all going to try to catch up with the rent. I didn't want to lose my lovely home in the country, where I had found such happiness. I had to find a job that fitted in with the school hours, that I could work around home commitments, my animals and garden.

So I ended up taking three cleaning jobs. One was in a doctor's house, a specialist actually, who was to help me in the not too distant future. Another was in 'the big house' where I had to iron the master's shirts, then button them up and fold them and put them in a drawer to look as though they were new, as you would buy them all packaged up, pins and all. Thinking this a waste of time, I hung them all neatly on hangers and put them in a wardrobe. I got dismissed. Another place was a farm with loads of kids – not the goat variety. So filthy was the place that the mother used to throw the dirty nappies into a heap in the corner of the kitchen, right next to where they had the bottle cap machine for the milk they sold!

Another posh mansion I went to had its own cook, who used to give me loads of food, especially ham, meat and tongue, because the employers couldn't carve it into neat slices once it got down nearer the bone of end. My dog had a great feast and I was given so much good food that would otherwise have been wasted. I cycled everywhere in all weathers. What with working, running a home and managing my menagerie, it was little wonder that I became run down and tired. I awoke one morning feeling too ill to do anything. I had caught brucellosis. It was confirmed by a portable x-ray machine brought to my home by the specialist doctor I worked for. He really helped me to get the care I needed to be nursed at home.

By now, Matthew was too intelligent for the village school and would sit there with nothing to do as he'd finished all the work for the lessons of the day. He was so clever that the teachers didn't know what to do with him. The other kids hated him for being so far ahead of them. They bullied him and tore his schoolwork to pieces. As Peter had left that school and gone to senior school he was no longer around to look out for his young brother. So Matthew went off to a special residential school that had an Outward Bound basis, out in the wilds of Devon. There was no more trouble. He flourished.

Things were breaking down, no matter how hard I worked. I was waking up from my dream of a home to a nightmare of eviction. Six months' notice to quit. All I had worked hard for, the garden, the animals, the wonderful way of life, the sense of achievement, was now in ruins, pissed away in a pub.

As my father lay dying in hospital, his last words to me were, "I told you a leopard never changes its spots." So now, on top of everything else, I had a funeral to arrange and a mother to comfort and help.

By a strange twist of fate, my mother gave me enough money to buy myself a motorbike, as I had so much travelling around to do. I ended up getting a Honda Goldwing. Unknown to me at the time, that motorbike would be the key to my future, to happiness overflowing, to dreams coming true. Instead of a four-mile trudge from town to home I had now passed my driving test and it took only minutes to get back to the cottage that I had spent the last seven years making into a home.

Seeing smoke on my ride home next day I thought that the place was on fire. It was Ken in the garden. He had chopped up our lovely piano and was burning it in an almighty rage. Next, he piled on my wedding dress and veil and precious books. On and on it went, he was wielding a pitchfork and swearing. Even the poultry had gone into hiding. Next to go were the Bibles and hymn books, even his old Masonic regalia. Where would it end? As he threw a flaming book through the cottage window, I rushed in to stop the place burning down. I was so calm. Maybe that was my trouble throughout life. I never lost my temper. I would always stay quiet for the sake of peace. I would rather think things through than shout at someone and later regret it.

By now the farmer and his wife were on the scene, shortly followed by the police and fire brigade. I felt truly awful. These people had found us a home in our dire circumstances, all those years ago, and this is how we thanked them. Social services turned up, as if on cue. Peter was taken into care because we had nowhere to go. He didn't seem to be bothered; at twelve years old he was testing the water of life anyway in the senior school. His innocence had been swallowed up in the unruly masses. My blonde, curly-haired blue-eyed boy had become an almost teenage croaky-voiced stranger, wearing the same tracksuit for months on end, like a second skin, and repeating the same Abba record until it became an ear worm in my head.

It was my mother who found us a winter let, not far from where she lived in Croyde.

"For goodness sake keep that rent paid up as I know too many people here," she warned.

I vaguely knew some of the villagers from years past and my parents had been well respected, as chairman of this and that, treasurer of the dance club, a finger in every pie in a quiet and unassuming way. They had other property in the area, so I believed at the time, but their main residence was a posh bungalow and it was here that my mother lived, now on her own. It was a lonely life for her but her only complaint was that after all the years that she and her husband had helped the community, no one now helped or cared to enquire as to how *she* was.

I now straddled three lives. Living in a flat, helping my mother and holding down a job. By living just a few doors from the local pub, it became Ken's daytime residence. Oh, what a mistake! As the drinking grew, his bad leg got worse and he went on the sick.

With my swimming qualifications I got a good summer job as a lifeguard and would think nothing of running the length of Woolacombe beach and back before work, plus the training. I became good at long-distance swimming and went to the Lake District with a team to take part. It was much colder than our local sea!

I had also kept in touch with the navy reserve section and went away on various refresher training courses including the diving. My motorbike worked overtime, packed to the limit with panniers and kit, off on one mission or another, be it shopping, training or work. I was also part of the cliff rescue team, dangling precariously from a Sea King helicopter off various rock faces.[5]

I mixed with lots of aircrew and went to Gloucester airfield and eventually did 35 hours solo, after much studying and training. Ken was out of mind for much of the time and, when I returned home to our winter let, he was hardly ever there. Rather, he was propping up the bar around the corner. I couldn't have the children back because we were still only in temporary accommodation.

Barnstaple

Another Easter, another notice to quit. The council had found us a three-bedroomed house in Barnstaple. As I rode away from the beauty of Croyde I pulled up into a layby overlooking the vast expanse of Saunton Sands. I really didn't want to live in town on that soulless, dreary council estate near the stinky lace factory. My heart sank at the prospect of it all. This was 1980, the start of a new decade. What would it bring? My motorbike would be the key to unlocking my future, but not quite yet.

I transformed the overgrown garden, a huge corner plot, at our new home. I managed to grow potatoes and veg and built a little pond and made a lean-to affair to grow tomatoes. Ken had the largest bedroom, the only one with heating in. He went to a

---

[5] While there could well be an entire book of stories to tell from this time, there are too many people still alive who might not want them published. Perhaps at some point it may be possible.

neighbour's party one night and got so drunk that I had to help him upstairs to the bathroom. He fell into the bath, so I put the plug in and turned the cold water tap on, full gush! He was fully dressed. I just couldn't help myself; it was payback time.

Ken joined the library, but he also joined the company of fourteen pubs in town. By now, he was on invalidity benefit and raking in more money that I was earning doing a 48-hour week. His leg was one big suppurating mess oozing through the dressings. I was not allowed into his bedroom but one day the smell was so awful I thought I should see what was causing the stench that was filtering underneath the door.

It was a large pile of soiled and bloody bandages and pus-laden dressings. The flies all lifted as one cloud from this dreadful heap as I walked in. There were piles and piles of unreturned library books amongst many booze bottles. Discarded fag ends were everywhere, with scorched surfaces where an ashtray had not been used. I was shocked and ashamed. I was glad to escape to work each day and his parting shot from his bed would be, "Have you got fifty pence for the meter?" and, "have you put the rubbish out?"

I worked partly at a leisure centre, teaching schools and also for the mentally handicapped and disabled. The work was hugely rewarding and I studied hard to get more qualifications with higher pay. With the award of merit under my belt and advanced resuscitation and first aid, I was progressing well. I also held private one-to-one swimming lessons in the water and was able to get people swimming who had been trying all their life. I never had a failure.

In the summer season, I returned to the holiday park in Woolacombe and was in charge of the pool, the chemicals, and was the sole lifeguard. I couldn't just stand or sit there doing

nothing, so I taught people to swim in a casual way and they were thrilled because some had been trying for years. The oldest was eighty-four! These people returned several times a season and became like a large family. I would receive all sorts of gifts as a thank you. Some of the children would cry when it was time to go back home; some even had a crush on me, promising to write!

Sporting Endeavours

Time moved on into 1981 and I entered my first triathlon. I was the only competitor with a Sturmey-Archer three-speed bike; everyone else had racers with drop handlebars. I was first out of the water after the one-mile swim, but a tiny Japanese lady overtook me at the start of the twenty-six-mile cycle race on her flashy expensive bike. I never did catch her up but on the ten-mile run we were neck and neck until she took a shortcut through some bushes to re-emerge appearing to have completed a whole circuit of the local park. There were ten circuits to do and the stewards should have been doing their job but weren't looking.

I got the triathlon bug! I went to various competitions. After all, I wasn't needed at home very much as Ken now had regular visits from a carer. I came World 6th in an international long-distance swim held by the BLDSA. I still have the little cup tucked away in a box somewhere, along with other awards and medals.

I did my annual training stint with the navy and trained in a dreadful claustrophobic tank at Portsmouth plus mock escapes in deep water from a helicopter. I spent six weeks on Drakes Island at Plymouth, teaching survival techniques in the water and training canoeists for their bronze awards. I went sailing, right underneath the overhang of the Ark Royal and as near the nuclear subs as allowed. I went onto various warships; it was fantastic being shown over these fascinating vessels. My old life seemed never to have existed as I basked in this sparkling new adventure. I was a very fit 40-year-old, bronzed, feeling and looking good in my sports gear, swimming costume or wetsuit and being appreciated for what I had achieved. As autumn approached I returned home to a hopeless heap of house and spouse.

When I had left, the carer had assured me they would take care of everything, yet no one had bothered to dig up my potatoes or pick the runner beans, tomatoes, or peas. They went out and bought the stuff instead. There was dog mess indoors as no one had let the poor dog out, let alone a walk. Had I realised this so-called carer would not do anything they had promised, I would never have gone away.

Now Christmas was approaching. I got up early on that morning and walked around the square in Barnstaple as it was only just getting light. The festive lights on the Christmas tree and the guests at their breakfast tables in the Imperial Hotel made me feel quite depressed. The familiar sound of the clock tower chiming out was like an old friend, still there despite what has gone before. It was a dead Christmas. I thought back to my old days in the church choir and it brought a lump to my throat. How I longed for a little piece of nativity with old chorister friends. Instead, I trudged back to that dreary house on an even drearier council estate. No Peter, no Matthew, just nothing.

Never had I felt so down and joyless as I did in that house of dirty dressings, foul smells, and depressive atmosphere. No matter how hard I tried to clean it up, it never responded to treatment. Stuck down in a dark part of town with the cemetery close by, it seemed to gather a miasma of horrid feelings flowing down from the graves of the dead.

The leisure centre closed as the building underwent repairs, so my swimming job was on hold. I would be stuck without an income for at least four months. But I had saved and for once was not destitute. Even so, this didn't do much to relieve the feeling of being in such a negative situation, a cheerless existence. So, with life going down the drain, I responded to a request from the MOD to update my training at Portsmouth.

Not long afterwards I was on my way to Ascension Island, re-fuelling on that bleak volcanic rock thousands of miles from anywhere, eventually ending up in a support role in the Falklands War. My underwater training was put to use and that's all I am able to say on the matter.[6] It didn't worry me to die here: there was nothing left to live for back home.

---

[6] The first we (and possibly anyone else) knew about this was during a writers' group meeting in 2019 when it happened to come up during conversation and, the moment Anne mentioned it, she clammed up and said

Returning Home

"Oh, you're not dead, then!" was the greeting I got as I entered my home.

So many things I could have said but I kept my mouth zipped up. I had that strange feeling of someone having been here and left in a hurry. A faint perfume lingered on the air. I had smelt it before, when the carer had been, but evening wasn't her time. The hastily left meal and tea still in the pot on the kitchen table said it all. I followed the scent out of the back door and saw a cigarette glowing in the dark in the corner of the garden. I said nothing. I just let Ken simmer on the hotplate of deceit as he got more uncomfortable not knowing if I suspected anything or not. I got changed into my running gear and jogged to the Pottington Industrial Estate, on the edge of town, in the dark. Here, I did five circuits plus the return run, which made ten miles, to unwind.

Back home, I picked up my sleeping bag and mat, my emergency kit, and some food. I had been having trouble with my Goldwing; the electrics had been allowed to get damp, so I had been using the kick-starter. Luckily, it started first time and I went off to Braunton Burrows, along the toll road, and sat and looked at the stars. The moon was glinting off the River Taw and, looking towards Barnstaple, the sky reflected orange from lamps in the town. It was another world out here, amongst the marshes, the hiss of incoming water on the sand and the sound of oystercatchers amongst the mudflats. The smell of the clean air filled my senses as I laid out my gear inside the old fishing hut. I needed a clear head and space to think and take stock. In the morning, I made myself a cup of tea on my old camping stove. I hadn't felt so happy in a long time. I was in my own space, in my own time, cooking my little breakfast and communing with nature.

---

that she couldn't tell us any more. Perhaps it may come out in a future book but, presumably, this will involve at least one letter to the M.o.D.

I reapplied for my summer lifeguard job at the Woolacombe holiday park. I was put in sole charge of the pool and chemicals. One day I had to shift an eight-gallon container full of chlorine with the lid unscrewed; it was dangerous to move it when closed because of a build-up of gases. The floor was wet and slippery and at the top of the steps to the ancient, rusty boiler room the container slipped from my grasp and the chlorine flowed down towards the naked flames of the temperamental boiler. At that point, thankfully, the boiler went into its turn-off phase and I had to work like heck with a hosepipe and water to sweep out the offending liquid before the boiler re-ignited itself. I tied a towel round my face to keep the gases out. The boss would be round soon, just before opening up time, to do his inspection. The whole place stank very strongly of chlorine. As he came in, he remarked on how clean the place was looking, in fact extra clean, and to cap it all he said I appeared to have made an even better job than usual as it smelt really fresh!

New Bike, Same Old Problems

As my Goldwing was drinking up too much petrol on my daily trips to work I traded it in for a much smaller Honda C90, which was so economical. I was getting fed up with life at home and Ken rifling through my personal things. I also had my suspicions about the carer. Some of her toiletries were appearing in the bathroom so I left them both to wallow in his filth together. I set up my little dome tent on the campsite on the holiday park. This was on a very steep slope, but I managed to find a tiny flat piece under a hedge at the very top. Then I was offered the loft space above the boiler room.

"It's nice and warm in there," the boss said. Oh yes, a bit too warm when the rickety old boiler finally blew up underneath me!

I finished my season there, went home and lived a separate existence from Ken, who was miffed, I could tell, that the carer couldn't stay at night. They thought I was oblivious to what was going on. Peter had gone into a bedsit prior to going into the army, so I never saw or heard from him. Matthew by now had started college and lived in various friends' places, 'sofa-surfing'. We all appeared to have gone our different ways.

I resumed swimming teaching, at the now refurbished leisure centre, and looked forward to the forthcoming season at the holiday park in Woolacombe as I had been promised a staff caravan for the duration. This was a good turn of events. I had a big plan in my mind. I would save hard all summer as I had no travel expenses. I could have free meals from my friends who ran the campsite café and bar, in return for cleaning their kitchen. Belonging to the Youth Hostel Association, I studied maps and journey times and terrain and planned to leave home for good. Yes, this time forever, no going back.

It would take me two and a half weeks' motorcycling to reach Wick in the far north of Scotland, where I was promised a job with accommodation by a lovely family I had got to know. They had a holiday caravan on the park at Woolacombe and I had taught them all to swim. We all got on well together so, when they learned about my circumstances, they wanted to help.

During the course of that summer I went home from time to time to sort out personal effects and to gradually bring back to the caravan the things that I would need for my new life. My heart was lifting as I also now had a good reason to file for a divorce. I had all the evidence. I said nothing about my impending departure.

I decided to purchase yet another Honda C90. No, I didn't want a powerful bike anymore; I wanted a reliable workhorse that I could gently potter my way on, complete with top box and maximum panniers for all my worldly goods. Besides, I could service a Honda C90 and change the oil. I knew it inside out, quirks and all. I changed motorcycle suppliers as my usual one hadn't any Honda C90s in stock. What a blessing that I did! This was to become a pivotal moment in my life.

Chapter 10 : Meeting Mr Knight

Entering the motorcycle shop as a new customer I was met with, "Yes, Madam, can I help you?" from a really kindly man behind the counter.

He actually recognised that I was a female form, despite my biking gear. In those days not many women went into motorcycle shops, especially on their own, to buy a new bike, cash in hand, or even to part-exchange as I would be doing.

The bike mechanics eyed me up and down, one wiping an oily rag suggestively up and down a spanner, his tongue sticking out. There were pictures of naked ladies on a calendar on their workshop wall. I felt slightly uncomfortable. I was to test ride a new Honda 90 but needed to swap helmets.

"Just put your helmet down there, on the floor," instructed the leery mechanic. As I bent down I got a pinch on the bum.

The mechanic suddenly found himself on the floor. That nice man from behind the counter had felled him and said to me that he was sorry about the misconduct from a member of staff, who would be dealt with later.

After test riding the bike I decided to buy it and all the paperwork was concluded by the kind gent whom I now knew was the sales and shop manager. He made it so easy. Not once did he treat me as a second-class citizen because I was a female. He even said I could have a new helmet for free.

After running in my new bike I returned to the shop for the first contractual service. I went to collect it later and that nice kindly man looked at the job sheet that the mechanics had left and promptly ripped it up.

"Madam, it doesn't take two and a half hours to service a Honda 90 and that's what you are being charged for, here."

Of course, I had to have it serviced by the shop for the first one; being a new bike it was all part of the contract otherwise I could have done it myself.

"No charge," he said as he pushed the paperwork across the desk towards me, holding my gaze.

We had hit it off when he had sold me the bike and it was obvious there was something between us. A spark; an instant rapport.

He placed his hand over mine and said, "You do know that I love you, don't you?"

"Yes," I replied, but we can't do anything about it!"

In that instant I felt an upsurge of love. This was real; I'd never felt like this before. I knew that from now on our lives were somehow inextricably entwined. We were in love. This was serious. I told him where I worked and the following week on his half day off he paid me a visit. He sat by the pool as I worked. I was walking on air. I couldn't stop smiling and the clock seemed to move oh, so slowly towards knocking off time!

That summer season at the holiday park had me torn in two, emotionally. My new-found love, John, made me feel wanted and we shared lovely times in my staff caravan, but the time was drawing ever nearer to September when my job would end, and I would be departing for ever to a new life in Scotland. As I made my final preparations for my journey, not wanting to leave my newly found happiness, John gave me a farewell gift. With tears in his eyes he watched as I unwrapped an all-in-one motorcycle suit, knowing that he was saying goodbye to me. He wanted me to be safe and warm as I drove out of his life. We had a last wonderful night in the caravan, and we drove to Mullacott roundabout, where I went one way and he went the other.

Tears blurred my eyes as I reached Blackmoor Gate. I had a long ride ahead to reach my first youth hostel at St Briavels, beyond Chepstow, by nightfall. On and on I rode. I should have been excited by this new life I was going to; I'd been planning it in minute detail for months. Instead, the further I rode away from John, the more miserable I felt.

At Brent Knoll, somewhere on the road to Bristol, I pulled into a layby for a cuppa from my flask of tea. I leaned over a five-bar gate and looked up at the big hill. Suddenly, to the amazement of the people around me who had parked up for a break, I shouted out, "I'm coming back, John! I'm coming back!"

All the plans I had made were now gone. I was not afraid of making that trip, but I was afraid of losing the only true love I had ever known.

Turning around, I drove into a fierce storm. Hailstones rattled on my visor and the crosswind threatened to throw me across the road. On and on I drove, becoming colder and stiffer. It took several hours and on my approach to Barnstaple I had to think of a way to contact John. No mobile phones then! I wrote a note to put through his door, hoping no one would see me deliver it and also praying that he would get it.

"I am fishing down on Castle Quay around 7:30pm. Care to join me, Mr Knight?" Mr Knight was my code name for John, my knight in shining armour.

With two hours to kill and a heavily loaded bike, and hoping that no one would see me, I made my way there and waited, watching the tidal River Taw make its way up from the sea. I was hungry, anxious, excited and in love. Would he see my message? Would he come? The stormy sunset glowered over the water. It was almost 7:30pm and the date was 10 September 1983, a day that would change my life forever, for around the corner came John on his old MZ motorbike. He leapt off and we rushed towards each other. I was in his arms saying over and over, "I came back," and, "What are we going to do, John?"

He was crying with joy, "My girl in the blue suit; I thought I'd lost you forever," and, "Wait there, I'll be right back with some things, for I've had enough too."

With that, he was gone. I knew that his marriage had broken up a long time ago, but his wife would insult him by hanging around his workplace on a Friday, waiting for his wages for her to spend in the pub. John and I never drank.

An hour later John reappeared, plus his old, battered guitar over his back. We stocked up on some essentials and at my suggestion we went to a holiday park near Instow and hired a nice caravan for two weeks under the name of Mr and Mrs Knight! By now it was dark. I cooked a great supper. We had a fantastic bath and lots to talk about and to plan our future together. I melted into dreamland in John's arms and awoke next day to see his wonderful smile beside me.

We were on the run! No one knew where we were. Our happiness overflowed. As we walked the old railway line to Bideford one morning a police car pulled up. Oh no! A police officer unfolded himself from the car.

"You alright, John?"

"Yes mate, never felt better."

"That's fine then, your secret's safe with me. Good luck, you deserve it!"

He was an old friend of John's, a fellow snooker player and dog handler. John also had been a dog handler and they often met up with their German Shepherds during the course of their work.

Several weeks later we moved onto a residential caravan park and John had no trouble in providing a reference to the site owners as he was well known and liked in the area. By now, the game was up, and our respective spouses knew where we were. We had a nice little caravan to rent and we were both working. There was never any problem with money because we shared everything. I'd found a true friend and soulmate. So certain were we about each other that we went to a solicitor friend and I changed my name to John's by deed poll. We were henceforth known as Mr and Mrs Beer and looked forward to the day when we would finally marry.

But so much was to happen before then. It was not an easy journey, but we had each other. We were a rock solid unit. We had a bond that no one could break. True love, no matter what they tried; and oh how they tried!

When Ken thought John was at work he came and smashed the caravan windows with a brick and limped off to the bus stop. But it was John's half day off and I watched, in fascination and horror, as he caught up with Ken and grabbed him by the collar, lifted him up into the air and then changed the shape of Bickington bus shelter for ever as he threw Ken against it, threatening that worse was to follow if he should ever come near me again. John was very strong. Now we had the embarrassing task of telling the residential park owners about the broken windows. How much would we have to pay to repair the damage? Would we have to leave?

The residential park owners were on our side. They knew John and they were on friendly terms as they both belonged to the same martial arts establishment. Ken had done us a favour; we were put in a much nicer caravan, tucked away down in a corner amongst the trees. It was a perfect love nest. I built us a cosy little home that autumn. Although we were working hard we had enjoyable evenings before the daylight went, cycling the lanes or to the beach with a picnic tea, returning home along the Tarka Trail from Instow with the sun setting behind us. As the tide pushed the River Taw in full flood, we would race the laden sand barges and return home glowing with energy.

On our day off, we went to my mother's home in Croyde, where John would do lots of jobs for her such as mending gutters and repairing windows and roof tiles. I would cut the hedges and do other things. My mother was mellowing in her widowhood and really warmed towards John. She was so pleased that I now had a real man that loved and looked after me. She actually invited us inside her home for a meal one day, something unknown before, and from then on she would cook us lunch and the three of us would sit around the little kitchen table on that one day we had off each week.

It was on one of these occasions that John leaned across the table and said, "Mrs Smith, there's something I want to say."

"Call me May," said my mother.

"It would do me a great honour," John continued, "if you would say 'yes' to my marrying your daughter one day, when we are both free."

"I couldn't be happier," she replied, "and the sooner it happens, the better!"

The three of us sat there with tears of joy and I felt closer to my mother then that at any time in my life.

"There's a special dress you can wear for your wedding. I'll show it to you just in case I shan't be there." A year later, she was dead. She must have known.

We accompanied her to the hospital to hear the specialist's verdict of cancer of the bile duct and six months left to live. She was so calm about it all as we helped her to pack up her home and sell her belongings. We couldn't look after her in a small caravan as she soon needed specialist nursing care. She was so sad that she had to sell her home to pay to go into a care home. She kept saying that my inheritance, her place, was being sold, kept saying sorry, I would no longer have what was supposed to have been handed down to me.

She passed away in Castle Rock, Mortehoe, on 19 December 1984 and the last thing that she had struggled to write in her diary, hours before she died, was, "I know that you and John will be happy. I want you to know this: I see a great future for you both…" and the writing got faint and went.

How strange life can be. The irony of it is that I felt such a bond, such love, flowing between my mother and myself just for those few short months under her death sentence. As I looked at her body in that nursing home bed I thought how sad it was that she wouldn't see us being married. I placed a chrysanthemum between her hands and left her in the hush of that room, which had a beautiful view out across the sea to Lundy Island, although she never saw it. I collected her things and went to the matron's office. I walked away from a mother I had only just found and into the arms of my future loving husband.

We had both filed for a divorce. Our respective spouses had got together and hatched a plan to bring us down. Nasty character-crushing letters of untruths were sent to our respective employers. That didn't work, as our employers were forewarned that something like this would happen. They valued us as we were good workers. Next, they tried malicious phone calls and that was no good either.

On 2 January 1985, Ken sent me some freesias with a nasty note. It was our twenty-fifth wedding anniversary and freesias were in the bouquet I made for my wedding. He also sent a death threat and texts cut out from a Bible and stuck on a card about fornication. Our solicitors were ahead of him, however, as when my mother had lain dying she made an affidavit in her will to say that Ken should receive nothing, as she remembered all the troubles he had caused and how badly he treated me. She was certain that he would try to claim any money after she was gone, and she was right. I bet he was hopping mad, as no deal!

We cycled away on that January morning and put our bikes on the train to Penzance. We did a week's cycle tour of the Land's End peninsula, all round West Cornwall. We even got onto St Michael's Mount, where it started to snow! I remember brewing up our tea on our little stove and thinking how happy we were, doing what my mother suggested, not to mope but to, "Get out there, go away for a bit. Life is for living; you're a long time dead!"

I still kept up my training plus renewing my flying licence at Gloucester, which was very costly. Things had become very difficult as the instruments were being modernised and I had a problem seeing them. I needed glasses and nothing but perfect vision would do. No more solos, but I could still be a co-pilot, and practised with the helicopter travelling at the same speed as the Oldenburg (the Lundy supply ship), winching up a casualty from the deck and down again. Fantastic stuff! It was really exciting; I loved every minute. I was fit and strong and practised all sorts of mock emergency exercises with the Sea King helicopter, also with the police and fire brigade. I was still teaching swimming and doing orienteering. I was being encouraged every step of the way by John, who did not want me to give up just because we were living a new life together.

Ken went to the County Court for failing to pay the rent and rates. We sat in on the hearing, unobserved. He walked in on crutches, specially borrowed for the occasion, and pleaded that his wife had left him and he had to bring up two children. Well, *they* had left home a long time ago! He came up with so many lies and was sentenced to two months in prison. At least we would be left alone for a while. By May, he was released. A letter arrived from his solicitor. Ken thought I had been left money when my mother died and demanded I give him some.

We became increasingly fed up. He sent a private detective to spy on our caravan. The site owners knew all about it and backed our latest plan. We were going to spend two months cycle touring around Britain, camping en-route. The site owners would temporarily board our place up and no one would know where we had gone. We finished our jobs having practised cycling with loaded panniers every night. Yes, I did have some money left from my mother. Not enough to buy a house but enough not to worry for a bit.

So in the morning of 27 April we set off very early, having paid up our rent for two months, and went off on our exciting

adventure, the adventure of a lifetime. John had only ever been as far as Taunton and once to Margate. I had planned the whole route. We had also joined the YHA to fall back on, in case of emergency.

As we used up our maps en-route and gradually shed our winter clothing, we would send these home to the site owners along with the latest postcard of where we had stayed. We had a Vango Force Ten tent. It withstood tremendous gales on some exposed campsites. Ours was often still standing when all the others had gone down in the night. We had a Trangia stove that used meths as fuel, plus a mini Globetrotter gas stove.

We had a fantastic trip, very hard at times. Mid Wales was memorable for its vast beauty. We camped at the foot of Snowdon. I remember doing the Snowdon Run a couple of years before in under three hours. I think the proudest moment was cycling around Loch Ness and then onto the ferry to the Isle of Skye. We met so many interesting people.

Norfolk was a particularly wonderful county of large skies and reed beds, crumbling coasts and friendly people. We eventually revisited Land's End and spent two weeks camping on one site at Marazion, opposite St Michael's Mount, that we had visited previously. Little did we know that we were camping just a couple of yards away from what was to be our home!

We did have the most amazing trip, never arguing, always loving one another, in what at times could be very difficult circumstances. All day battling with a headwind, only to arrive to find the campsite that was listed in the book no longer existed; having to find the reserves to pedal to the next site miles away and then to find the energy to pitch tent and make a meal. So in love were we that we could conquer anything.

Returning home to the residential caravan park, we couldn't settle, so unwound by cycling and camping on Exmoor for a week. Whilst we were away our decree nisi divorce papers were served to us. We now had to wait up to a maximum of three years, as it was back then, before we would be free.

I resumed my seasonal lifeguarding on various North Devon beaches and John did lots of odd jobbing. We did another cycle tour to Marazion, as we were drawn to the place, and stayed at the same campsite as before. The campsite owners showed us a beautiful mobile home for sale, with three bedrooms, fitted kitchen, all the furniture there ready to move into at a moment's notice. Oh, how tempted we were! The garden, although becoming a bit overgrown, had three waterfalls and four ponds and many garden statues. We were given a couple of weeks to think about it; Mother's legacy would easily cover the purchase.

The idea bubbled away inside us. I had moved many times, but John had never lived anywhere but Barnstaple. The matter was settled for us whilst having a massive plate of fish and chips in the local Marazion café.

"You look excited," commented the friendly owners and we told them about our big decision of whether to move or not.

They were nearly as excited as us and said, "We'll move you for nothing; we've got a van. And the meal is on us!"

We returned to the campsite, I signed the papers with my souvenir Isle of Skye pen, and we were now home owners! Neither of us, in our wildest dreams, would ever think that we would own a home.

A fine October day in 1985 saw us, riding our separate motorbikes, following the van all the way down to Marazion. We had left the past behind to make a new start. So much lay before us: new places to explore, new people and new employment. We were a happy couple, and everyone assumed that we were married as we had the same name. We were invincible. Our home was with several others on this campsite in a beautifully landscaped setting. Besides camping, there were holiday caravans as well.

John applied for many jobs without success as there were a hundred applicants after one job. I was fortunate as I taught swimming and could lifeguard any of the many beaches. After several anxious weeks and with winter setting in, the problem was solved from an unexpected source.

I had a temporary position at the local heliport, serving the Isle of Scilly, just for a few weeks and was about to take up a lifetime dream, to go to art school. John was thrilled that this was going to happen and encouraged me so much. As I was about to start, and we were both so happy with life, the campsite owner said he had something serious to discuss with us and could we meet that evening in his house. Oh no! Please, not now things were going so well. Did he want us to sell up? Had we done something wrong? Whatever it was, we had each other and would face it together.

As we entered the owner's sitting room, his wife brought in drinks on a tray. As neither of us drank we had some fruit juice instead. Official papers were spread out on a large table. John and I glanced at one another; this was serious. He squeezed my hand and I felt stronger. The site owner was also the mayor and his wife was well up on the local council.

"Ah, John," said the site owner, "we know that you have been trying so hard to find employment and we have come to a decision…" Oh, here it comes, I thought. "Would you be willing to consider working for us as site maintenance manager?" Wow, this wasn't what we expected! "You can live here and no longer pay us ground rent for your home. Keep the site grass cut, roads and paths swept, empty the camping bins, clean the shower block and laundry rooms. Also, we have plans…" Here he indicated the papers on the table. A swimming pool was to be built just yards from our place and all the holiday caravans were going to be replaced with brick-built chalets and help would be needed to paint them. In winter there would be plenty of upkeep that would be ongoing. I thought John would jump at the chance but, after he gave me a double hand-squeeze, he said we needed time to think about it, which we did.

We already had a job that we both enjoyed on a Friday evening and Saturday, doing holiday lets, cleaning fourteen flats in a mansion. We had a great boss who said we could keep all the 'perks' left behind. We did an excellent job and for the entire holiday season we collected enough perks to keep us in toilet rolls, washing-up liquid, soap, washing powder, cooking foil and Brillo pads to last a year and enough flour, sugar, margarine, cooking oil and eggs to keep me cake baking for another six months. A lot of people on holiday in those days used to arrive by train and couldn't take home what they hadn't used. But this job was only part-time and only for a few months in the year.

At home, we talked about it well into the night because, once the swimming pool was built, I would be given the job of setting up a swim school and running it. John and I had also given consideration to setting up our own art business and becoming self-employed, so we were torn as to what to do. Take a chance on our own business, becoming successful, or having permanent full-time jobs on site, on our doorstep?

I was going to the Penzance School of Art three days a week, doing homework and paintings to sell of an evening. John was very good at framing and I had taught him to draw and paint well. So well in fact that he had begun to sell his work and we had things for sale in various galleries. We had also acquired a camper van which served as a mobile studio and we would park up at a beauty spot, set up easels and interested people would buy what we 'just happened to have on board'. Then we would get out our guitars and, if staying somewhere overnight on a holiday park, others would join us with their guitars. It was wonderful, around campfires, meeting people from all over the world and sharing experiences.

So, we were torn between our rather happy but uncertain lifestyle, where we could up sticks and go off somewhere for a night or two, sell paintings and go to art school, or settle for a job that was certain but tied us down to be on site most of the time. And the biggest problem with that would be if there was some kind of fall out and we wanted to leave. Living on top of the job, would it work?

John was given a month to think about it. I definitely wanted the freedom side of our life: to go daffodil picking in the spring and pack them for market, or ride out on my cycle to a quiet spot and sketch a mine stack that some passer-by would immediately buy; to be able to take off on a fine day with a picnic and paints, to meet all kinds of people on holiday, tend our garden and waterfalls, enjoy our new life and wait for our decree absolutes to come through.

In the end we chose security. A steady, 'safe' income. John was happy cutting and strimming the site grass. He took a pride in it and it had never looked so good. The campers loved him and would spend ages yakking to him. One of his jobs was to replace the black bin bags that sat in a metal ring with a rubber lid that came down on top. One morning, a bleary-eyed camper strolled down in flip-flops and shorts, lifted the rubber lid and poured all the contents of his waste bucket into what he thought was a black bin bag. There wasn't one, as John was changing them, so he got all of his own rubbish back, down his bare legs! How they laughed.

We met some great people from all over the place who came, mainly, to visit St Michael's Mount, which I jokingly called Mickey's Pimple. But all good holiday seasons come to an end and winter came, the building started on the swimming pool and chalets and I saw John at lunchtimes in between art school, heliport training, re-taking my bronze medallion prior to teaching and we still kept our holiday flats job, which lasted until Christmas.

January 1986 had me laying mosaic tiles in the swimming pool floor. This was a picture of a Cornish Engine House. I was very pleased with my efforts. It was only slightly marred at the special grand opening night, with all the local dignitaries in attendance. The local reporter had given credit for the design to the site owner's wife, and apparently nobody saw fit to put them straight.

The site owner's wife wanted me to teach swimming. When I do something, I like to do it properly, through the ASA and their approved lessons which are, or were at that time, six-week courses.

"Oh no," she said, "I just want someone to go in the water and help people, you know, just casual like."

Her husband got her to see sense and I set up a course for beginners with everyone passing after six weeks and gaining a certificate. This led to improvers, then one for pensioners, then a school class came in and by this time I was having trouble trying to juggle the things that I had really moved here to do: my art and setting up our own thing. I couldn't let John manage our holiday lets job of cleaning fourteen flats on his own; it was a joint effort that we both enjoyed, and we didn't want to disappoint our really great boss or lose our perks.

We no longer had time to go cycling, my training was slipping, we had a job to keep up our painting commissions. What started as a straightforward job for John got extended into the evenings as we were asked to stand in and manage the site and pool until 11pm whilst they, the site owners, had some time off and went out. It was a huge responsibility. There was no lifeguard. There was just a murky video fed into the owner's office, showing what went on in the swimming pool. Too late if someone was drowning, but the wife could see what I was doing and started to criticise my actions when teaching. So I enlisted her help and got her into the water, which she was none too happy about, being such a large person.

One day, she told us to give up our cleaning job at the flats because she wanted me to squeeze in another lesson at the weekends, on changeover day. This we refused to do as we had that job first. She got very angry. She was jealous that we had another job and we found out that she had a long running difference of opinion with our laid-back boss. It didn't bother him, and he gave us a rise!

I was excelling at the art school. I took part in an open-air exhibition at Newlyn, where paintings were displayed on the seafront railings. I was showing with famous artists either side of me and did well. Then I was invited to submit work for an annual exhibition in the great Newlyn Gallery, which was world famous. To get something chosen was an accolade and I had done it. I did not go to the preview as I hadn't got any high heels to totter about on and I couldn't talk la-di-dah language or stick my little finger out when raising a glass of wine that I didn't want. But John and I did visit at a later date and he was so proud of me, as we carefully trod our way around the exhibits and spoke in whispers in that grand building.

Another season got underway at the campsite. Visitors came and went. They would chat to us in our garden on their way to and from the pool or shower block. Then the wife didn't want us to chat to people. Well that was the whole point of it: people came and relaxed and enjoyed a casual conversation about their home life and problems and we were on our own patch in our own little garden and people came in to buy our paintings. The wife wanted to put a stop to that as it was on their land. A conflict of opinions came about. John got fed up with it but at that time could do nothing about it as more and more work and little extra duties got piled onto him. Just as things were getting us down, our divorces came through. Finally, we had made it!

That July evening we strolled down a country lane, hand in hand, with the fragrance of wild flowers filling the air. We reached a little stone bridge with a stream flowing through. Long-tailed tits were flitting in and out of the willows and John picked a wild pink rose from the hedge. I could see the sunset reflecting in his loving eyes as he knelt down, tenderly kissed my hand and formally proposed to me.

"Yes," I said. "Beyond all doubts, for ever and ever."

We strolled home in the dusk as the moon rose and the owls called in the woods. I placed the rose in a book, and we named that bridge 'Marry Me Bridge'.

John got a special licence. That way, no one would see our names in the list of forthcoming marriages displayed on the town hall noticeboard. Everyone assumed we were married, as I said before, because we had the same name. We were to be married the following Monday at 9:30am. We wanted a few days off to go away and be back by Friday to clean our holiday flats. The wife was very put out that we wanted some time off without much notice. The evening before our wedding I made some beautiful buttonholes of flowers from our garden. I removed the tissue paper from the dress that my mother had given me and did a dress rehearsal in the shower block as I did not want John to see!

The morning of 21 July 1986 started out misty. A taxi took us to St John's Hall in Penzance. As we waited for the weekend deaths to be registered, John left me and went to find two witnesses off the street. They were on holiday from Exeter and they thought that John was trying to sell them something.

"No," he said. "There's my bride-to-be, up on the steps over there!"

They thought it was the most romantic thing that had ever happened to them. They had two children: a very little girl and a baby in a papoose. I asked the girl if she would like to be my bridesmaid and hold my bag and lace gloves. She was thrilled.

The registrar had a brown paper bag and inside were some roses which we put in a vase for our wedding. We went into the little office and as she locked the door and took the phone off the hook I finally realised that this was it, the day we had longed for had come. There was no big mistake this time. No jumping out of the frying pan and into the fire. I had found real love and support. I knew beyond doubt that I was doing the right thing. It was a wonderful intimate moment as John placed that ring on my finger.

It didn't matter that we had no official photographer or grand reception. We just took some photos of each other and exchanged addresses with our witnesses, who were still quite overcome with it all. Then John and I had a wedding breakfast across the road in the Buttery. Yes, we had an all-day breakfast fry-up!

"Oh, are you going to a wedding?" asked the proprietor.

"No," replied John, "We've just been to our own."

"Then your meal is on the house. Have anything you like!"

So we followed our fry-up with apple strudel and ice cream. What a combination!

Then we did a bit of shopping in the local supermarket and people were eyeing us up and down at the checkout, all dolled up at 11 o'clock on a Monday morning.

Returning back home, I couldn't wait to get my tights off. No, it wasn't that I wanted to fall straight into bed, it was because the crotch was killing me as I'd bought a size too small! We took some

private photos and then set off on our motorbikes to stay with friends who had a B&B at Crackington Haven in North Cornwall. They gave us a champagne evening dinner, plus strawberries from their market garden. We strolled down to the beach as the sun set and a band played on the little seafront as if specially for our day. The stars came out as we climbed the hill back to our comfy room in the B&B, where we immediately fell fast asleep as we were so tired.

The following day there was a royal wedding. We went to look around Bude but all the shop people were watching it on TV at the back of their premises and it was a job to get served. Our marriage, with a simple wedding that only cost £45 for a special licence, outlasted the royal one that was full of pomp in Westminster Abbey and cost millions. We had a couple of lovely days with our friends; all their B&B guests had clubbed together and bought us a wedding present, a lovely vase. We said we would be back next year for our anniversary but that never happened:

tragically our friends that ran the B&B died. It was a great shock and a reminder that nothing stays the same. It reinforced our determination to make the most of our lives.

Returning home married, we appeared to the outside world to be no different but inside we were: stronger, bonded, even more committed and in love. But as the summer wore on and we wore out, with so much extra work piled on by the wife, we had to seriously take stock of our situation. It couldn't go on like this as the wife was now trying to drive a wedge between us. No hope! No one could do that! John had become her obsession; he could do no wrong and I could do no right. She was jealous of what we had: perfect harmony and true love. We were a unit and nothing was going to separate us. The atmosphere between her and her husband was tense and we heard their constant bickering overflowing onto the campsite.

We soldiered on for the rest of the season but I was getting dreadful headaches teaching in the swimming pool. It got so bad that I became unwell and had to stop because, I told the wife, the air ducting was not big enough to tackle the fumes from the chlorine.

"But what about my reputation as a first-class swim school?" was her response.

They had to close the pool, as I had said they would all along. That's right, no one would listen to a mere female or the builders' warning during construction. It was shut for over six months, which meant I was able to do more painting and sign on for another year at art school. At first, John had enjoyed his work around the campsite but now the cracks were appearing as the site owners were falling out with each other. A big family conference ensued. We could sense a change. Were they going to sell up? We loved our home and where we lived. It was beautiful.

Then came the bombshell. It was all over. Our dream out in the west had ended. New owners took over the site. Everyone's ground rent went up. John lost his job and free rent with it. We sold our motorbikes although, thank goodness, we still had our campervan. Our home went up for sale and we made a massive profit. People were queuing up to buy places in West Cornwall. We got four times the price we paid for it. Ten per cent of the sale of a mobile home goes to the site owner but we had done exceptionally well out of this sale. We purchased a bigger campervan as we would be living in it for some time to come.

It was impossible to still attend the art school as we could find no permanent pitch for our campervan. We hadn't enough money to buy a house but we did have enough to purchase another mobile home or a caravan. I also collected a considerable amount of interest on a savings account that had matured. We weren't broke but we were careful. We stayed around the Penzance area for a bit, until on one site we met up with a group of people who were travelling around the country, working on farms or market gardens on the way. The spring of 1987 was a varied and interesting time as we joined this group. The other members came from all walks of life and between us we could turn our hands to anything. There were around twenty of us, with five vehicles.

The first job we went to, and where we were expected, was on a remote farm. We all parked up and were made welcome. Our job was to completely empty a huge barn of all its machinery and bales, fencing and drums. Luckily, I found I could still drive a tractor, even though it was an ancient Fordson. I moved thousands of bales. John was mending fences. Everyone was singing. It was great. A massive cauldron of stew would turn up at midday, provided by the farm, so long as we provided our own plates and cutlery. One lump sum was paid for our work which was divided amicably amongst us. In the evening guitars came out. It seemed as if anyone with a campervan owned guitars as well! There was no drinking or drugs, but plenty of books. One van was like a mobile library. We were like a bunch of middle-aged students. We had writers, musicians, and artists amongst us.

We all got on well together but never delved into each other's histories.

This was the life! Our next job was picking daffodils, being sure to wear the gloves provided to avoid a nasty rash from the juice of the cut stems. I soon got more pay as a packer as my experience all those years ago on the nursery stood me in good stead. We had another barn job in another county, to decorate it in a rustic style for a wedding. Our men scaled ladders and tied sheaves of corn to the rafters. We made posies and set long trestle tables with flowers. The bride-to-be came to inspect it just hours before the wedding and promptly burst into tears! Didn't she like what we had done? She did, but her florist had let her down and had not produced her wedding bouquet or the bridesmaids' flowers, nor the gents' buttonholes. Half an hour later, John and I were at a market garden, buying up most of their flowers and greenery. We raced back to the wedding venue, armed with raffia, tape and wire and once again my past experience was put into action as I quickly made all of the required floral items. With a half hour to spare before the ceremony I sat down exhausted but elated. It all looked wonderful and went off extremely well and we were handsomely paid for our efforts.

Reaching Dorset, we were expected at our next unromantic venue: a pig farm! Ah well, you couldn't win them all! We had to dismantle lots of pig shelters on an organic farm high in the hills. It was 'high' all right! The heat beat down and the smell came up. The corrugated metal of the curved shelters was so hot we could feel it through our protective gloves. I had the bright idea of hosing the metal down with cold water. The pig farmer leaned back, scratched his head, replaced his cap and said, "Gor, darn it, mother; you's got somethin' there. In all the years us 'as been doin' this, us as never thought o' that!" and he went off chuckling and slapping his thigh. We all just rolled about laughing, it was so funny.

We were a happy band of workers. Life was never dull. We did hedging and ditching on the Somerset Levels with Glastonbury Tor looking down on our efforts. The bird life was amazing as we toiled amongst the reed beds. It reminded us of our cycle tour in Norfolk, where the cold wind whipped across the fens and the dry reeds rattled in response. We got black and boggy smelling but the basket maker's farm where we camped provided us with showers each night and invited us all in to share their huge inglenook fire. There were rugs and sheepskins on the floor, roast potatoes passed around and happy contentment after a hard day's work. Our guitars came out and my eyelids would droop whilst performing until I was playing by instinct only. Back in our campervan we knew that this couldn't last; something was bound to break it all up.

It did. Peter, our 'leader', who knew all the farms and places where his travelling band of workers could earn some money, became unwell at intervals. He had been abroad a lot and had contracted malaria. This kept flaring up and other things were ailing him too. He got worse as we made our way towards Bristol. He looked dreadful and was taken into hospital. He never came out. He instructed us to sell his campervan and divide the proceeds between us. It was such a sad, sad time. John played a lament on Pete's guitar as we all met up one last time before going our separate ways. I was crying and John had a lump in his throat as we tried to force down our final meal as a group. We all promised to write but never did. It was best remembered as it was, a truly wonderful close-knit band of like-minded people that just happened to meet along life's road for a short time.

Autumn of 1987 found us wending our way from Bristol onto the Quantock hills. Parking up on a ridge under some beech hedges, we awoke early one morning to the sound of tapping on our campervan. Was some angry farmer trying to move us on? Peering out into the thick mist, we discovered that it was red deer with their antlers in a twist. They had added some dents to our battered vehicle. They went off, roaring and bellowing, in an autumn rut, vying for females.

We were due at an artist friend's farm in a few days' time to goat-sit for a couple of weeks. We would have to make a decision soon as to what we were going to do. We couldn't spend the rest of our lives travelling, however romantic it seemed to any onlookers. It was a tiring life at times, like living in a constant doll's house as cold nights set in and the van would run with condensation. With not much room to manoeuvre and having to constantly put things securely away before moving off, it was becoming more of a chore than a pleasure. We missed the company of the others but cherished our love and solitude with each passing day and night.

As we wound our way down off the Quantock hills, with brown beech hedges damp and dripping with fog, we had a puncture from hedge cuttings left in the road. As John lay in a wet ditch, changing the wheel, I thought we were doing the right thing in thinking of finding a permanent base.

We drove on towards Wheddon Cross on Exmoor, almost back into home territory, but first we turned left and descended into a colourful autumn riot of trees. We followed the wooded valley winding its way towards Dulverton where, stepping back in time, we purchased provisions and then were told by a 'horsey set' to move on. John told them to remove the manure that had lodged beneath their noses and to, "Speak prupper, like us Devon volk!" With that, the owner of the gun and country wear shop came out and told the horsey hunt set not to treat us like scum as we were also his customers, who had purchased the same articles as they had. Well we had bought, quite some time ago, good fishing and walking gear. With that, they rode off.

We stayed at a farm at Brushford. I milked the goats like mad whilst John held their heads in an arm lock and fed them. One morning we couldn't find them and got very worried. Why do things go wrong when you are looking after someone else's stuff?

We needn't have panicked. After searching several fields we found them near the farmhouse, grinning at us from on top of a horsebox! Perhaps they didn't like their new teat squeezer and arm locker!

Returning up onto Exmoor the once purple heather now dripped in blacks and browns on each side of the road. The further we rose, the thicker the driving wet fog became. Descending into Withypool, we got fuel at the little pump and made a few purchases in the post office-come-village shop. Woodsmoke curled downwards, clamped by the miserable damp conditions. As we continued up to Sandyway we seemed to be forever chasing and joining up the big geographic circle that we had made: we were instinctively returning home, to Barnstaple. How had it come to this? Our dream in the west had now gone. Who would have thought that we had had another existence and so much adventure packed into the last three years?

With nowhere to stay in Barnstaple we parked up in Rock Park. We carried our cycles on our campervan plus our sea and trout rods. We cycled out to Newbridge and did some fly-fishing on the Taw. I used a good old black and silver fly at first, until I remembered the trout fishing season was now closed. What were we thinking of? We should have known better, so undid our sea gear instead and caught a few late mullet by Rock Park. They were uneatable, gone over. Like everything else in our life lately, gone over, but not our enduring love and faith in one another. Why on earth had we landed back here when there were so many other exciting places to live in? Were we mad? Perhaps we needed to come down from our dream and get normal and find somewhere to rent.

Fate now stepped in, so opportune. A jogger tapped on our van, which we called 'Calendula', and had an orange marigold painted on the side.

"Is that you? John?"

"Yes, you old bugger."

"What are you doing back in good old Barum? Thought you'd vanished for ever," said John's old mate. We spoke of our search for somewhere. An hour later he had directed us to a residential mobile home park near Landkey, where he lived. A home had just come on the market. The price was very low because it needed lots of work done to it, including a new roof. I fell in love with it and its little stove that heated the water and burned coke, coal and, if you were careful, some wood. A beautiful view stretched over the hills one way and across the estuary in the other direction. It was tiny with one mini bedroom, a galley kitchen, a bath and living room plus a sunny greenhouse porch. An apple tree guarded the garden, lawn and veggie patch and an old shed stood at a drunken angle, filled with wood and coke to last for years.

We were to spend the next nine years in this place; we named it Little Sanctuary and had that sign put on our gate. It lived up to its name most of the time. It was here that we became self-employed, painting and framing, working towards my first solo exhibition, which was a huge success. My next exhibition, containing thirty-six pieces of work, was at the Elliott Gallery in Braunton. John had done much of the framing and we secured a selling spot in that place for years to come. Our work was on sale throughout the south west. We had a very productive few years, based in that tiny mobile home with its little stove, and in addition our campervan still served as a mobile studio. We met all sorts of customers en-route and were exhibiting and selling in many galleries, cafes and shops.

We were the perfect team, the perfect couple, bouncing off one another, always ready with a pun. Practical jokes were the norm. I bought a pair of false teeth from a sweet shop, the edible sort. I got up just before John one morning. He had left his dentures to soak overnight in some frothy liquid cleanser. I quickly emptied it away, removed John's dentures and replaced them with the much smaller false teeth from the sweet shop. Oh!

When John got up, all bleary eyed, minus his glasses, groping around for his dentures… "They've *shrunk*!" His face was a picture and I was doubled up laughing.

Our business was doing well and making a small profit. I supplemented it with lifeguarding and teaching, but this time at my own pace and not someone else's. I took up my training again and co-piloted from Plymouth to Hartland Point with Castle Air and thence to Lundy, in winter, where I would work for a few weeks at a time. Although I would be away from John he didn't mind; in fact he positively encouraged me as the extra money was useful and he could progress unhindered, whilst I was away, making frames for our pictures. He was always waiting on Bideford Quay on my return and our reunion would be a joyful celebration. After he had driven me home, I would find that he had carefully arranged a meal for us. If it was a salad it would be artistically laid out, with fancy lily-shaped tomatoes and scored cucumber slices. Brown and white bread slices he would make into alternate colour triangles. Later, our loving would be intense after time spent apart. We were so in love. We cycled and swam, we went to various galleries, swapping work around, chatting to the owners, collecting money to put in our work account. Life was wonderful.

On 30 November 1985 I celebrated my fifty-fifth birthday, using two free entry coupons given away by a local newspaper to go to Clovelly. This was an ideal time to go, free of tourists, after which we were going to Bude for lunch and a gallery visit, then a quiet ride home to put a match to an already laid fire and have tea. It was a cold, crisp day. We took a few photos on Clovelly Quay and started the climb back up the cobbled street. John was very quiet. I glanced across to see that he was pale and sweaty – on such a cold day too.

As we neared the top he sat down. "Do you mind if we don't go to Bude? I just feel a bit off colour, that's all."

I'd never known John to feel unwell; he was always so fit and robust. We had a quiet drive back home, put an early match to that already laid fire and listened to some music before going to bed.

There was a subtle change in John leading up to Christmas. He became irritable and spent more time out in the shed, where nothing seemed to go right with the framing. I could hear cursing and swearing, and stuff being thrown about. On Christmas Day we cycled to Instow, where we ate our turkey sandwiches and collected two saddlebags of wood from the beach for our store. John got very cold despite wearing the right gear. He seemed to withdraw into himself but said he was okay and asked me to stop going on. That hurt; he'd never spoken to me like that before.

Then 1986 arrived and our idyll was about to end. On 2 January I was up and about while John was still in bed. I went outside to fill the coal bucket and my 80-year-old neighbour was shifting furniture. I asked her if she needed some help. It was lucky that she didn't because at that moment John called out from the bedroom. He was feeling very unwell. He looked dreadful. He was having a heart attack.

I dialled 999. I kept absolutely cool, running through all the first aid procedures that I had done many times before at work. As he stopped breathing I did CPR and mouth-to-mouth with not a single moment of panic. The ambulance crew took over. I had written down the time of onset, pulse rate and symptoms. As he was taken away I wondered if I would ever see him alive again and, if so, what would he be like. Left alone, standing in our little home, I looked at a half-finished portrait of Exmoor that John had been working on. Would he ever complete it? I would leave it there as a talisman in the hope that he would return.

Oh, my darling husband, my strong, ever-faithful lover, had I driven you – ourselves – too hard? Our zest for life and adventure, had it been too much? You, the one always helping others, cheerfully lending a hand wherever needed, coaxing me along in life, what now? Without you… What if…? I must not think like this, I told myself. I must be positive for your sake, send healing thoughts.

Maybe we should never have cycled so much, or swum so many times. I should have taken into consideration that John, now sixty-six, was eleven years my senior. But he never flagged, never slowed down, until that day in Clovelly.

After two weeks in intensive care, John sat out on the ward, weak and helpless. I was summoned to see the specialist. John had had a coronary and was lucky to be alive. I said that it was probably all my fault because of the active life we had led but was told that if we hadn't been so active it would probably have happened much sooner.

"There's something else…" The specialist revealed that John also had type 2 diabetes, "…probably for quite some time." He asked about our living arrangements and was aghast that we lived and worked in such a small, and now unsuitable, place. We had to move, and urgently, as we needed carers.

"We can bloody well do without them!" John yelled.

"But they wouldn't even be able to get around the bed," I replied. "Even we have to climb over the end to get into it."

"Oh f***, f***, f***! Get on with it then! Ruin our lives!"

His language was dreadful. My kind and loving husband had changed. I was warned that this would happen.

"There's a bloody awful diet I'm supposed to be on, too. I might as well not be here." With this, he tried to rip the tubes out of his arm. I pressed the alarm and the staff came running. The ward was in uproar.

"Go on, leave me! Get a better life!"

As a sedative took over, he looked so peaceful. Staff were kind and quite unperturbed at this outburst.

I had been given thirteen years of happiness. I had no intention of leaving. I would be staying, no matter how rocky the road ahead. Had I but known it then, the rocks had already started to fall and we would be sorely tried as we moved into our next place.

As I stood in our now empty 'Little Sanctuary' and remembered the last seven years, encapsulated in the dust motes drifting across the picture window, I wept. There was my little galley kitchen, where so many meals had been made, and the scorch mark John had left on the worktop from an experiment with a blow torch. I caressed it now. I had cursed it then. Then there were the notch marks on the pull-down table, where he had missed, and the craft knife had slipped off the drawing board.

The geese in the field behind were looking up expectantly for their piece of morning toast to come sailing out of the window. Now no more. They loved to listen to country and western music and our guitar playing, heads cocked to one side. Now no more. As I took a last look around I turned the key in the lock for the last time. Now no more.

Oh dear God, help me. I so loved this place.

Chapter 11 : Misfits in God's Waiting Room

The day we moved into a grey flat, surrounded by very old people, a community room, and a warden, was one of the most soul-destroying moments of my life. With buzzers and emergency 'light pull' alarms in every room, grab rails and walking frames, it made your mind up already to quit this life.

Even before all our bits and pieces had been moved in, in the middle of the kitchen amongst the boxes, John promptly passed out. It had taken twenty minutes to get him up the stairs to this first floor flat. It must have been too much.

The removal man was one of John's friends from schooldays and fishing. With his typical black sense of humour, he said, "Just as well he's 'dead'; he wouldn't like this place anyway!"

So the ambulance came to take John away before he had even seen the flat properly. I was left standing once again in a strange place to call home. 'Old before our time' kept springing to mind. I emptied boxes whilst my mind was elsewhere, at the hospital. I had to get some semblance of order in case he would be back soon. There was a positive side to this place though; it was a large flat and had a storeroom. The downside was the dark north-facing lounge that looked out onto a grotty grey council estate of dumped prams and mattresses and the hulks of burnt out cars.

Demolition music blared out; half-naked, snotty kids were screaming up and down the slopes on scooters and un-helmeted teenagers roared up and down on trail bikes. What a contrast to the rolling hills and birdsong of Little Sanctuary.

There was a kindly and helpful on-site warden who came to make up a file of our illnesses, medications, doctor, and which funeral director we would be using. Oh, how cheerful! So encouraging, I must say. Funeral director? No way. I would get away from here before we'd even begun; this was God's waiting room! I was to get away, not just yet, but in the most bizarre of circumstances one could ever think of.

Dishonesty, Lies and the Arm of the Law

There was a community room with a library and the warden's office joined onto it. John had returned from the hospital but was not fit to go out yet. I was invited to bingo in the community room. This took place every week. Not my scene, but I went just to be sociable. It was run by two of the residents, who also collected the weekly 'subs' and acted as treasurers.

One day, not long after moving in, I went to look at the library books. I chose a book and sat out of the way in one of the high-backed wing chairs. It was quiet: no one in there and it was the warden's day off. The treasurers-come-secretaries of the bingo crept in. They didn't see me there, so I sat tight and watched in amazement as their fingers felt along the ledge above the warden's office. They located the key and entered, coming out a minute later with the residents' diary and personal data, which the warden always took around with her when visiting each flat every day. It contained private information, medical histories, and the medication needs of each resident.

The next day, the warden was in a flap. I dared not say anything because of any lashback. Those nasty people were clever though. They pretended to have found it 'dropped' by the bush outside the laundry room and gave it back, after looking through everyone's notes.

One night, soon after this, I couldn't get to sleep in our flat and ended up kipping down on the sofa in the lounge that overlooked the residents' parked cars. Looking out of the window, with the light off, I saw a woman with a hoodie placing what looked like glass under the wheels and a brick on the bonnet of the car belonging to the man who lived opposite us on the landing. He was always horrid to me, for no reason that I could think of. Little did I suspect that this was to be the start of an increasingly bizarre set of circumstances that would lead to me being arrested and wrongly accused of criminal damage.

A few nights later I saw flour poured over the car by the same hooded woman. Next, it was notes stuck under the windscreen wiper, then soil. These strange occurrences went on for a couple of weeks until the warden gave in to our neighbour's insistence that cameras be put up to catch whoever was doing it.

This neighbour left his flat door open one day and called out, asking me to go with him and look at something downstairs. As John was in our flat I didn't close our door; I would only be gone a minute. When we returned and our neighbour went back into his flat, he said his TV remote was missing and accused us of stealing it. John was in bed, but sure enough there was the 'stolen' remote on my armchair. We had numbered wheelie bins out the back. At five o'clock one morning a woman in a hoodie was seen by one of the residents we were friendly with, going down what he knew was our wheelie bin and taking out what looked like old papers. This woman lived in the flat below that nasty man across our landing. They were friendly with one another and she spent much of her time in his place. I often wore a parka with a hood and the only way in and out of the building was past that parked car.

Every week I had a stall in the market, selling our paintings, and would walk wearily home at the end of the day with my backpack on and my hood up as it was dark and cold. It was a hard walk back up the steep hill with a heavy load and one night, just as I got outside our flats, I happened to miss my footing and fall against that blasted car. Picking myself up, I staggered upstairs and into our flat where John, bless him, had attempted to make a meal. Before I had time to remove my parka there was banging on our door. Police! Whatever could have happened? Had someone died?

It was me they had come for.

"I am arresting you on suspicion of criminal damage." With that, the handcuffs were on, not plastic ones this time; not an ambulance either as in those far-off days when I was carted off to the asylum. This time it was a police car.

"Have you anything on you that you can harm yourself with and are you on medication?"

Well, my parka had many pockets! I had a penknife, scissors, a couple of weights (to keep my papers down, on the stall), pens, cash and a wad of notes from my takings that day, plus keys and some gold jewellery swapped in lieu of money for a painting. Oh yes, and some blood pressure tablets!

Poor John, recovering from a heart attack, nearly had another as I was taken away and police swarmed all over our flat. That man across the landing and his fancy woman from the flat below looked positively gleeful as I was led away.

At the police station I was divested of my shoes and clothes apart from my underwear. I was put into a cell where I promptly had the runs and stunk the place out and myself, as there was no paper. I was marched out to an interview room and made to watch a video film of 'night vision' scenes of a woman in a hoodie vandalising that car. "That's you, isn't it? You can't deny it." I said it wasn't and that you couldn't see the face. They said I was going to do it again as I had penknife, scissors and other 'utensils of malice' in my pockets and the police had found my writing on a threatening letter to that awful man across our landing.

John knew the police who 'raided' our flat. They kept apologising and saying that it was all wrong. They were looking for samples of my handwriting and pens. Well, being artists there was plenty of both to choose from! Back at the station I was having a bad vertigo attack. I felt unwell and lay down. A female doctor was sent for as my blood pressure had rocketed. She told the duty sergeant to send me either home or to hospital and to drop the case as it was obvious I was innocent.

The copper who arrested me drove me not home but out of town. I said this was the wrong way but we kept going along the link road towards South Molton. I kept asking why we were going the wrong way.

"I shall keep driving until you confess," was his response.

Soon we were going through North Molton; this led up to the moor.

"Go on, say you did it and I'll turn back and get you a fish and chip supper and take you home."

I refused and still he drove on, up to Sandyway then down to Simonsbath where he parked up.

"You haven't a clue where you are. I can deal with you and dump you out and no one will believe you because we close ranks in the force!"

Well I did know where I was, but I didn't want to be 'dealt with' and he was a big man. So I said, "Yes."

"Yes, what?"

"I did it."

He drove me back, laughing his head off. He was mad, I thought, as he was carrying out some very risky manoeuvres with his driving. He appeared to be off his head.

Nearing the police station he said, "Sign this."

I said I wanted to go home. I didn't sign anything, and eventually he gave up and drove me home.

"No one will believe you, you know, so it's a waste of time trying." He obviously meant the drive and the threats on Exmoor.

The man across the landing, we learnt, wanted our flat for his fancy woman. She had forged my handwriting, copied from the bits of paper from our wheelie bin and 'sent' a threatening letter from me to the man across the dratted landing. Between them, they had set me up to appear to be vandalising his car. She had done all the 'work' to look like me in the hoodie but not actually damaging the car. The man's son was in the police force, which gave them more leverage. It was she who placed the remote in our flat. They had concocted this whole affair just to get us out of the flat so that she could move in closer to him!

John and I recovered from that event, John more slowly than myself. The other residents really thought I had done it. They revelled in this juicy morsel of gossip, adding embellishments of their own so in the end you would think I had committed a murder.

We made an official complaint to the warden about the cause of my arrest. She didn't want to follow it up for fear of losing her job and the home that went with it. So John said, "Okay, we'll take it no further so long as you find us somewhere better and out of this town, soon. Bloody soon!"

Once again, I stood in an empty room as the removal men decanted our belongings. I was more than glad to be rid of this place, the people, and dishonest goings-on. It was Christmas Eve 1997. We were off, this time to Watchet in West Somerset.

We were in another first floor flat with the same housing association. It had a store room as well so we still had somewhere to stash our paintings and art gear. John visibly improved, living here in this charming little town with boats in the harbour and the West Somerset Railway at the back of us. We'd walk along the old Mineral Line and marvel at the wildlife, or up to Daws Castle on the crumbling cliff top. One day John got the bikes out and serviced them. He was looking well. Our new doctors were the old-fashioned sort who had plenty of time for their patients. John was put on different medication and was given a proper diet sheet and cookery book for his diabetes. The change was amazing. John had a new lease of life and we were able to go for gentle cycle rides. He loved to walk around Watchet and chat, or lean over the harbour railings for a man-to-man chinwag. All the dogs knew him as he carried dog biscuits around in his pocket. There was a friendly library in what was the old lifeboat station and every day we would walk out to the little red lighthouse, where we would place our hands, one on top of the other, over the red flaking metal.

We studied the peregrine falcons past West Beach and marvelled at the fossils and ammonites revealed by yet another unstable cliff fall. Our painting took off: I had several successful exhibitions. We acquired two allotments, which were balm to the soul. How proud we were to see the fruits of our toil and only two minutes' walk away from the flat. We donated produce to the Red Cross for their local meals service. My herbs I used to sell to the hotels and cafes and made enough money to pay for our seeds and small rent for a year. We even drove the campervan to Bude, for a week at a time, where I did locum lifeguarding and John went painting. As much as the flat's warden tried, she could not get us to join the social club in the community room. No way!

I was getting expert at diabetic cookery and got chatting to the local health food shop owner. Soon I was baking for her, making diabetic cakes and biscuits, jam and marmalade, as well as making posies of flowers and bunches of herbs from our allotments. She paid me well and introduced me to some interesting courses on herbalism. I took it further and two years later got my diploma. This was to stand me in good stead in years to come.

Watchet harbour was made into a marina. John and I were commissioned to do pen and ink drawings of the construction, from start to finish, by the National Maritime Archives. We could easily fit this in with our other work.

I still had a motorbike and started doing an indoor car boot market in an empty factory in Minehead. Every Sunday I was up at 6am to load up our artwork. This had to be done with precision regarding balance and safety. I had to include cloths to cover the tables, packaging, bags, cash and cashbook, sales record book – and pray that it was not raining or there wasn't a sidewind from the sea. In winter it was dark and sometimes slippery. I would arrive with numb fingers. Everyone else seemed to be in couples but being on my own I had to have my wits about me and eyes everywhere when unloading and going back and forth outside to the bike. It was the same in reverse at the end of the morning, but even more so as late punters came in to pick up anything left that was going cheap. Going to the loo was a problem as other stallholders had their own things to keep an eye on.

There was no heating in the building and no water to wash your hands in the defunct washroom but there were twenty-four toilets! The cigarette smoke got so thick it made my eyes water and my hair and clothes stank. I did well most of the time. I would just fall into my chair, exhausted, when I got home but my ever-loving husband had a cup of tea ready and a simple cooked meal. We had a ritual. We would eat our meal then clear the table and I would teasingly count out the takings bit by bit. It varied from week to week but in the summer the Butlins brigade would really boost the coffers. The counted-out money we split down the middle. No squabbles: everything we did was shared. It didn't matter if it was a 'John week' for artwork sold or if it was an 'Anne week'.

John was always full of surprises. He would say he was going out to get a paper and would return with a bunch of flowers for me or something I might have spotted in the charity shop window, even a pebble off the beach to paint on. The rest of the Sunday, we would take a quiet stroll, look in on the allotments (but we never worked them on a Sunday) then if the tide was right, fish off the harbour wall. Failing that, we would amble up to St Decuman's well. After tea we always enjoyed Scrabble and listening to relaxing music, or we would play our guitars. We avoided the other residents as much as possible, except for poor Paddy. Many a time we found him down by the harbour, head in his hands, unable to stand up properly, so we would take an arm each and help him back to his flat.

He would sway and stagger and say, "Holy Mary, mother of God, how much longer are ye keepin' me here on this perishin' earth, walkin' in hell?"

Back at the flats you could hear the residents tut-tutting and saying, "Drunk again!"

He wasn't drunk, he was suffering from vertigo and I fully sympathised as I used to get unannounced doses of it that came when least expected.

By now we had 'officially' retired. John had also got a problem with his diabetic feet. He came home from the doctor after a routine blood test and overhaul and the doctor advised he should give up cycling and also to see a specialist. Later, as he was getting his bike out, I said I thought he was supposed to stop.

"Oh yes, I'm stopping alright!" and with that he was gone. Whatever was he up to?

One of his fishing mates found our flat and said I had better, "...come down the harbour, quick!"

My poor dear husband was bent over, weeping, with a bunch of fishing chaps trying to console him.

"Here mate, have a drink of tea from my flask," and, "We'll get it back for you."

"I don't bloody want it back!" cried John and there, in the muddy sludge of Watchet harbour, lay John's bike, his beloved bike that he had cycled round Britain on, that he cherished, polished, cajoled. He had apparently, with a mighty roar, lifted it above his head and thrown it and then collapsed in a jibbering heap.

For the rest of that week he went quiet. We didn't do the allotment. All he wanted to do was play snooker with me at the club. No one else was in there of an afternoon. It was, of course, played in a dimly lit room. We were quite good players and were in the league when we lived in that far-off dream in the west. I think he felt safe that afternoon, cocooned in the womb of the snooker room. He played some master shots. But then he deliberately left his sacred cue behind in the club rack along with the pack of chalk I had given him.

"Don't ask," he said. "I won't need that anymore."

I nearly said why don't you throw it in the harbour to join your bike, but I didn't. This wasn't my man at all.

Night-times were a trial in our double bed. His feet kept kicking out and he had terrible night sweats. Something was going wrong with John. Now he could barely manage the seventeen stairs up to our flat.

On 11 August 1999 I observed the full solar eclipse alone. We had planned to share this event at our special spot, with our hands linked on the little red lighthouse, but I had to walk up there without him. As the sun disappeared and birds started roosting, thinking it was night-time, I was surrounded by hundreds of people, but I felt so alone. Alone in a crowd.

Watchet was gearing up for a big celebration as the new millennium approached. The harbour was being decked out with illuminations. John was still in a deep trough of low pressure. He didn't want to join me on the harbour at the stroke of midnight as 1999 turned into 2000.

I went. Everyone was in party mode, fancy dress and hats, lanterns, and streamers everywhere. Flashes from cameras reflected in the water along with the coloured lights. Free hot food was passed around. A couple with champagne were kissing. Everyone was happy and toasting each other.

Then the moment came. I thought to myself I will remember this, the exact spot where I stood with my hand placed on the corner of the shelter of the esplanade in Watchet, as Big Ben, via a link, boomed out and a new century and a new millennium had begun. Everyone was kissing and hugging and as I stood all alone in the lamplight I felt the chill wind creep across me and wondered if this was a warning, a sign of things to come.

"Come on love! You all on your own?" and one of the boatmen lifted me off my feet and gave me an almighty whiskery kiss, "Happy New Year!" and was gone into the seething mass of revellers.

I wished it was John.

So I walked to the harbour in 1999 and returned home in 2000. John was asleep, unaware of the milestone in history that had just passed.

The next thing to go from our lives was our beloved Calendula. It was becoming too expensive to run and anyway the housing association wanted us to shift it. There was nowhere to shift it to! Residents had got up a petition behind our backs as they thought it was an eyesore. It definitely was *not*! There was no rust, it was cleaned and polished every week, the little curtains were neatly tied back and it had recently been resprayed and looked really nice. John always kept it in good order; everything inside was stowed away and we used the correct numbered parking space allotted to us. We had been stupid enough to provide excess allotment produce to the people of the flats by placing it in the warden's office to put in the community room. We left a voluntary donation tin. No one ever donated.

One week, when there was no surplus veg to spare, people were going around saying, "Where's the free greens this week?" et cetera.

I'm so glad that we didn't get involved in the community room social club. Once bitten, twice shy.

We got a Ford Escort, with which John was familiar. He had one when driving on patrol with his guard dog in a previous job. He wore it 'like a coat', often driving 200 miles a night, in and out of it, shrugging into the seat then out, all night long.

I noticed he had an occasional problem with the clutch and he would blame his foot as it was getting numb and swollen. Then we had to start carrying sweets everywhere as his sugar levels dropped. Then the regular meals; oh how he hated having to do as he was told, that as a diabetic it was important to keep those levels up and not go into a 'hypo' and collapse.

I still went running and swimming but not so much. At sixty I now had other demanding things taking up my time and needed all my energy. Even the allotments were now my domain. One pleasure we had left was the free Sainsbury's bus from Watchet to Bridgwater. The top deck was ideal for this fabulous scenic ride through the Quantocks, stopping at pretty villages en-route. Even that became too much for John and he got so frustrated that he couldn't help to carry the shopping. So I went alone and wore a backpack.

My knee gave way and I ended up in hospital having it 'washed out' of loose cartilage. The doctor said he wanted to see us both.

"I'll write a letter," the doctor said. "I will recommend that you need a ground floor property from the local council housing stock. Oh, and a small garden for you to potter about in. No more allotments!"

John looked resigned.

"And come back to me after you have seen the specialist," the doctor said.

We knew that date was looming the following week as a hospital car had already been arranged.

John's face had become bloated. His body was now collecting fluid. As we sat in the dreary waiting room in Musgrove Park Hospital a right snotty kid kept staring at him. I could feel John gearing up. His language of late had become embarrassingly rude. It was his illness making him tetchy.

"What are you staring at?"

Wiping his sleeve across his snotty nose the boy replied, "Your face; it looks like the moon gone wrong."

With this, the boy picked the snot up and ate it, so John said, "*You'll* go bloody wrong my boy, eating that, you will be dead in half an hour!"

I wished the floor would swallow me up. Everyone was staring at us.

"And you lot can wind your necks in!" John said. It was rather funny, really, as whatever magazine or paper people had looked up from suddenly got extra rapt attention as they went back to pretend reading, ears flapping.

The boy's mother said, "I'm going to report you."

"To whom? God? He's not listening this week."

I didn't know whether to laugh, cry or give John a dig in the ribs. We were saved from further embarrassment as our number was called.

"I give you five years, my boy," the condescending specialist said.

"Five years? What's that, a jail sentence? I thought this was a hospital, not a prison," John replied.

"To live. Five years left to live," said the specialist. Time stood still. The 'live' word went round the room, full circle. It rested on John.

"To *die*, you mean. Five years to *die*," he said.

The world carried on outside the window. The sun shone. It shouldn't have done. It should have been raining. It should have been dark and dreary. Anything but this. Whenever I found something good in my life it always got snatched away.

As we were driven home, not a word was spoken between us but we could feel each other's thoughts going round and round inside the hospital car, trapped, knotted, what ifs, how long and when.

I had to make a decision before I got out. Do I keep bemoaning the outcome of today's findings and feel sorry for myself and the life we have lost, or try, no matter how sad, to make the most of what life John had left, bad language and all? I decided to be strong for his sake and at journey's end I got out of the car with a fixed smile on my face, determined to make the best of a bad job.

John improved on new, different medication. His swelling disappeared and he drove okay again. On his seventy-fifth birthday I gave him a workmate bench as he liked to do a bit of woodwork. As he sat on the end of the bed and unwrapped it, tears of joy streamed down his face and we hugged for a long time.

As John was so much better, he drove me to Bideford to board the Oldenburg as I was due to do a stint on Lundy.

"I'll be fine," he said.

He never wanted to stop me from doing those things that I loved and he sent me off with a good heart. My time away refreshed me and as I neared Bideford Quay on my return I searched longingly, looking at the people lined along the quayside. Where was he? Where was John? The ship's crew had the usual familiar banter with me but I only half took in their remarks as I kept searching the crowd for John. I saw an old man, leaning on a stick. Suddenly I realised that my husband had aged. There was no turning back of the clock. Our time together was ticking away. Our former life was gone.

His thoughtfulness never failed to touch me though; he had brought a flask of tea, turkey and cranberry sandwiches, and fruit, which we ate parked up, overlooking the high tide as the Oldenburg craned stores on and off the quay.

On the way home I sensed an air of excitement about John. He was happy and whistling our old guitar songs. Something was afoot! I knew him too well. Reaching our flat he opened the front door with a flourish.

"There, my lady! Welcome home!"

He had decorated the place with flowers. The table was laid for tea and a parcel was waiting for me on the bed. He rubbed his hands together with glee and couldn't wait for me to open it. I did, and there it was: a beautifully made wooden box for my art materials. It was big, with many compartments and well thought out extras. It was an amazing piece of work, beautifully sanded down and varnished, complete with a leather carrying strap made from one of his old belts. The box was made from pieces of old motorcycle crates and the catches were made from brass fittings.

As I was thinking it would be far too heavy to carry, he came out with, "That's for when we go out for a day in the car with our picnics on the moor. The other one is in the other room."

He had made a smaller version for local trips on foot.

"This week and last week had flown past, wondering if I would complete this project for my lady in time," he beamed.

Gosh, this new medication he was on certainly helped his concentration if not his appearance of ageing! After tea he went to bed, worn out.

John was getting up much later these days, at around 11am. I would take him breakfast at eight. I then used this time to continue my studies until preparing lunch. I had already gained a diploma in Bach flower essences and was currently doing crystal healing and herbalism, all recognised professional qualifications. I needed a few more before I could practise, in the future. Somehow, I couldn't see us living in a block of old people's flats forever; it was depressing. Although physically impaired, our minds were still surging ahead and young. I must have been seeing into the future.

A letter came from the housing. We were to go for an interview this coming week.

Not only was it an interview, but we were driven out to view a property by the housing officer. I couldn't believe our luck. There, in a beautiful little village situated inside the Exmoor National Park, was a small semi-detached bungalow. It had roses around the door, fabulous scenery, with Dunkery Beacon before us and steeply wooded hills behind. One couldn't wish for a more perfect place. It was on the bus route to Minehead, nine miles away. The walks were varied and stunning, just as well as I was now on blood pressure pills and was doing the recommended two miles brisk walking each day, taking the doctor's advice seriously.

Once more, I stood in an empty flat waiting until the final boxes were loaded onto the removal van. We had dug our last golden treasure of Charlotte potatoes from the allotments that we had made from a wild overgrown piece of land. That was the worst bit, saying goodbye to our 'digs' as we called them. "Us 'digs' the ground…" as John would say. We left the harvesting to others and for nature to enjoy.

The bungalow was tiny after the large flat. It had no bath but instead had a shower with a weird pump that was so loud that everyone else knew when you were using it, as they had the same. The shower had no sides so you couldn't use much water but it did the job, just, before overflowing onto the floor. There was no room for a wardrobe as the double bed took up all the space. The living room had a quaint alcove where I could put my desk and do my studies and John made a bookshelf for all my course work and to put a lamp there. There was no store room so our art gear and frames were in tea chests that also served as tables when we put a piece of wood on top. I made a small lean-to greenhouse and also a tiny lawn.

Every Monday we went to a pensioners' special lunch at the one pub in the village, where an old lady cooked proper, un-messed-up British meals for little charge. Of course, it was 'collect your pension' day at the post office, which used to be a front room parlour. Classical radio music was always playing amongst the dust and cobwebbed shelves that had half-starved cacti leaning at drunken angles on the window ledges. Often there was the smell of cabbage water or yesterday's dinner floating on the air, plus a cat, or two, or three…

It was so dark in there, I wondered if enough takings had been made to put in the meter for a light and when it did come on it must have been the lowest wattage light bulb ever invented.

I loved this little village, with its pinky-red coloured local stone cottages and a jewel of a church. I spent many hours in there when things got a bit stressful at home. How reassuring it was to hear its clock strike each hour, especially during my sleepless nights. Those nights! How one could see the stars so clearly, there being no light pollution, just as on Lundy Island. I saw meteor showers and sudden streaks of light that began and went nowhere, space beyond space, beyond comprehension. What was I? Just a speck of dust. Something touched me in this place.

I passed all my exams at Master's level and was qualified to practice holistic medicine. I flew to Glasgow to spend some time at a unique place, on the Isle of Arran, that specialised in holistic medicine. From there I took a special boat one day to visit a tiny community on an outlying island. It was the Buddhist Centre of Light. It was unbelievably peaceful, it was as if nowhere else existed; it was so remote, calm, and loving. Untouched.

Returning home, I soon discovered that our neighbour was a reiki master and I started to meet other like-minded people. My credentials got me into a clinic share, where an old and mellow building had been converted into a healing centre. Here, I practised things that the local vicar might not have approved of, but they were natural, relaxing, and healing things and people went away feeling refreshed. I always made a 'free' session each week for those unable to afford it. I didn't set the price. We were a happy cooperative. Ah ha! But I still spoke to the vicar! I saw a pair of shorts streaking past my window one day and the pair of shorts stopped by and put something through my letterbox. By the time I looked down the road I saw the vicar's bottom vanish around the corner as he had been delivering the parish magazine. I wondered if he was wearing his dog collar as well as his shorts! He and his wife were to help me in weeks to come.

The one big mistake I made in this village was to enter every class possible in the annual flower and craft show, sweep the board and win the perpetual challenge cup. I only did it for fun. I didn't realise how deadly serious it was until the winner was announced (me) and a huge and horrified gasp went up from the crowd of villagers collected in the hall.

"But I usually win that!" an indignant voice piped up.

Then muttering turned to raised conversation and the vicar saved the day and suggested that applause should be given to a worthy winner.

"Hear, hear!" I heard from the back of the hall. I didn't see John creep in!

As he helped me to collect my exhibits someone was heard to say that the exhibits are usually auctioned off. I'll spare you John's reply.

I went to a few services at the lovely church and found that the vicar was not God Almighty but a really interesting and sincere speaker. I could not mix with the congregation though: it was my past re-emerging. I was okay at being an individual doing things that I knew and was in command of myself. As I sat in that church, I could almost feel the happy times spent in the choir in that far-off distant past. I wondered how many in the congregation knew that a ley line passed through the site of the font in the church. I had done much dowsing with my copper rods that had served me now for many years, ever since our dream in the west.

Since then, I had found water where the water board had given up searching, even with their technical know-how, also numerous wells that had been closed up for years, pipes, electricity and gas mains, objects, even a body, which I located on an Ordnance Survey map, aided with my pendulum. It is not so-called magic; it's an ability we all had naturally years ago. When people say it's stupid, I put water in a bowl, place my rods in their hands and they are amazed that it works for them, too, as they walk towards the bowl of water and the rods cross above it.

I started up two more allotments, this time at the back of Dunster. The view whilst digging was phenomenal, right across the Bristol Channel to Wales, ships going to Avonmouth, big skies and ever-changing, far-reaching weather patterns. All this, with the backdrop of Dunster Castle, pine forests and St George's clock playing tunes on the hour. The castle lawns spread out and made a contrast to the main road in the distance, where cars looked like small Dinky toys, busy zooming along. Dunster Marsh was beyond this, where I would see little egrets in winter, searching amongst the reeds for food.

I grew all the herbs needed to make ointments, creams and medicines, teas, and pot pourri. There was a large call for these items at the clinic and I wrapped them in pretty handmade paper to sell.

I still continued doing the car boot sale on a Sunday. Sorry vicar but needs must when the Devil drives. When the factory shut and went up for sale, I and many others had to find somewhere else, but it was outside and summer only, in a field called 'Twenty Acre'. It was dodgy, as I had to use my motorbike on sometimes wet and boggy ground and use it as a display stand, covered with a sheet. It would gradually sink, and I would hope it would last the morning before keeling over altogether. Weather was another problem. I had no proper stall or cover, no car to dump things in if it rained. Sometimes the sun was so strong that my paintings that were in mounts inside a see-through bag would start to get condensation. Not good for watercolours! There were mainly John's work. My acrylics and oils were okay but transporting framed work with glass in was a risk and so much bubble wrap was needed that it took up too much space.

I found that I only sold work if I took along a few bits of worthless bric-a-brac, stuff that caught the punter's eye, then they would spot the paintings. These had to be local sea or Exmoor scenes, where punters drove to and didn't get out of their cars, such as Porlock Weir or Watchet Harbour. Paintings of beautiful remote places, however well accomplished, hardly sold but Dunster Yarn Market, a well-known landmark, couldn't do enough of them! Eventually I gave up on Twenty Acre field, with its one chemical loo between thousands of visitors, and John drove me to Dulverton market each week, where we had a stall undercover on a Saturday.

He loved it! But not the early start at 7am. It was really good to have him with me, to watch over the stall if I needed to go anywhere and he was so good with the prospective buyers. He was an excellent salesman. We couldn't understand, though, why we had to have the stall up and running by 9am when the rest of Dulverton didn't wake up until 11am. We had to finish by 1pm and then drive home and unload, by which time it would be 2:30. This was awkward as the whole day threw John's diabetic eating routine out of balance, despite taking snacks with us. Much as we loved doing it, after two seasons we abandoned the idea; it was doing him no good.

By now I had to give up the Dunster allotments. Despite paying a high rent for the privilege of using them, the association had failed to put high fencing around the whole area. There were many allotments and money had not been spent on upkeep. The deer, pheasants, foxes, and rabbits destroyed everything. It was so disappointing after all that time and effort. It had produced some excellent results for my 'pharmacy'.

John was beginning to get irritable again, and bad language started flowing. It all started out when leaflets came through our doors from a well-known pharmacy in Minehead, stating that they were starting up a free delivery service of prescriptions. I thought this was a great idea as it would save an eighteen-mile round trip plus parking fees. No, John insisted on collecting his prescriptions himself. It all came to a head late one morning when he borrowed my motorbike to save paying for parking in Minehead if he had used the car. I just said there was no need to collect it if he signed up to have it delivered, as others in our road had already done. He rode off in a strop. Diabetes was getting to him.

At five minutes to one o'clock I went cold all over. I suddenly knew that something dreadful had happened. Our meal was at one o'clock and I knew that John would never eat it. We had no phone or mobiles then. Everything went on hold.

I saw the police driving up to our place. They had a woman police officer with them. That's what you see in the films when bad news is told to a female. A sort of woman to woman thing I suppose.

Yes, John had been scraped off the road, having been knocked off my bike by a druggie driver shooting out of a side lane at a place called Nutcombe Bottom. There were plenty of witnesses, following drivers all keeping to the thirty mile an hour speed limit. A tractor coming in the opposite direction stopped within inches of running him over. Now he was in hospital.

John had nasty injuries. At home, he was laid up for six weeks as the district nurse visited each day to dress some awful wounds all down his right side. He couldn't write, paint, or do some personal things and needed help most of the time. He had stitches in his hip and lost the feeling in his finger on the left hand, which made guitar playing difficult. He was an utter miserable wreck and the more I tried to sympathise the worse he got.

Now I was trying to sleep on the floor in the tiny living room between my desk, the front door, and chairs, to give John a more comfortable chance of getting better in our double bed.

During this time I decided to help myself to some beautiful apples going to waste in a millionaire's orchard. It was surrounded by a substantial wall and it irked me that I had to buy when there were so many just lying there going to waste. There was never an answer when I rang the bell. I could hear it clanging away somewhere in the bowels of that huge house. With my backpack on, I clambered over the wall after taking a running jump at it and hastily put a number of apples in my pack. It was a different matter trying to get back up the wall with all that extra weight! Then I saw him, the owner, half snoozing in a deck char.

He looked up and said, "Oh, have you lost your way?"

I said, "Yes, sorry, seems like I hit a dead end when I thought your drive was the footpath." It was a lame excuse.

He pointed at the gate and added, "By the way, help yourself to some apples; you backpackers are always hungry!" and with that he went back to snoozing. I had to laugh!

It took me back to an incident just a few decades before, when I was broke. There was a shooting club in some dense woods, in the middle of nowhere, that I knew about. After a weekend of shooting I would go to the shooting enclosure, which was securely locked with a big wall all around it and barbed wire running along the top. With the aid of a piece of corrugated iron, which I placed over the top of the wire, I would get inside and pick up all these spent cartridge cases that had brass on the ends and sell them to a dealer in the market. He never asked me where I got them from, but he paid me well. One week I had an extra-large haul, but he was no longer in the market. I was told he wouldn't be returning as he was now residing at Her Majesty's Pleasure for receiving stolen goods! Oops!

* * * * *

My mangled motorbike was picked up from our place and went to a dealer for assessment for the insurance company. The 'dealer' was a friend of John's from way back. John had helped him to set up his workshop and it had a very good reputation over the years. My bike was theoretically a write-off and I was well compensated. John, on the other hand, had to wait nine agonising months before his insurance claim was settled. We had to take a long and arduous bus ride to Bridgwater to see an insurance doctor situated at the top of a musty old building accessed by a narrow, dark, and steep spiral staircase. How ridiculous if you are less than able bodied! We had to get a taxi home, at ridiculous expense, as John was feeling unwell.

When the final judgement came through the payment for all of those injuries was considerable, stuff you only dream of, but we would rather it had never happened. It was all downhill from then on.

One day in the autumn of 2003, John said he would sit outside in the last of the late sunshine. There he was, happily looking at the view, mostly recovered from his injuries apart from a painful right hip. He looked contented and more like his old self. He smiled at me and I felt happy again. Then he slid off his seat and fell to the ground, unconscious. Unresponsive, he was blue-lighted to Musgrove Park Hospital, Taunton. To visit him was a five-hour journey on the bus and the same when he was transferred to Exeter. It wasn't the distance that took the time, it was the indirect route. John wasn't happy that I was then starting to do the journey by motorbike instead, especially around the city centre. It worried him, so I stayed in one of the hospital flats for a month whilst the medics got to grips with John's problems. He had swollen so much that his testicles were the size of a small melon. He had several operations to prepare him for dialysis as his kidneys were failing fast.

I got to know Exeter a fair bit and the flat I was staying in was really nice, with a communal kitchen and a connecting phone to John's ward day and night. That flat, in a secure block, faced the main hospital building. It contained memories and moments of past occupants. It was tangible. Even in the communal kitchen, where I met no one, the window I looked out of as I drank a cup of tea was the same glass seen through by hundreds of people before me as they also passed through on a temporary stay, waiting for outcomes of friends and loved ones, good or bad, living or dying, rejoicing or grieving. It was so real, the thoughts bounced off the walls. I opened the window, hoping that they, the thoughts, would escape but they were like ghosts not wanting to leave.

I had to return home and leave John in the hospital as I had necessary things to do. I was feeling quite drained and weary. On my way to the village post office I saw that cheerful vicar who asked how I was, so I told him about John and from then on either he or his wife drove me to the hospital, a good hour away, until John finally came home.

The doctor visited each day. He was worried about our living arrangements and said that we needed two bedrooms, not one. I did *not* want to move from this lovely place but had to see sense. On a freezing cold day in January 2006 I once again found myself in a familiar situation of standing in an empty room and seeing the last of our belongings onto a removal lorry. John had been taken by ambulance to spend the day in the Minehead Cottage Hospital until I had moved all of our things into our new home. This time it was to be in Porlock. There, as the snow came down, I got colder and hungrier waiting for the removal lorry, which was now two hours overdue. It was only a twenty-minute drive at most from our old place to here. The smell of hot pasties drifted through the snowflakes from the bakery in the high street, but I couldn't leave to get one in case the removals turned up in my absence. I couldn't contact them. I didn't own a mobile phone and I couldn't see a public phone box to use.

At four o'clock they turned up and had the cheek to hand me a box containing all the tea-making stuff and demand a pot of tea! They were late because they had 'stopped for a lunch break'. What they had really done was to sell some of our things to a local dealer. I got the things back because I knew the 'local dealer': we met up from time to time at various markets and car boot sales. One day at a sale I spotted my walnut sewing box on legs, for sale, on the dealer's stall. Going over to have a look I saw that it still contained all the things I used for sewing. My parents had given me that sewing box on my twenty-first birthday, filled with enough equipment to last me a lifetime. I got it back. They were horrified to think it was stolen and I didn't have to pay the mark-up price of £50! They had no idea that they had been dealing with people who filched possessions from removal lorries. The law caught up with the removals in the end and they went out of business.

Our new place was a terraced bungalow. It had an open fireplace that heated the water. Although it had two bedrooms, it was quite small, but it had a proper full-sized bath and shower. The kitchen was miniscule and led onto the back garden. The backs of these bungalows were used as the fronts, for access. The front doors were seldom used: they were for officials and strangers who didn't know better. Someone had kindly driven our car over from our previous place. There was a large separate outhouse, which used to be used for coal, and an outside WC. It was a pretty little place with yet more roses to come around the front door, bare for now but I could imagine the potential. The previous disabled tenant had left behind a filthy blue fitted carpet but, on the plus side, a mobility scooter in new condition.

I made John's bed up, tried to heat his bedroom, and put hot water bottles in the bed. This was my priority, as the temperature was still dropping. He was too tired after the ambulance returned him home. He went to bed, just as well as there wasn't much room to move with boxes to unpack.

Next day, the warden came to see us and to take details. She would be making a daily visit as this was sheltered housing. Imagine our surprise when she said that the neighbours either side had said that we were making too much noise and they had put in an official complaint to the council. This was beyond belief. It was only normal moving in sounds, no banging or hammering or slamming of doors. In fact, we were a very quiet couple, but woe betide if you got John wound up in his present state. There could be an expletive explosion!

Oh, it was so cold. Porlock in winter meant ice and snow, and the wind straight off the Welsh mountains, non-stop across the Bristol Channel, depositing shards of sleet, stinging one's face and making the eyes water. It was in such weather a week later that I took the battery out of the car, strapped it to my motorbike and made a treacherous ride to Minehead to get it charged. It was a hair-raising journey as my back wheel kept slewing with the unwieldy weight and a mighty crosswind threatened to keel me over. I could hardly unfold myself at journey's end, I was so frozen. But I did it and managed to get the battery back into the car. I had to wait all day in Minehead, so had done a lot of shopping. Porlock was dreadfully expensive, up-market, with most shops being gifty, touristy honey traps.

The best place in Porlock was Miles tea and coffee merchants. Their loose tea was the finest and I had been drinking it for over thirty years. Sometimes the roasting coffee would permeate the whole of Porlock. Occasionally, I would have to shut the windows if the coffee got over-roasted; a blackish haze would roll up the high street. The smell of this, combined with burnt out brake linings from vehicles descending Porlock Hill, would get trapped at the bottom.

The parish church had a chopped off spire and folklore has it that the chopped off bit was carted off to make the spire at Culbone's tiny church just a few miles away. I went to the parish church sometimes as I loved the organ and choir music and the atmosphere. I also went to the Methodist church, where there were none of these things but there was a non-boring speaker, the atmosphere was really friendly and the outreach was thriving. What I hated was that, at both places, you had to dress halfway smart and I hated getting togged up and squeaky clean.

Back at our little bungalow I had worked hard and as spring came all the bulbs I had planted made a wonderful show. But in a bizarre rerun of previous neighbour difficulties, we kept having bad trouble with the neighbours either side of us. We had done nothing to upset them, or so we thought until we found out that their relatives had been promised our bungalow and we had got it instead.

We had been advised by the warden not to put bread out for the birds on the grassy area at the back of the bungalows because it would attract the rats. One day, when John was feeling much better, he went for a little drive, leaving me at home. I was sitting quietly beside the open window when one neighbour came out and spread bread all over the grassy area.

She then went in to get her husband out and said, "Look what the neighbours have done; they've put all this bread out for the birds. We'll have to report them."

As our car was out, the neighbour must have presumed that I was out as well.

Next, they got a tape measure to measure the distance that the front wheel of my motorbike protruded onto the communal path.

"Three inches. That's dangerous, we could fall over that. It needs reporting!"

They wanted the plants that the previous tenant had left behind and thought it was their right to dig them up as they'd been promised them, but I said no. Then they came in and started picking my runner beans, later in the season.

I said, "You only had to ask." John was all set to have a war with them, but he saw reason when I said that is what they are waiting for, an almighty row to enable them to report us. Why ever were we stuck in the middle of all this?

Rocks on the roof and a cut washing line were the next things to happen, then plants turned out of pots and trampled on. Both sets of neighbours were huge people and would sit all day boozing in the garden. One couple were completely nude, shuffling their overweight bodies around, their fleshy overhangs stained with spilt drink and food. They needed a navel clean out! Snide remarks were cast in our direction. Any tourist visiting this pretty showpiece village would be aghast at what was happening just fifty yards off the holiday route. This chocolate-box picture-perfect place was not all it seemed.

I loved to escape down to the marsh and shingle ridge, away from it all, and to watch the miniature creeks and gullies between the fields gradually fill with water as the tide crept in. I liked to sit by the 'lagoon' below Hurlestone Point and see the reflection in the setting sun, then walk home past the cottages at Bossington, the thatch like lowered eyebrows looking over the whitewash and pink roses. Then the evening mist smell of dank marsh and straw rising from the cold seawater that had met the warm land. Oh, how I loved it all and wished that John were there to hold my hand as he would have done not so long ago. My emotions rose up like a pain. All that we had shared was just a memory. Nothing would ever be the same again. The lantern moon lit my way home, guiding me through what was left of the raised pathways now being submerged by the incoming sea.

We had really caring doctors here. They actually walked round the village to visit patients. Sometimes they would call in unannounced, just to see how you were doing. They were kind and they knew everyone by name without prompting. By June 2006, John's body was filling with fluid and he could no longer put slippers on. The fluid was on his lungs, which was making him very ill. He had taken to his bed for a week and was looking extremely unwell when the lovely lady doctor happened to drop in to see how he was doing. She decided at once that he was dangerously ill and within half an hour he was rushed off to hospital in Taunton. Another week like that and he would have been dead, the doctor reckoned.

The fluid was drained off as he received dialysis. It was now decided that he should be on dialysis for the rest of his life. He had several blood transfusions straight away. After some procedures under local anaesthetic to set him up to receive dialysis in the future, he remained in hospital for several weeks.

At the end of July he returned home and was glad of the mobility scooter that the previous tenant had left behind. We set off into Porlock high street but it was a bad place to be on a scooter, with no regular footpath and many kerbs and having to go into the road in places. Eventually we would go to Porlock Weir, quite a long walk for me, but John liked to look out to sea and take a few photos and have a picnic. The sparrows in the pebble beach bushes would share our crumbs and chirp to us. It was a long haul back, mostly uphill, and John would be way ahead of me.

One day I put a very realistic model of a lookalike snake on the back of his scooter. As he drove along, or hit a bump or a pothole, the snake would move. He was unaware of this practical joke and as I was lagging way behind on the journey home up the long draggy hill, I was laughing my head off as motorists slowed up to do a double-take at a snake slithering on the back of a mobility scooter. John was getting annoyed and looking in his mirrors, kept beckoning for them to overtake. As they did so they would lean out and shout something at him.

When I caught up eventually, he was saying, "What an ignorant lot of f*****s, don't they understand what a hand signal means?"

At least it amused me on that endless, tiring walk, trying to keep up with him. He never did find out about the snake as I eventually thought he would not be very amused, so I detached it and left it hanging on someone's windowsill, which created a few screams in Porlock high street!

A Shock Letter and a Rapid Move

John had always kept our name on the North Devon District Council housing list as a safety net. It had been on there for years. He was doing a 95-mile round trip in an ambulance three times a week to the dialysis unit at Sedgemoor. The journey time was two hours each way, picking up and setting down other dialysis patients, plus the four hours on the machine. It was very tiring for him.

Out of the blue an offer came from the housing people in Barnstaple. A sheltered bungalow had become vacant and we had one week to inspect it and make up our minds. John would be in a different catchment area, with a different health authority. Instead of a ninety-five-mile round trip to dialysis, he would only have an eighteen-mile one to South Molton and back. He was champing at the bit to return to Barnstaple, his birthplace. Oh, how he longed to go back! Oh, how I *never* wanted to leave West Somerset! But I didn't tell him that as he was full of the idea of returning to his roots. I had found mine in West Somerset, it suited me, the moor and sea with so many friendly people (apart from our present neighbours) and places to paint plus selling outlets. Also the slower pace of life, the caring doctors, the warm pinky colour of the cottages and walls beneath the thatch and window boxes overflowing with flowers. Just everything about the area was so pleasing and I loved Minehead.

On a boiling hot day at the very end of July, when the tar melted on the roads and heat haze shimmered on the moor, we turned up in Barnstaple to inspect our proposed new home. We met the housing officer and after a few explanations he left us to take a good look around. My heart sank. The noise was the overriding thing. The main road lay below, an artery to the hospital. Ambulances and police sirens echoed around, bouncing off the walls, then there was the fire station as well. Diesel fumes were really noticeable as vehicles chugged away up the hill. How could I ever give up the sweet air of Exmoor, the tang of the Bristol Channel and the sound of the buzzards rising on the thermals above the woods?

It tore at me, the grief of it all, when I saw John's face light up as we entered the bungalow. He was 'home'.

"Home at last," he sighed. Never had I wanted anything less, ever. But I couldn't tell him that, he looked so happy as he said, "We've landed on our feet here; what a lovely place!" It was on a very steep hill; why build old people's places in such a hilly area?

John and I were always so close but this time he didn't pick up on how unhappy I was. His own happiness had overridden the moment. I knew then that his mind was made up when he said that dialysis wasn't so far away if we lived here.

"You have a week to make up your mind," the housing man said.

"It's already made up, with a resounding yes!" announced John.

We had two weeks to moving in day. I was back and forth on my motorbike getting a new floor covering put down and making arrangements, collecting keys, packing, lugging and carrying heavy boxes. It was a frantic, hectic time as I was doing most of the work.

On 9 August 2006 we moved in. It was like being in a massive car boot without end. Stuff all around but out of all the debris I managed to cook us a roast dinner. A cuppa tea never tasted so good!

The following morning I awoke to traffic noise at 4am then at 6:30am it started for real. It was something I would have to get used to after the silence of the country. I didn't like it one bit, but the view was surprisingly pleasant. At 7am I got up, knowing that I must make a home out of this muddle. Then the flooring started to buckle, and I had to get the firm that laid it to come out and re-scree the floor, this amidst packing cases, unhung curtains, and boxes. The hot water system failed and then the WC wouldn't flush. It was one thing after another.

A few days later I had spent the morning lovingly preparing a meal including John's favourite of blackberry and apple crumble. I was sitting at the table waiting for him, as I usually did, when he said, "There's no need to look like that at me, like you want me to hurry up. You *know* how you look, like it's all my fault," and he didn't want the blackberry and apple. The day was spoilt, and the mood became a horrid silence. This dreadful atmosphere lasted for days. Where had our wonderful life gone? I had so much to do. I was doing miles on foot, tramping around Barnstaple sorting things that people had failed to do or deliver. Was this the attitude of living in a town? I queued up for ages at the doctors to register us, amongst all the coughs and sneezes, so very different from our tiny practice in Porlock. I also queued for over half an hour in the germy, smelly post office, where no one else spoke to you, and I was finally served by a sour-faced grumpy woman, not like the country post office I was used to where there was a friendly, "Good morning!"

Back home, if I could call it that, the constant noise of traffic was driving me mad and I took the shortest possible route to a walk into the 'country' by Bradiford Water. I felt quite at home there, shrugging on the green cloak of the trees, watching the trout rise whilst I was standing in a field of bullocks. Herons and buzzards soared above the water and the steeply wooded valley. I enjoyed this, even if it was just for half an hour, and wept at what I had left: my heart and soul in West Somerset. As I walked back home, the traffic sound and smells and sirens of town just got me more and more depressed. How could I find any peace? What had I come to? A nice home but at a price, hubbub, and I had always wanted peace and quiet. John was happy to be there and said he didn't hear the noise. I was nearly going off my head! I went to bed that night hoping John wouldn't be so bad-tempered in the morning.

But he was. He went ballistic at me in public at the shops. People were staring at us and he told them to mind their own business.

I felt really stung and said, "Don't shout at me, please."

I remembered when we used to hold hands and now he was blowing up at me with hatred in his voice for no reason. How I kept my temper I don't know. I was so fed up I felt like forsaking everything and sleeping rough. Suddenly, the next day it was as if nothing had happened and John drove us to Braunton to collect a plastic form of double glazing to keep the noise out of my bedroom. I had the only bedroom and John had his bed in the lounge. He was laughing and joking in the shop. Then he took me for a drive and a cream tea. We had a nice day and I had to remind myself that John was blowing up because he was ill and couldn't do the things that he used to do. The so-called double glazing made no difference.

I had to keep an appointment with the new doctor as a new patient. I told him I was tired and low and that I had a strange spot on my arm, that it was sore and tender. However, he said there was nothing untoward, but it was oh, so 'ouch'!

A few days later I was off to Lundy. This had been booked many months ago. Just what I needed, to get stuck into whatever job I was given there. It was the worst crossing I can ever remember, really bad, but I was always okay on rough seas whilst everyone else was heaving up.

People were passing me on the way up to the top of the island. Very unusual as I was always the first up to the Tavern to register. I just felt so tired, I had to keep stopping. I got to my digs at 2pm, had a shower and went to bed. My arm, neck and chest were in agony. I couldn't sleep. The spots on my arm were now blotches the size of cucumber slices. I'd never had so much pain and kept shifting positions, but nothing would relieve it. The next day I felt tired and unwell but went to inspect the wall I had built eighteen months previously and found that it had settled in well. I was due to do some gullying work but thank goodness was detailed to do some easy work inside the church, although I don't know how I did it in all that pain. I went to bed at 8pm, much worse. I tried to get NHS Direct on my phone but had no signal. I knew I couldn't go on like it so I left a note in the Tavern at 1am, "I need medical assistance please," as I knew that someone would see it at 5am.

At 8:30 I was carried in a makeshift stretcher of a blanket held by four people at the corners and was airlifted off the island courtesy of the same Sea King helicopter and crew that I had trained with. They gave me some blessed morphine. At the hospital they said it was bites. They filled me with painkillers, x-rayed my neck and then sent me home. How I walked across the road and down the hill to my place I do not know. First I was on Lundy then suddenly I wasn't. It was all so bewildering.

It got worse as the day went on. A doctor came and asked me if I had ever had eczema and gave me diazepam! Feeling even worse the following day, I described the symptoms on the phone to a lady doctor who came immediately and diagnosed shingles. She gave me the proper medicine for it plus morphine as all the other pain killers made me sick. For four days I couldn't get out of bed and when my arm got paralysed I went into hospital. The shingles had got into a nerve in my neck. A few days after returning home, John drove us to Braunton to get a recliner so that I could rest in the garden in the sun. I couldn't get out of the car as my neck was hurting so badly. I put a cushion under it and curled up to wait. John, hardly able to walk, got a shop person to bring the recliner to the car. After that, the car wouldn't start and we had to go through John yelling and swearing and people looking, plus skateboarders getting in the way, thinking it was funny and me unable to do anything.

For several weeks my insides felt as if on fire. I had to use my fork right-handed and drink through a straw as I couldn't bend my neck. My left hand began to swell so much that I had to remove my wedding ring. I'd never taken it off since the day John had put it there. Each time I swallowed it was like dragging across a severe burn in my throat. John was swearing at everything and the traffic noise was driving me mental. I felt so low, so lonely in my isolation. There were thousands of people living all around me, yet I might as well have been living as a recluse on the moor.

My heart started playing up and going 'tachy'. I was wired up in hospital for several days, undergoing tests. I was a wreck. I was assaulted by a dementia patient in the opposite bed who thought I was the police! I was told by the medics that I was bored and had depression and was shoved out of hospital with three antidepressant tablets and told to go home. Within an hour, an ambulance was at our door. I was to go back, they had made a mistake and had discharged the wrong patient. No way! I wasn't going back in there if they made mistakes like that. They might think I'm dead when I'm only sleeping and I would end up in the chapel of rest!

A few days later, John drove us to Combe Martin. Oh, how wonderful I felt as that blue line of the sea hove into view! I did a doddle toddle on the beach and peered into the rockpools. A face looked back at me. My face, on my body, that had carried me all this way through life. In that moment it all rewound. I only had myself to blame: my decisions had got me to this place. I had turned back for John all those years ago in that gateway at Brent Knoll on the way to Scotland. It had been worth it for all the beautiful and wonderful times we had spent together. He had lovingly placed a wedding ring on my finger but now it was no longer there. I had to get well again to be able to get it back on!

With renewed determination I knew that, although things would never be the same again, I had to make the best of a bad job and get on with it. It was hard. There were several nice days in October and John drove us to Minehead and our old haunts and shops. As the skin started peeling off my hand and chest, after taking some recommended things from my friend in the health food shop, I began to feel better. I bump-started my motorbike down the hill and rode to Baggy Point then walked out to the end. It was warm for the time of year. There's nothing like the smell that wafts up from the sea over the rocks and warm cliff grass in a particular spot along that path, all the way, so warm, so meltingly lovely, and Lundy clear on the horizon. The sound of the sea, the air, so clean, was refreshing my lungs.

I did feel better after my escape to Baggy! I went again the next day and felt much stronger after another afternoon by the sea.

When I returned home, John had bought me roses, carnations and a trifle; life wasn't all bad after all.

I took up my coursework again, distance learning. John drove us quite often to Minehead and I increased my walking distance. I was feeling happier than I had been for some time now; at last maybe the awful sense of loss and heartache which I'd had since moving was passing, albeit slowly.

I decided to go to a long-established art group. All I wanted, really, was an escape hatch for a few hours on a Monday morning at a drop-in session. This suited me as one could do one's own thing and not join in with everyone else. No one was aware of my artistic accomplishments, so I had no expectations to live up to. The mornings were peaceful and the old school by the church was only five minutes' walk from home. I worked in all mediums but here I could use pastels to my heart's content and would complete three pictures in a morning and frame them on the spot. Where everyone else was taking weeks over one picture with a photo to copy from, I was doing mine from memory, mainly of Exmoor. I was in my own little bubble. The only sounds were people's brushes on canvas, the creaking floorboards and the occasional run of water in the sink as someone cleaned a palette. I could wear my oldest clothes and not dress up.

There was an annual fee to belong to this group plus an annual exhibition. I submitted several good pieces of work but none were chosen. This surprised me but at the annual general meeting I discovered how cliquey it was. There were many at the AGM whom I'd never met before, all dressed up in arty gear, including the carefully placed brushes sticking out of a jacket pocket and the haw-haws drinking wine. The hubbub of buzzing conversation and not being included soon had me heading for the exit. I couldn't join in and pretend I was someone I wasn't.

I still went on a Monday morning on an informal basis. There were formal courses on other days. I did attend one for a whole term, just to lend moral support and boost the funds, but I found it very constraining and I couldn't flow as I had to paint as if in a straitjacket! I could have finished in a day what it took a whole term to complete. Then there was the talking. Yak, yak, yak! As I listened to everyone's illnesses of, "I've got a worse back than you!" type of thing. I couldn't join in, so just like schooldays I let the class buzz on as I did my own thing in my own little world.

For two days a week I used to share a studio with two other artists who were nothing to do with this group. One was a world-famous wildlife painter who was so laid back he could fall over his own easel! His beautiful paintings were published in books and made into cards by a well-known maker of greetings stationery. His scenes were commissioned to appear on limited edition bone china plates by a famous company. It somehow leaked out that I was working alongside this artist and the art group I went to suddenly started being nice and gushing towards me, almost to the point of 'climbing on the bandwagon' of my success in knowing somebody that was famous in his field, but they were unlikely to ever meet as he loathed all that snobby stuff!

These people were flaunting art degrees but had no artistic talent except splodges on a wall or 'works on paper'. Lavatory paper, more like! There were a few 'careful' painters in this group though, whose work was so tight it would take a whole term to complete a picture as they re-worked it numerous times. The snobby few spoilt it for the normal, especially if you were hard-up and had little money. It served its purpose for a while and gave me the chance to have a wry smile at how the other art half lived.

I would pop into the church on the way home. Here, I found peace in its very dark interior (there were no lights on during the week). The previous day's Sunday service still hung in the gloom. I could feel the voices, the organ, the now whispering echoes of a hymn. Out into the bright daylight I soon reached home. John would say, "You've only to press the switch," as he had primed up the kettle for a welcome cup of tea, then we would have some lunch – if he was having a good day, that is.

On Tuesdays, Thursdays, and Saturdays he went to dialysis. We called these days D-Day. The days in between were spent recovering. He had up to four pints of blood 'cleaned' by the machine and was very groggy sometimes, to the point of passing out if too much was taken off. Our whole week revolved around dialysis. Appointment, visits, outings and even food and drink had to be carefully planned. He was allowed only one litre of liquid a day; meals had to be punctual and diabetically suitable. There were so many foods that were not allowed. It was a cook's nightmare, me of course being the cook! At first I took a list of the no-no's with me when shopping and had to look at all food ingredients before purchasing. After a while I was well-practised in this art and didn't need the list.

John could still drive, so long as his foot wasn't swollen, and we'd carry an alarm clock with us to prompt him into remembering that it was time to take his tablets. We were queuing up at a checkout once when the security man on the door casually strolled over. He asked me to place my backpack on the floor. "Can everyone move back, please?" John cottoned on straight away, it was the loud ticking alarm clock that the security guard had probably heard, so John with his warped sense of humour said in a loud voice to me,

"What time did you set it to blow up?"

"Any moment now," I replied, quick as a flash.

First of all there was a queue and a checkout person, suddenly they had all disappeared! Including the security man. There was an ominous puddle where he had been standing! Oh, this was how it used to be between us, John having a joke. There we were, creased up laughing, tears running down our faces as out in the carpark everyone was staring at us, not finding it quite so funny.[7]

---

[7] Publishers' note: It is worth bearing in mind that, until they had made their rather dubious joke, nobody, including the security guard, really believed there was a bomb in the backpack. If they *had* then the least likely course of

If he was recovered enough on the in-between dialysis days, John would often drive over the moor and we would relive happy times with a picnic and do a sketch or two, then drop down into Minehead. These were precious times as, very soon, there would be no more driving. John gave me and himself a big scare one night coming back in the dark. On a road that we knew well, just a mile from home, and a wide road at that,  he drove round a bend on the wrong side, causing oncoming traffic to swerve dangerously.

"Stupid f*****s! Why don't they look where they are going!" he yelled.

"It was you, dear. You were on the wrong side of the road."

"Don't you tell me how to drive!"

The lovely day evaporated in an instant. At home, the car keys were thrown in the road and the pre-prepared meal wasn't wanted as John stormed off to bed. Another smashed day. From heights of happiness to depths of despair. Illness does dreadful things. I felt wretched and despondent as there was nothing I could do.

---

action would be to approach and calmly ask her to remove the backpack and place it on the floor.

Next morning, the car keys were on the table instead of the key rack. As John was being wheeled out to the waiting ambulance to go to dialysis he said, "Find a buyer for the car, will you? A couple of hundred should do it." And with that, he was gone.

Gazing at the dear Green Goddess, our Skoda Felicia, I was sad. This was the best vehicle we had ever owned for road holding, economy, and room. As I emptied out the side pockets, memories came flooding back. There was a car park machine ticket with, "I love you, darling," written across it. A bunch of old dried-up moorland heather, some shells and pebbles and John's emergency glucose tablets. An old shirt, now used as a rag, reminded me of those far-off days when we were first in love and he wore that and hugged me to his fine chest. I felt his heart beat as he kissed me. Oh, those beautiful days, endless, that stretched out before us. We were invincible, nothing could come between us. Now it had. Illness. Shadow. The valley of the shadow... We were starting our walk through the valley of the shadow of death and not knowing how far into it we would go before the hills would close over our heads.

Someone came for the car. I needn't have bothered to clean it up as a farmer wanted it for his son to practice in, around the muddy acres. He didn't even want the seat covers I had washed and pressed. Goodbye, Green Goddess. Goodbye Exmoor rides. Goodbye sunsets on the beach, seaside picnics, the open road, wide spaces, and views. Hello to being hemmed in, halted, stuck in a rut, humdrum and limited. John's view was even narrower. I should feel sorrier but each time I helped I got pushed away. Now I had to dress him, and he wouldn't let me wash those parts that he could not reach. Then he refused to take his shirt off for a month at a time, then it was his pants. I was ashamed to send him off to dialysis in this state.

A Wonderful Diversion

Maggie, our first black greyhound, came into our lives from Dogs Trust. John fell in love with her. She gave him affection, which he didn't want from me. Best of all, she gave me a reason to escape and go for regular walks where I met other dog walkers in the park or along the Tarka Trail. John started to go out again on his mobility scooter and having a dog with us was a go-between as people struck up a conversation, admiring Maggie. I would take her on the bus to Croyde and look around my old haunts and where my parents used to live. Maggie was so gentle and won prizes at the family dog shows. I made a few dog-loving friends at these events. It was a welcome diversion. Maggie, slender, dainty, her coat like black satin in the sun. She knew the routine. When it was a D-Day she didn't get up until I had done breakfast and made John's sandwiches. Corned beef, ugh! I hated it, thought it smelt like dog poo, but Maggie loved it and she knew when I had finished making them there would be a tit-bit waiting for her.

One of the biggest trials centred around the ambulance service. Sometimes it never turned up and John would miss the time slot at the kidney unit. Then he would often be two or three hours late getting home, by which time any meal was spoilt. It was very trying for everyone. I couldn't go out in case the ambulance turned up in my absence. In the end I got a key safe fitted.

Maggie loved her walks and I loved her jaunty attitude to life. We went to the woods and fields but these were being nibbled away as building work began. All those wildflowers, the bluebells, primroses and garlic, gone for ever under a digger truck. Rubbish was bulldozed into the stream, old prams and mattresses, the trout disappeared and the nesting ducks vanished. As the woods were cut down the buzzards roamed the roof of the sky unable to use the thermals that used to rise up as the day grew warm. Now they mewed in distress, their calls echoing around the once-green valley.

My studies were going well. I was getting 98 per cent passes. They helped me to focus on something and having Maggie was the best thing to happen in a long time. I had a daytime companion and was never alone.

In December 2006, John got very puffy. His face was swelling and he was breathless. He couldn't do his trousers up. I was having to lift his legs onto the bed as they had got so big he couldn't do it himself. The doctor came and said it was his renal failure causing it and gave him some water tablets. What a job it was to get John to the toilet. He kept having accidents. John took to his bed. By 21 December we were still waiting to hear from the specialist. John had been in bed for three weeks. Extra water tablets did not get the swelling down. Now an oozing sore was opening up on his leg, the start of an ulcer. His middle was badly swollen.

I got some bird feeders to hang outside his window. I was finding it hard, keeping up the unrelenting tempo of shopping, cooking, washing up and worry and trying to walk Maggie as well.

I had once been a wonderful lover but now I had turned into being a reluctant carer. On Christmas Eve I walked around the local housing estates, just to see some Christmas lights as Christmas this year would be a non-event for us. At least other people's lights were a sort of company and comfort as I walked back to my bleak house.

On Christmas Day 2006, after a bad night listening out for John, I got up at 8am, at dawn, with the church bells ringing out, removing the final cobwebs of the night. Maggie and I went for a long walk. It was midday when we returned and John had not eaten breakfast, which I'd left him. Neither did he eat any dinner. He slept on and on and on... He went hypo in the night. The ambulance crew saved him.

I saw in the new year of 2007 on my own, in bed listening to the radio and wondering what it would bring, as John was getting more and more swollen and was too ill to go to dialysis. The next day our warden was so horrified at the state of John. We couldn't even wake him up and still the doctor didn't come. The following day a nurse came and begged the doctor to visit. It wasn't until a week later that John was admitted to hospital, where he remained for six weeks, far away in Exeter. During this time the whole bungalow was rewired by the housing people, or rather their contractors. They managed to smash the lintel above the front door with the step ladders, put their foot through the ceiling twice, mix up plaster in the sink and left the residue to go rock hard. They used my nice flooring to cut things up on, managed to break a new toilet seat and leave muddy handprints on the wall where they leaned whilst having a piss. They lost my keys, so I had to get a new lock put on the door. They took three weeks, with almost every day another disaster. They broke the cistern up in the roof space and so it went on. They even stood on my bed with muddy boots on and plaster landed in the dog bowl. The warden came and saw the damage and mess the workmen had made and I was eventually paid £200 compensation.

I had so much worry going on, but Maggie saved me from going mad. I was very glad of her company. As a distraction, I made use of the time to catch up on my exam papers.

By now, the hospital wanted me to visit John pronto. It was a tricky journey to Exeter, but I made it. I spent half an hour with John, although he was unaware of my visit. He had to lose sixty-three litres of fluid, they told me, but the machine only took off three at a time, so it was going to be a slow process. A few days later I got a bad cold, probably caught in the hospital.

I eventually had six weeks on my own. Time to myself. I had a tidy home, a dripless WC pan, the lounge no longer resembled a hospital ward. I slept well, got up and went out as I pleased. I wasn't tied down. In fact, I was quite enjoying my existence of not being tied down. For the first time ever I was being *me*. No kids, parents, husbands. As sorry as I was that John was ill, I had found a new freedom of not having to cook every day, or watch the clock, worry about getting here and there on time. I discovered I was capable.

John came home. The meal I had lovingly prepared he had one mouthful and started retching. He had nothing to eat for two days. He was so frail. I was up all night as he kept wanting the loo, shivering, and sneezing, wandering in his speech and mind, and wanting me to leave the hall light on as he was afraid. It was a dreadful night, followed by having to get up at 6am to take him to dialysis in Exeter. The driver was none too pleased at John's frailty and inability to walk and said they were not trained to handle bodies.

He went away and had more procedures done. When he came home, he promptly fell into a diabetic coma, so it was back to hospital. He caused a huge disturbance. He refused to get undressed, wash, eat or drink. He was swearing and ranting and the staff wanted me to come and calm him down.

When I walked in he said, "What the f*** are you doing here?"

He was in a strop and demanded to come home, where he promptly messed the bed, the bathroom mats and walls.

* * * * *

During this time I was doing a project for Exeter University on the consumer landscape during the 1950s. I found it to be a life-saving mental diversion, along with my other course work. Working towards exams and passing meant so much to me. I had all my papers laid out for a final exam when the housing sent round an inspector to look at the rewiring. It was unsatisfactory. The whole lot would have to come out and be done again. Another month of mess and dust, drilling, plaster, and upheaval. That, combined with John in a sick bed 'being sick', was news I was loath to hear.

I got permission to have a shed and a greenhouse. The shed was big, and I planned to use it as a studio with heat, light, et cetera in it, an escape area on bad days. I laid a concrete base and also made steps out of paving stones which I found dumped under some trees after highways had not bothered to collect them after a road job. I also made steps to a balcony and sawed a gap in the wooden balustrade so that I could open the lounge door and John could sit in the sun. A greenhouse was a wonderful addition as well. I knew by then that I was stuck there for quite a while to come, so I wanted to make it half bearable.

I did loads to create a beautiful garden from what was a piece of waste land, full of six-foot-high brambles. I made two ponds, one had goldfish in by the kitchen door so that John could watch them as he sat there to eat. I even got a fountain going as well. The other pond was a nature one, which I put frog spawn in and for years afterwards the emerging frogs came back to lay eggs and start again. Some palmate newts arrived as well. These ponds matured and gave me great joy as did the greenhouse. The neglected pear tree bore fruit after I pruned it. It gave me 600 conference pears that year as a reward! My garden, I was so proud of it. It looked a picture, a haven of peace, but it wasn't. It was too noisy to sit in. It was impossible to hold a conversation above the traffic noise. The bird bath on a pedestal was a source of amusement as two resident pigeons tried to bathe in it together. The inverted dustbin lid on the 'lawn' was also a bath: a dust bath for the sparrows.

I decided to enter a national competition, run by McCarthy & Stone, to name a new block of retirement flats in Ilfracombe, yet to be built. A reason had to be given for the name, which had to have a historical background. I asked to see some artist's impression drawings of the completed complex. I wrote the 500-word article and gave the name of Lantern Court, because it faced across the harbour to the building that has the flashing light on Lantern Hill. I won a £150 prize! A taxi was sent to fetch me to go to the presentation on a building site. Lantern Court would not be completed for another five years but I vowed to go to the official opening and when I did I met Mary Peters, who opened it. We had run together at the White City and there was only two days difference in our ages! She remembered me.

By now I was also ghostwriting for a well-known naturalist who had a column in a national newspaper, but only when he had a big workload or was unwell. I could never reveal this to anyone at the time as I was sworn to secrecy. It just so happened that I had a similar writing style and was knowledgeable on wildlife.

Our twenty-first wedding anniversary passed without John noticing. He spent the day on dialysis. He was always a romantic and, until then, had never failed to do something special. To think that just the year before he had driven us out from Porlock to an inn on Exmoor for a meal.

I had a very successful stall selling our paintings at the Green Man festival only a stone's throw away from home in the local park. It looked gloomy all day but stayed dry as thousands of people packed the event. Just as I finished packing away the heavens opened: what luck!

Building work commenced in the front garden to put a ramp and scooter store in place. For me, this was almost the final nail in the forthcoming coffin. It meant that we would be here forever, stuck. I found it hard to comprehend that there was nothing else left in life, no adventure. Even my beloved garden was being wrecked. Hydrangea bushes uprooted, rockery dismantled, herb garden and carefully laid paving stones, heathers, bulbs, all sacrificed for the six-foot-deep trenches. I wondered if John would even survive to see it completed.

I had the afternoon off, so I motorbiked to Combe Martin via Whitefield Hill. Oh, what joy to see the Hangman hills come into view! As I approached Combe Martin the sun shone and the sea danced a million crystal glances of turquoise. I struggled up the lane of mud and stood and marvelled at the sheer beauty of Wild Pear Beach below me and an uncluttered sea horizon. The gentle scrunch of sea on shore was soporific. How I had missed it all! The smell of the ferns, the gulls wheeling and crying, the warmth as I sat on the springy turf and the feel of a hot smooth stone baked by the sun. I was made for this, not for the town. What an amazing couple of hours I had. I cleaned off my muddy shoes in the stream. The water carried away my negative thoughts. I was refreshed.

* * * * *

The church wanted me to do the altar pedestal for a wedding as the usual flower ladies were away. I was well pleased with what I had done and so was the church. My old floristry skills were not forgotten, and I was asked if I would do the whole building the following week. I must say it looked fantastic. Then I was asked to go and shop around for the flowers myself. This was difficult minus transport, on a D-Day with a dog in tow. I paid for the flowers, thinking that I would be reimbursed. Muggins me, too scared to ask, never got paid. The flower ladies returned and didn't like the professional touch I had brought to the church.

"Oh, you don't get paid; it's part of your donation to the upkeep of the church!" I was informed. Well, here endeth the first lesson!

Things changed, the choir and robes were done away with, evensong disappeared as did the processional before a service. A piano was hauled into use and the deep tones of the organ that thrilled one's very core no longer played. Then there was the sign of peace during a service, where people hugged and kissed each other. I absolutely cringed at this, I couldn't bear it to be kissed by a stranger. As people walked around to do this it broke up the flow of the service and one lost the thread. I wished the pew would swallow me up.

* * * * *

In August I had a day to remember. I did something new and so enjoyable that I couldn't wait for the next time! We went on the train, Maggie and I, to Umberleigh Dog Show. Maggie won two blue rosettes, second places for veteran and best rescue. She rode on the train as if well-travelled and strutted her stuff in the show ring. Other family dog shows were held locally, and I went if I could get there on a bus. At one event we won so much stuff plus a large sack of dog food I had great difficulty manhandling it all to the bus stop. As I was wondering how I was going to transport it at the other end, someone from the dog show offered to take me home. What luck! Most of these shows were on a dialysis day so I wasn't missed. So long as I was back when the ambulance arrived it was okay or, failing that, there was the key safe.

The ambulance crew became friends who knew their patients over several years and one by one these patients eventually died as they were all under a death sentence, including John. Of course, I loved John and as I cleared up yet another load of vomit or back-end disaster I tried to remember the good times that we had had. I didn't sleep at night for worrying about him getting in and out the toilet, and falling down; he was so heavy to lift. I was all the hospital staff rolled into one: the cook, the dietician, nurse, cleaner, occupational therapist, laundry maid, housekeeper. What would it all bring forth? A catalogue of disaster, that's what.

It was like having a child to look after, the difference being that this child had a thinking brain that's unable to dress itself and walk properly. This child was once my lover who had thrilled me with endless nights of passion. Now I had to get down on the floor with my legs apart to put his footwear on, not make love to him. I felt so sad. I felt like crying but only when I was alone … and Maggie was there, my beautiful Maggie.

Most people would have families to help but mine could have been living on the moon, detached, somewhere floating in their space. What did I matter when they had so much to occupy them? In another world, another time, so long ago, they were my precious bundles that I nursed, protected, brought through tough times to maturity against all the odds.

I was sad, so sad, but as I put my arms around Maggie and wept into her coat I knew that she understood. She was my all-enveloping comforter and friend. She looked stunning, standing in a field of yellow buttercups on a spring morning, her delicate black shape enhanced by their colour. With the Bradiford Water running past it felt as if all the troubles I was enduring were being washed away. The blackbirds were singing and lambs were calling across the valley. Perfect. I could stay forever but my trap beckoned. The only way out of this trap was when John died. His five years to live were well and truly up.

I was worn out in my head. No end to it, being a full-timer carer was taking its toll. One drudge after another. No reward. No thanks. Where was I heading? I felt like bashing my head against a brick wall until all the pulp oozed out. I needed help. My blood pressure rocketed. The new medication made me worse. Then my tinnitus and Ménière's disease reared its ugly head. I couldn't get the noise out of my head and life became a merry-go-round as I lurched giddily from one task to the next. I went to the mental health clinic. At last! Help was on hand without having to resort to antidepressants. I was not depressed, just worn out. I met with practical help, suggestions, and sympathy.

On dialysis days a mentor would come and have a chat and we would run through any problems and peruse them. I would then be driven with Maggie to a place of my choice and then be picked up a few hours later and returned home. What precious hours I had, walking along a beach or Braunton Burrows, along the toll road, Mortehoe, Woolacombe or Putsborough. Big skies, wild seas invigorating me, with Maggie by my side enjoying an outing, which she deserved. She kicked up the sand and laughed, tongue lolling, eyes shining. This was freedom. Sun, sea, and air. But even this did not last as the mentor was to be moved to another department. Before she went she asked if I could take part in a film to be shown to doctors and mental health workers. I did. It was fifteen minutes long and starred me and Maggie, also John in our kitchen. I was so proud to think that this was being made to show that stress could be overcome minus medication. It was part of a scheme called 'Time for Life'.[8]

The film showed us in various locations enjoying a walk, also in my studio painting, as having given it up I was encouraged to start again. I was put forward to attend Art in the Park. There were so few places I was honoured to be chosen. There were about eight of us, all with 'issues', but we never spoke of them. We met in the little lodge in a park where we did a structured art programme for one term. How I enjoyed this! Out round the park with cameras, taking pictures of lines, shapes, and curves, be it road markings, decorative railings, or the curves of the roundabout on the play area. We were all shadowed and looked after and we made interesting interpretations of what we had

---

[8] You can find this video on the Vimeo website at this address https://vimeo.com/5291248

photographed. The tutors and helpers were so kind and caring, they made drinks and snacks for us and laid out and cleared away all our gear. This was all part of helping us to heal and cope. If someone broke down, everyone else sympathised. It was a remarkable experience. Someone actually cared about *me* and understood my situation.

A week towards the end of the term we were given canvasses nailed to the wall. They were about five feet long and two feet wide. Such a strange, oblong shape in a vertical position. Our folders with the term's work were given out and we had five minutes to pick a photo we had taken and one-and-a-half hours to reproduce this in acrylic on our long upright canvas. Being an autumn term I had no hesitation in choosing a picture of some orange bunches of rowan berries on a dark and sultry ultramarine / black background. It had to be finished in the allotted time.

On the final day of term, the following week, we were taken up to the college to the art room. Imagine our surprise when we walked in to see that all of our canvasses had been made into deck chairs! There they all were, lined up on top of the art tables, our photos and folder beside each one. What a sight and a proud moment for us all as we devoured a nicely laid out buffet. Such kindness. I met with such understanding people who cared and made you feel not worthless anymore. The deckchairs toured the south west, to be shown at mental health conferences.

Everyone had the opportunity to take up the spring and summer term at the college, doing a certificated course in art and craft one day a week, a sort of O level. I signed up, skidding my way up the steep hill into the college on my motorbike and promptly got a parking ticket for parking it under the window of the art room on a path that nobody used. The tutor was very angry at the jumped-up trumped-up so-called college traffic warden, saying, "These students have issues you'd never dream of, mental health ones, and you are not helping by issuing a petty ticket!"

The ticket was eventually waived but in future I had to park my bike in an awkward tight space inside the potting store where all the clay was kept. It was 'get it right first time' as I had to use a plank to get the bike over the door frame into the dark confined space.

It was all worth it though. It was on a dialysis day, which meant walking Maggie, seeing John off, then hoping the dog sitter would turn up via the key safe later.

The best thing of all was mingling with the other students, fifty or sixty years younger than me, in the eating hall where I was completely accepted and had the most gorgeous meals. I had to wear a student identity round my neck and got ten percent off in the local art and book shops! The young students, who were generally regarded as unruly and bad mannered, I found to be very respectful towards me and always helpful when I lost my way in the maze of corridors. They always bade me go first in the food queue and made sure that I had a chair, rather than a bench, to sit on.

I did so enjoy my time at the college, making things I only ever dreamed of and experimenting in different crafts. A running report-come-dossier was kept on our individual work and I ended the course with A-plus and a recommendation to go on to do an art degree. Oh, how this lifted me up, to go on to better things through my own hard work! I got a government grant and set my sights to start in September. I was shown where my place would be, and my name was put there. I went home full of excitement. John would be so pleased! But I didn't take account of his illness and how it had changed him.

"What the f*** do you want to do that for? *You* could teach *them*!"

At this point, he demanded I pass him his guitar, which I refused as I guessed that he would smash it. Those beautiful guitars... He wrote love songs and we played them together; such joy they brought us. We automatically knew when the other one wanted to play and we'd both pick them up at the same time and an hour would pass. Our extemporisation was phenomenal. John had a beautiful deep voice. He could impersonate any of the country singers. Now he could hardly croak a tune out ... and all my visions of college were blinded in one rant. I suppose it would never have worked out anyway as he got worse. I knew he would, but I had a dream, even if it was for such a short while.

His fingers wouldn't work in his left hand. They had been getting worse for some time, so guitar playing was out. His words were getting muddled and he refused an x-ray of his head. He had had a small stroke. The swearing was one of the outcomes and it would get worse. The swelling started up again, despite dialysis. A special hospital bed was installed in our living room, with a moving mattress that groaned at intervals as it changed shape. This was supposed to prevent bed sores. Sides were put on the bed to stop him falling out. Instead he fell out with me. I could do nothing right. I knew it wasn't the real John, that went when he got ill, but all the same, it was very hurtful. I felt so alone, no one to compare notes with, no advice, no support, so it was with interest that I spotted an advert to say that a carers' group was starting up. Although not a 'group' person, I felt maybe I could learn something with like-minded people. Fortunately, it was on a dialysis day. Maggie got an extra-long walk before I went, plus her dinner and she usually slept all afternoon.

The meetings were very informative, and I learnt that I could apply for all sorts of benefits and aids. Also, there was an interesting programme of events and one of these was a lovely lady who came once a month doing creative writing. I bless the day that I met her as it started for me a fantastic new interest that was to lead me into great things in the future. She gave us a subject to write a story about and to read it out to the group next time. I was on fire with the project! I had so many ideas just rolling out of my head that the story would be there before I reached home. I could get a story out first go, without any alteration, just as I'm doing now. It was like sketching or drawing. I just 'got it' straight away down on paper, no rubbing out.

Then John's dialysis days got changed and I had to do a rethink of my activities. I had to get help as things were getting worse. I kept asking social services. It took three months and I had to pay nearly £100 insurance for my helper. It was all so complicated. They couldn't help me with the things that I really needed doing. They weren't allowed to do anything above head or below waist height, so cleaning windows, or under the bed; reaching for something in a cupboard, or under the sink was out. I put up with it for a short while but it all came to a head when I went outside to get the washing off the line and came back in sooner than expected to hear the supposed home-help saying, "It's okay, the old bag is out in the garden getting the washing in, you can speak now."

She was crouched down behind my bed, talking into her mobile phone. "She ain't 'alf an old cow, I'm slavin' me guts out 'ere."

(*That* wasn't true!) I held my tongue and bided my time. I made a pot of tea and when we had sat down and she had the cup poised to her lips I said, "I'm so sorry you are slaving your guts out but the old cow made a nice cake if you would like a slice?"

In mid-swallow she half choked on her tea and spilt it all down her front and it was the day that she had forgotten her apron! I didn't sign her work sheet. She was gone, never to return.

A reliable friend of mine from long ago came for half a day and took Maggie out, cleaned up and kept an eye on John. Those half days I took the bus by the country route and went to Ilfracombe. I just loved the place, the friendly people, scenery, and independent shops. So much to see in one place, different views, and harbour scenes. I just felt so relaxed there. I enjoyed the ride, too. I knew that John was in safe hands with a trustworthy friend who understood his 'language' and turned a deaf ear to it.

Walking around Ilfracombe brought back memories of seeing my first trapeze artist at the Gaiety Theatre there. I must have been around nine or ten years old. The trapeze artist seemed to fly right over our heads and his silver skin-tight costume sparkled in the spotlight. I was wondering if he would fly off into the audience, maybe into our coach party. That would be dramatic, I thought, as it would delay the outing a bit longer as body parts would be scraped off people's laps! Afterwards we always had a fish and chip supper at the Capstone Restaurant. I was the only child on the outing, which consisted of squeaky-clean grown-ups in evening attire. I kept my mouth shut, but not in the restaurant! I was served a baby sized portion, and someone spoke up for me and said I was a fast-growing girl. When nothing was forthcoming some people in the party did the unthinkable in those days, they put chips on my plate from theirs whilst my parents disapprovingly looked on. Even worse was to come as I was served some ghastly drink full of bubbles called cherryade. It got up my nose, made me sneeze and produce the most almighty burp, which I could feel coming up and couldn't prevent. I could also sense a similar feeling in my nether regions as I tried to sit tight on it and not let it out.

This was an annual outing from that blasted holiday camp in Croyde. As we journeyed back in the coach in the dark, everyone started singing irritating, meaningless songs, *I've Got Sixpence* and *She'll be Coming Round the Mountain When She Comes*, plus *Ten Green Bottles Hanging on the Wall*. I thought that there were nicer songs to sing and wished I had some ear plugs as they were singing it all slur-like and at journey's end were a bit unsteady on their feet, having had a few drinks.

Now though it was time to return home to John and Maggie. John was fired up and happy and Maggie was pleased to see me.

It was through Maggie that I met two lovely people and their dog, Sam. In the years to come they would be my lifeline and support in desperate times. I will refer to them as the Winden

Wood couple. Maggie and Sam became great friends. I would be doing a circuit of the local park and the unmistakeable sound of Sam's bark, as he stood on the park steps entrance, would announce that he had arrived.

"Here I am, everybody, take notice," and then he would trot off and find us. Over time, his owner, one half of the Winden Wood couple, got to know me as we chatted on park circuits and I peeled off to my own place on the way home, leaving him to continue on to Winden.

Yet again, my childhood past reared its ugly head as, invited to visit, I approached their beautiful house in its glorious setting, overlooking vast acres of stunning scenery and beyond to Hartland Point. I, living in social housing, felt degraded and on the bottom rung. How could I live up to this lovely home and lovely people? Why had they asked me here, with my dog as well? Well I needn't have worried. Here I was valued for who I was, not what I had, or where I lived, or what I wore. The lady of the house was impeccably turned out with well applied make-up and nice hair. I might have felt quite shabby, but she wasn't like that. She was the most welcoming and kind person who made me feel like a family member as she showed me around the garden. I had found out that not all people with big houses and two cars were snobs!

* * * * *

It was well over five years since the specialist gave us that gloomy prediction of John's life expectancy. He had survived far longer, but at a cost. His quality of life was awful, drifting in and out of sleep, suppurating legs, and now a dreadful swollen fluid-filled eye that kept weeping. He was blind in this one. The light kept interfering with his vision, so he had a greasy baseball cap practically glued to his head day and night. Dialysis was becoming a trial as the journey shook him up. As time went on, instead of being wheeled out he was stretchered out, his thin frame felt every jolt. It was now August 2014. His weight had dropped to eight stone. When he was fit and well it was around twelve stone. He was beginning to look like the other patients that had gone on before him and the ambulance crew agreed with me that this was the beginning of the end.

Maggie too, now thirteen, was getting thin and frail. She had an incurable open sore on her flank that was impossible to cover and the flies kept landing on it. At night she could no longer make it outside and became incontinent. She slept by my bed, always, but I knew in my heart that this was now the beginning of *her* end as well as John's. One morning, she didn't get up. She just looked at me, tired and dull of eye. I rang the vet who had been treating her and we agreed that her time had come. It was a beautiful sunny day as Maggie lay on her favourite blanket in the sun patch by the open door. John was in his bed, watching and waiting for the vet and his assistant to arrive. I explained to the vet about John and his unbalanced state of mind.

Maggie's rosettes and medals surrounded her. She didn't raise her head as the vet came in the room. He examined her and said that she had had enough and was ready to go. I looked into her eyes, my head close to hers, she looked into my very soul and drifted off peacefully into eternity, her head in my hands. The vet withdrew the plunger. His stethoscope confirmed no heartbeat. My darling dog was gone. I would have to relive this again. This was a practice run for the main event with John.

Dearest, sweetest Maggie, I loved you so. You never did anything wrong. Always by my side. I would miss her.

Suddenly, "You've murdered my dog!" John, witnessing, suddenly exploded.

The vet and his assistant, with dignity, carried Maggie outside. I apologised for the outburst. It was okay, he said, and I had done the best thing and made the right decision.

John weeping... The lump in my throat threatening to make me do the same. Under control Anne, cup of tea. Horrendous... Weather too nice for such a horrid day... In a daze. Empty space where the sun patch had been by the open door...

Forever after my gaze would go to that empty space as the sun journeyed across the gap. John crying. My dam yet to burst. Comfort him. No one to comfort me.

Next day, rain streamed down the windows outside, echoing my tears on the inside.

August blurred into September. I went on empty, futile walks that had no purpose now Maggie was gone. No nose to nuzzle into my hand first thing in the morning as I lay in bed. I was devastated. The Winden Wood couple eased my loss. I'd never missed anything so much, *ever*.

By the end of September John couldn't keep any food down and was put onto special vitamin drinks, on prescription. He definitely took a turn for the worse after Maggie went.

With due respect to Maggie's memory, and knowing no other dog could be the same, I still went ahead and rehomed another black greyhound that no one wanted. Ruby came from the Retired Greyhound Trust at Honiton and was driven from there by the Trust's manager to meet me at home. My sorrowing heart melted towards Ruby. The manager and I had a long chat about Ruby and her background, and we all went for a long walk together. Ruby was bigger than dainty Maggie and she wagged her tail a lot. It was like a whip if you happened to be in the way! The manager had some sandwiches and we all had our snack together, after which Ruby settled into Maggie's old bed as if she had always lived there! She had wormed her way in and stolen my heart. She would go back to Honiton if there was a problem. Black greyhounds, I learnt, were always difficult to rehome. People preferred the ones with the tiger markings. After completing the paperwork, Ruby was signed over to me and it was reassuring to know that I had support if things didn't work out. John was at dialysis and when he got home, he would once more have a loving dog to stroke.

Much as I loved Maggie, I was bursting with excitement. She would have wanted me to rescue another greyhound. John came home in a good mood and Ruby went to John's bed where he stroked her and called her Maggie. Ruby was a bit of a trooper, strong, and I had to calm her lead-walking down. She soon got the message. She was seven years old and in nice condition.

By the beginning of October John was gurgling up blood after his vitamin drink. I still rubbed his pressure points three to four times a day with surgical spirit, to prevent bed sores. This was a difficult operation as each move now caused much pain. Dressing him was just as bad. It got to the point where he didn't want to remove his clothes because of the pain it caused. He had a constant pain all over, but his hand would be there for Ruby. He spent the next month in hospital, just up the road. He begged me to have a break and spend some time away as he said he was in good hands.

I stayed in a holiday cottage on a farm near Watermouth. It was by the bus route; if I had to get to the hospital urgently in the daytime, the bus passed it. The farm had its own private beach, plenty of beautiful views and fields to wander about on. It was a breathing space. I even did a few watercolour sketches. Ruby loved the beach and I spent much time just looking out across the Bristol Channel and enjoying the fine weather. I met no one, which suited me fine. Peace and tranquillity: medicine for my soul.

When I returned home I found the contrast overwhelming. The traffic noise and smell, and grumpy people with their noses to the pavement grindstone were depressing. Even more depressing was seeing John in that hospital ward. It was 4pm and his untouched lunch was still on his locker. No one had given him his vitamin drink.

"They don't have time to open it," he explained.

He couldn't open it as he hadn't got the strength. There was old, dried blood down his front. His teeth were lost and so was his mobile phone. I went to the sister in charge.

"We just don't have enough staff to sit and feed a patient," she said.

I explained that on his notes it said that he could no longer eat solid food but had these special drinks on prescription and that I had left a whole box full of them in his locker.

"He needs someone to open one and put a straw in it. The straw is attached to the bottle," I explained.

I looked everywhere to find his dentures and mobile phone. Even his clothes had disappeared.

Sister said, "Can't you get him some slippers?"

What a stupid question, when John hadn't walked for weeks and his feet wouldn't fit in them anyway.

"No," I replied. "They would probably disappear along with the other missing articles!"

John's thin hands were cold. It was hot in that ward. The window was open. An air ambulance helicopter was coming in to land. Switches, buttons, dials, and vibrations fleeted through my thoughts as it finally touched down. The noise and smell drifted in briefly. Huge skies remembered. Now back to the narrowed vision of this claustrophobic death ward. Men like skeletons, the harsh lighting shining off their skulls. Teeth gone, cheeks sunken, eyes mostly closed. Tubes and bags leading from who knows where? Urine smells, vomit and sweat. Beds are moved. John's bed, without warning, is shunted also.

His cries of pain as it is roughly handled with, "Come along now, it's not that bad, we're only going on a little journey!" The journey, just across the ward, must have seemed like a lifetime.

"He's going home tomorrow, there's nothing more we can do." Sister threw this remark over her shoulder as she hurried off.

How was I going to cope? I demanded to see someone about this, and a hastily organised meeting was held. There were ten 'black suits' and some social workers, all trying to pass the buck and not spend money on putting John into a care home.

"He's dying anyway so it wouldn't help much. He might as well go home," one of them said.

Dying. Dying anyway. How casually it came out. No one told me that he was dying but I already knew. Supposing I was someone who didn't realise? How would that have sounded then? At least my experiences in life had prepared me for the one that was soon to happen. I just hoped that John didn't hear that remark. He was discussed as if he were not there, this old bundle of shawl-wrapped humanity in a wheelchair. I swallowed a big lump in my throat as I felt so sad yet frustrated. Social services were costing it out. How much would it cost to have a carer come in to help for fifteen minutes, twice a day?

John came home from hospital worse than when he went in, with big bed sores on heels, base of spine and elbows. I had kept all of this at bay all this time at home and yet the hospital routine was too busy to provide this basic nursing care… *"He's dying anyway…"*

Dozing off to a hoped-for sleep one night, I heard groaning. Was this it? Had the time come? Rushing into the room where John slept, all was still until another groan came… Not from an expiring body but from that weird hospital mattress as it did its job of moving around. Aaaaahhh! It groaned and gurgled. I had to laugh at myself.

The October leaves fell gently from the trees in the park, making a scrunchy yellow carpet for the dogs to investigate. Shiny conkers rained down and the little footbridge over the river became slippery with early morning frost, sparkling in the sun. Mist rose off the water. Such a lovely morning to enjoy all too briefly as the treadmill of the day loomed before me. The carer only had time to dress John. My back was too bad to get down to put his trousers and sandals on. By now he refused to remove his socks for days on end. His toenails were growing over the ends of his toes and he refused to have them cut: bad news with diabetes. How glad I was to receive helpful advice from the carers' group and to exercise my mind with the latest subject set for creative writing that month. Through the group I got some vital backing and found that I could demand two carers to come in twice a day and for minimal cost.

By now, John's eyesight had worsened and he could no longer read but enjoyed looking at pictures with a magnifying glass. I also used paper plates for safety. I had found that his old sense of humour was still there at times. He asked me to cut out a very realistic picture of some life-sized baked beans, which I did. Then he wanted me to glue them to a paper plate and put them on his tray with a slice of half-eaten toast, which I also did. Chuckling to himself, he waited for the carers to arrive for his evening bedding down for the night.

Sitting on the edge of his bed, looking mighty sorrowful and down in the dumps, he gestured to the carers to take his uneaten food away.

"Just scrape it into my waste bin," he told them, "by my bed. Don't want the wife to know…"

I was creased up laughing as I watched through the dining hatch as one of the carers couldn't get the beans off the paper plate as they were Blu-tacked in position!

Having my dear dog to walk was the perfect safety valve as I would let off steam and walk two to three miles, quite often meeting half the Winden couple walking Sam. It was good to offload to someone I could trust.

Halfway through November the district nurse came every day to change John's dressings on his ulcerated legs and feet. The wounds were getting bigger day by day. Poor John was rotting out. I had to collect an 'end of life' package, containing pain relief and syringes, so I was told.

As we entered the final week of that month, John stopped drinking and didn't know if it was day or night. I was shown how to use a wet sponge on a stick to moisten his mouth.

On the morning of my seventy-fourth birthday, 30 November, there was a different atmosphere in the room. John was in such pain he could not be moved anymore. His eyes were closed. He tried to say something but had barely the strength.

I had to put my ear close to his face and he must have remembered that it was my birthday as he whispered, "Candle... Must have can...dles..."

So I lit a large twenty-four-hour lemon-scented candle and put on his favourite CD of all time to gently play in the background. *Silver Wings*: he often painted to his music.

Nurses arrived to apply the end of life package. The morphine driver was in place. Pain subsided. The Winden couple were due to take me out for a birthday lunch. They went ahead without me and brought me back a hot roast carvery dinner on a plate, which I surprisingly ate with relish. After this, I suddenly felt too tired to stay awake. I was on my own, so I went to fetch a neighbour as promised, a surgeon off duty, and he came and watched over John whilst I fell into a deep afternoon sleep. He said he would wake me if there was any change.

At 7:45pm he called me. I stepped into the candle-lit room, which was heavy with a life about to depart.

I held John's hand. He opened his eyes. His face lit up as he beheld something that I could not see. He was radiant as he uttered his last words, "Yes! Yes! Yes!"

His eyes closed, his breaths became further and further apart, shallower. My finger was on his pulse as I held his hand. It got fainter and fainter and he drifted peacefully away at a few minutes to 8pm.

It was typical of John's sense of humour to pass away on my birthday. I certainly would never forget it! I went and got our dog from my bedroom and bade her sniff John's body so that she knew he would not be stroking her head anymore. A specialist nurse came and together we washed John all over, intimate parts, where I gave thanks for all the pleasure and love that he had given me, glad now that he was out of pain. He had been the most wonderful thing that had happened to me. I didn't break down and cry; I became strong in that moment. I would survive, move on, do great things. Power at that special time. I was buoyant! I even had a sense of humour, black humour: as I walked with the undertakers up to their van in the dark with John I said,

"Mind he doesn't give you any trouble in the back; he's partial to a practical joke!" And then he was gone.

I stood alone in that now empty room, empty apart from all the accoutrements of medicines, dressings and the hospital bed and wheelchair. Empty, yet it still held something. Finality. Sorrow that such a kind and fine man should suffer such a dreadful end.

I threw open the window and doors and let it all out into the night.

The lull before the busy week ahead. I was alone. No family to help me. Smile, Anne. John is no longer in pain! As I crept into bed I felt a great sense of relief and slept deeply.

I had much to organise but had already rehearsed the next few days ahead. I was in control of myself, completely calm and collected, and consulted the list I had previously prepared. As I could no longer bear the sight of that bare, empty bed, I placed a posy of flowers on it. There was so much to get rid of, and fast. A friend came and together we cleaned and scrubbed the room after all the equipment was taken away. Within forty-eight hours the living room was back to normal. I fully appreciated how quickly all that equipment and bed was removed.

My Winden friends got it just right; supportive in the background, but there in a flash should I want help.

On the day of the funeral I was alone, waiting in that bungalow, looking out for the hearse to arrive. I made that lonely walk up the path and kept myself together as I saw the coffin and an array of flowers. Solitary. Cold. Wind blowing off the estuary, the estuary we shared either by cycling, walking or fishing and lastly in a wheelchair. I wore the cross which I removed from John's neck after he died. As I fingered it, it gave me comfort.

Now the journey to the church. I sat in the front of the hearse beside the driver. So slowly we went. Everything around our bubble was going on as normal. Traffic, people; some gave an occasional glance and quickly looked away.

"This could be you one day," I thought. As we progressed extremely carefully over some speed bumps in the road, my ever-practical brain got to wondering and I asked the driver, "How do you keep the floral tributes from falling off?" "Blu-tac, Madam." I laughed inside as I remembered the baked beans joke with John and the carers.

My Winden friends were there and we walked arm in arm, myself in the middle, as we entered the church. I was so thankful to have their unfailing love and support. At the back of the church were John's paintings displayed on easels. On either side of the chancel steps stood our beloved guitars. I was surprised at how many people were present, including all the ambulance crews we had known over the past few years. That was a great comfort. I knew both clergy very well and felt at ease in a building that I visited most days. After the eulogy (which I had written) a poem was read out, also written by me as it just came into my head one night as I struggled to settle John down to sleep.

How do you love a skeleton?
I wish I knew
The withered arms and legs are but a trace of you.
I want to love you how I used to
But how can I love the skeleton I once knew?
The parchment skin, the sunken eyes
That used to adore me
The useless arm, the immobile hand, that no longer can
Pen a letter, paint a scene or play the beloved guitar
Where are you now? What land inhabits your mind
That once was so agile?
What people are you speaking to?
I wish I knew
How do you love a skeleton
So weak and frail?
I feed your open gape, like a baby
You greedily suck the straw like a nipple
I change your bed clothes
You revert to childhood
How do you love a skeleton?
Oh, I wish I knew!
And when the time comes to go
Will you still be travelling backwards in your childhood
To the place before conception?
Oh, my darling skeleton
I loved you so

A SERVICE TO CELEBRATE

the life of

John Reginald Beer

5th March 1930 - 30th November 2014

The Parish Church of St Mary the Virgin, Pilton
Thursday 11th December, 11.30 am.

There was a small, quiet gathering in the local pub afterwards and Ruby had singed herself sitting too close to the open fire. Just myself and one other person had been to the crematorium. My Winden couple had discreetly given me a drink on my return as I was very cold. What, me? Drinking? A double brandy, no less, straight down the hatch! It was lovely and I enjoyed seeing the folk I knew and valued their support. I was feeling very upbeat and happy.

The following day I didn't hang about moping. I had a new life to sort out.

As I was gaily striding it out with Ruby, someone spotted me and said, "Oh, you're smiling. But your husband's just died…"

"Yes," I replied, "I'm glad. Glad that he is no longer suffering."

I was free, too. What a terrible thing to think like that, but it was true. I could go out all day and all night if I wanted to and not worry about getting back by a certain time. No one to be responsible for except myself and Ruby. I could go on a bus ride or a train. But not yet.

Chapter 12 : Moving On

That first week I completely turned the whole place out from top to bottom. First to go were all of John's dreadful clothes in the wardrobe that he had kept for twenty years or more and hadn't worn for so long. Mouldy sandals and shoes, hooray! Get shot of the lot! No room for sentiment, best gone. I wasn't getting rid of his memory; I had those in the songs that we had recorded, his paintings and photos on the walls, the various plants he had given me and bulbs now growing in the garden. I got rid of the curtains and lampshade in the room where he had died as the curtains had absorbed unhappiness and bad vibes and the lampshade had picked up pain as this was the object he saw most.

As winter turned to spring, Ruby and I went on bus rides and, in summer, to various dog shows, where I made quite a few passing friends. We would meet up at the next show, either on the moor or in a field. As long as it was on a bus route I was okay. But we kept winning lots of prizes that were a job to haul home by bus and that entailed a long walk at either end.
Sacks of dog food were most welcome as my savings had diminished somewhat, having paid out thousands for a funeral and a headstone in the churchyard, plus solicitor's fees on top as I now had to leave a will.

Something had to be done. I had a free bus pass because I was ancient, so I used it!

Thank goodness I had watched John framing our paintings. I had all the gear and set to, in my studio shed, and framed many pieces of work. I also taught myself, from a library book, how to make jewellery from papier-mâché and other things, coupled with what I had learnt from that wonderful college course.

So one day I set off with Ruby and a shopping trolley full of paintings and craft work and had a free bus ride to Lynton and touted my wares, where I successfully sold and left pieces of work in some galleries. I then managed to get Ruby, plus shopping trolley, onto the cliff railway down into Lynmouth. The dramatic view was not enhanced by the railway operator muttering unkind things about bringing too much on board. Maybe he was suffering motion sickness; his life after all was a load of ups and downs!

In Lynmouth I met up with an artist friend in his studio shop. We had a good old yarn about past experiences. As he put his palette down, Ruby went and sniffed it and ended up as Bluebeard, with blue oil paint all over her whiskers!

Two members of the public came in and saw this dog with blue whiskers and remarked, "Oh, how unusual, a black greyhound with a blue muzzle!"

"Oh yes," replied my artist friend, "it is very rare indeed, probably the only one in the UK."

With that, the couple started taking photos. We kept a deadpan expression on our faces as they snapped away. Ruby was so placid and deliberately posed on cue.

"Oh, please don't stroke her," I said. "We find that too much of it tends to wear the blue whiskers and hair away!"

I thought that if they touched her they would end up with blue oil paint all over their fingers.

"You're lucky," said my artist friend, "we usually charge if people take photos, but we'll let you off today!"

With that they left, and we couldn't stop laughing when a few minutes later they returned, placing a £5 note on the counter, said

237

that they had just drawn some money out and then wished us well. The funniest thing though was their parting shot.

"By the way, you are a fantastic couple; you bounce off each other. We think you make a lovely husband and wife!"

I hadn't laughed so much in a long time. My artist friend was clutching his side. Customers came in, saw us laughing fit to bust, and it was contagious as they all started laughing as well and in the end nobody knew why or what we were all laughing about, but it was good for trade as they all started buying stuff.

I then trollied my wares to a lovely big hotel in a prime position overlooking the water. All my work was snapped up and I ended up with a commission to paint three large works for the residents' lounge.

I would go on the coast route bus from Lynmouth to Minehead and meet up with old friends from my West Somerset days. It was so good to be back, to leave more work in galleries and gift shops, and Ruby enjoyed the beach. Sometimes we stayed overnight at a friend's bed and breakfast. I was enjoying life, being valued as a person doing my own thing. I no longer felt a drudge, weighed down by circumstances beyond my control.

Living alone successfully requires routine. It's no use lying in bed of a morning or going to bed late. I found that keeping to a routine, no matter how boring, is the lynchpin to an ordered and rewarding life. Having a dog makes you do this. It too must have its routine, so walking it, feeding it at regular times, is a goal in itself; a goal worth having for all the love my dear dog gives me in return.

I continued going to the carers' group but only to do the creative writing. Although welcome, I felt that I had used up all that they could offer me as I was no longer a carer. Everyone else was discussing life as one; I had now moved on and needed to put it behind me. I just didn't turn up anymore.

My Winden friends never interfered with anything I chose to do. I always hesitate to ask for help from anyone but their help was gratefully received when once a month they would collect and look after my dog when I went to the South Molton creative writing group. But, as events transpired, it was not Ruby they would be looking after.

* * * * *

Ruby, my ever-cheerful dog with the softest of brown eyes started a slight drag in her hind leg. Two months later she was dead. The vet took her away for an ultrasound and I never saw her again. The phone call I was expecting, to tell me she was ready to come home after the examination, was actually to tell me that she wouldn't be coming home at all. The vet had 'found a vascular mass' and said he wouldn't want to send his own dog home in that condition. It was kinder to put Ruby to sleep while she was still anaesthetised. Did I have his permission to go ahead?

He said there was no point in coming to see her as she wouldn't know me anyway, and did I want her ashes back? Yes, I did, but I couldn't afford it. Already this veterinary practice had discontinued the PDSA scheme whereby you could give a donation instead of paying the full amount if you could produce certain paperwork. Now, I was up to the hilt financially, having to pay in full. Worse though, I couldn't afford the taxi fare to get to the vet hospital some distance away, to say my farewell to Ruby. I never ever had closure. It was to haunt me for years to come.

This was worse than when John died. At least I expected that and was prepared. This was different. Such a shock. My comforter gone. My reason for getting up each day. Someone who loved me, tail wagging, so full of life. Gone. Nothing to remember her by. No ashes. Just her rosettes and pictures and an empty bed. She was only ten years old and seemed full of life.

Looking back now, I could have asked my Winden friends to lend me the money for Ruby's ashes but I was too proud, too ashamed for them or anyone else to know that I was at rock bottom. When John died, I lost his pension and full carer's allowance. I had saved some of that, week by week, but it had got spent on essentials and unforeseen circumstances. I had to keep an emergency reserve for more serious things than my dog's ashes, but it still hurt.

Those wonderful Winden friends took me to lunch on my birthday and at Christmas in the same friendly little pub where Johns' wake took place. And later, when I attended the monthly creative writing group, they would send me a meal along with the returned dog! I often wondered if they suspected just how far I had sunk financially.

Walking around the local bit of countryside, Mannings Pit, was a joyless exercise minus Ruby. The trees appeared dull, the sky grey and the birds songless. The spring in my step became a drag. Just one foot in front of another, eating up the boring miles of sadness. Closure wouldn't come and it never did.

I went away for a bit, back to West Somerset to the clinic cooperative, and there I immersed myself back into all my holistic activities. I was offered a well-paid permanent position, but I couldn't get any local authority housing, despite being on the list. Anything local, to let, in the private sector was out of my reach, especially inside the Exmoor National Park. To think I once lived in it! I had never wanted to leave.

So, back to the traffic noise of home and the town smell. The empty bungalow, soulless Christmas with its cards still addressed to 'Mr and Mrs'. If it weren't for my Winden friends I would have spent it all alone; I did have one other kind offer but there would have been too many people for me to cope with.

* * * * *

In the kitchen, out of the corner of my eye I saw a black shape and my heart had a pang as I realised it was not a black greyhound, it was a black bin bag: as black as the pit in my stomach. I went out for an aimless walk to clear my mind but all I kept seeing was people walking their dogs. I'd got it bad. This really was the first time I had been alone with not a living thing in the place. Even the goldfish in the pond had sunk low in the winter gloom.

Very soon, I found myself responding to a call to give a greyhound a home. I was being driven down to the far reaches of Cornwall, near my old haunts of the dream in the west. The old familiar roads had once been conduits for my new aspiration for life with John by my side. What would they hold for me now? They were chopped off as a new road raced down the spine of Cornwall. Those familiar roads and villages were now blind backwaters, cut off and seen at a distance from that fast road. Blank-eyed buildings and derelict cottages were all that was left in some places, their roads coming to a dead end by the concrete artery. Petrol pumps gone, village shops shut, weeds in forsaken gardens. Livelihoods finished.

Our special greyhound van turned off the fast route and into tranquil countryside. The Cornish stone hedges bordered a long lane which meandered, seemingly, to nowhere. Fleeting sun and cloud shadows raced across the vast landscape. My heart raced with them, with anticipation. I was about to start a bright new chapter in my life.

The lady who drove me here was a greyhound rescue specialist and was able to vouch for me as being an experienced and responsible owner. We trod our way through a 'work in progress' extension to an already existing Greyhound Rescue kennels. I didn't see or hear any dogs and had a brief interview with the rescue people. The groundwork had already been done before I arrived and as I sat in the foyer-come-office I heard the rescue people saying quietly, "Yes, bring that one out, she's very affectionate."

A small black greyhound, off lead, came straight over to me and buried her face in my lap! She refused to leave me, looking up into my eyes, my very soul, begging to be coming away with me. We had fallen in love with each other.

She was an ex-racer, having completed eighty-four races at Swindon track. Her racing name was A Touch on Elle but she was known as Wotsit and was four years old. She was truly loved by the staff and as we completed the paperwork and payment I could see that they were sorry to see her go, but they knew she was going to a good home. I led her out to the van and as the sliding door opened she jumped straight in and curled up in a tight little ball on a comfy bed, her nose tucked into her body. Only her eyes moved, this way and that, as if she didn't want to get out until reaching home. We had to get out before then as it was a very long journey.

Stopping at Widemouth Bay, we went into a very crowded café and this sweet little dog was unfazed by it all and lay under the table. We then had a short comfort break by the beach and she jumped straight up into the van again and resumed her curled-up-in-a-ball position. The sun was setting as we pulled up outside my bungalow. She trotted straight in, had a drink, made herself at home in Ruby's bed and slept the night through. I didn't; I was too excited and relived the moment, over and over again, of when her eyes looked into mine.

She walked nicely on the lead until we saw other dogs. Then she would stick her face in between my legs. Perhaps she had only seen greyhounds, and these were a different shape?

She didn't respond to the name of Wotsit so, since her racing name was A Touch on Elle, I started calling her Ellie, to which she responded well. Walking into town I introduced her to a lady who kept a kennels and grooming parlour.

"Hello Ellie!" she said, as she greeted my dog.

My mouth dropped open as I hadn't had a chance to tell her the name yet.

"She was in my kennels for six months and I called her Ellie because it was like her racing name," explained the lady.

A double coincidence! Two minds with the same thought. No wonder she went to her so readily for a fuss: they had already met.

She had looked after Ellie until the Greyhound Rescue Centre had a space. It was only then she had been given that ridiculous name of Wotsit, along with some other dogs called Pringle, Mars, and Bounty.

I took Ellie every day for three weeks on the same varied walk with different situations at the same time in each day, with and without traffic, and she overcame her apprehension. She was so loving and affectionate, following me around the home and garden, sticking to me like glue. She had no 'recall button', knew no commands, and I didn't dare let her off the lead outside my secure garden. A few weeks later we signed up for the Kennel Club's Good Citizen Award at the Braunton Dog Training Club. This was the best thing that I could have done for Ellie as she got to socialise with all breeds and types of dogs at close quarters amongst all that barking in a hall, one almost needed ear defenders!

She passed the bronze award. I was so proud. It took me out of myself. I had a new purpose for living but it was bitterly cold waiting around for the bus in the dark on a January night to get back home again and, despite wearing a coat, Ellie shivered all over. I told the organisers of the club that I couldn't put Ellie through that, but rather than see us not finish the course, one of them offered to drop me off near home. Such kindness!

Before the next term, when we would be tackling the silver award, I took Ellie to her first dog show, way out in the country. There were several show rings for different breeds of dog, ferret racing, and scurry, hounds, marquees, all held at a posh equine centre. We entered various classes in the family show and then I entered her in the 'best hound' category. There was a large turnout and a very knowledgeable show judge. Ellie was amazing and did all that I asked of her. She shone in the sun, she stood proud, she trotted like a carriage horse. The judge asked about her background and I explained I had only had her for three months. He congratulated me on a job well done and, after conferring with the stewards, came back with a red rosette. First in the hound group.

That meant we would be eligible to enter at the end for 'best in show', where all the first placed dogs from each group line up and compete against each other. So Ellie, so calm and poised, did her delicate trot, and took the cup for best in show. Cameras clicked, reporters wrote, and Ellie yawned! I was staggered. When it was all over and everything packed away the judge, now off duty, came across to me.

"You and your dog are going to have a rewarding future together. She will stick to you like glue!"

My thoughts exactly. "She already does," I replied, "and thank you for making your choice."

"And thank *you* for rescuing her."

We had some wonderful, useful prizes, but most treasured of all was that trophy and the encouraging words from the kind judge.

We resumed going to the dog training club. Ellie passed everything on the silver award except 'stay' on a mat for two minutes. She wouldn't. She would not leave my side. She would stick to me like glue, as that show judge had prophesied!

Until we passed the silver award, we couldn't progress to the gold, which was just as well really as I was so hard-pressed to find the £25 for the term, plus the exam fee. With this thought running through my head, I was mooching along Barnstaple high street when the *Big Issue* seller looked questioningly at me. This was to be another pivotal moment on my life's journey.

"Sorry," I said, "I can't afford a *Big Issue* right now as I have to buy some dog food instead." His dog and mine were greeting one another.

"I know where you can get some for free; just say I sent you."

He explained where to go but I couldn't grasp where it was, so he packed up his pitch and took me there. Through the glass door I saw a room full of what I thought of then as 'down-and-outs'.

"I can't go in there!"

But I did and he introduced me to the people running the place. The down-and-outs were so respectful towards me and Ellie, who charmed everyone. I was given a seat, and someone filled my backpack with dog food. A mug of tea was thrust towards me, then a fry-up meal and Ellie curled up on an old coat. She then had a sausage and was wide awake, hoping for more! She went round to all the men, who stroked her. She melted their hearts and the raucous goings-on ceased and everyone became calm, such was the effect that Ellie had on these troubled people.

I got chatting to the volunteers. I had a need, they had a need. So every morning Ellie and I would go to this place, only open for an hour, and have a free cooked breakfast amongst the lonely and homeless. I was made so welcome. They were glad to see us. They made a bed for Ellie.

If things got noisy, the volunteers would ask them to calm down as, "we don't want to upset the dog!" and it worked.

My lonely life was now filled, and I had made the most unlikely friends. We all met up again at 4:30pm for another meal. All the food was donated, cooked, and eaten in one hour and cleared away by the men. Sometimes, some homeless women would turn up. I heard and saw things that should never happen in this so-called educated society.

I went round town and sat in shop doorways with Ellie alongside homeless people. I got spat on and told by some to go and get a job, but it didn't bother me. I sympathised with the unfortunate situation some found themselves in as I had experienced the same things in some cases, especially the women.

Eyes would light up when they saw Ellie coming as she would go up and love them. We would go round the riverbank and the park as we knew where various 'camps' were. I felt wanted and needed. Lots of these people had some tragic things happen, not of their doing.

Didn't I just know this? I had fled with a tent and lived rough, been through dire situations.

We all met up one day a week at a church hall, hired by volunteers who made a delicious three-course meal from donated food. There was a table of donated clothes and shoes as well, plus odd tins of food. An energy advisor was there, and she helped me pay less on my bills by changing tariffs and suppliers. The cooks would fill plastic containers with any spare meals and put them by my backpack with a, "Shh!" Ellie was put to work when it got noisy. We would walk around to each table and the noise would subside.

Everywhere I went, round town, down by the river or in the park, I was never lonely. I knew where everyone hung out. I didn't have to dress up, I could be me and hear the most extraordinary things about people's lives and how they came to be in their present situation. There was a respect, a code of conduct, and they looked out for one another; one day soon they were to look out for me, too.

I had an idea that Ellie would make a good PAT dog (Pets as Therapy)[9] and this idea came to fruition when a PAT dog volunteer came to give us a demonstration at a local event. I chatted to her and obtained details of how to go about it. She thought Ellie an ideal candidate. My Winden friends drove me out to Torrington Common, where Ellie's test was to take place. I already had the paperwork from Pets as Therapy and knew what to expect. Ellie did everything that was asked of her, despite all the distractions going on around us. My Winden friends looked on at a discreet distance. The examiner was well satisfied, and I was thrilled that Ellie had passed. All we needed now was the certificate in the post, the public liability insurance and Ellie's uniform. We were going places!

I had a smart uniform as well as Ellie. We looked and felt great as we visited our first care home together. It was a huge joy to see the residents' faces light up when they saw Ellie. It brought happy

---

[9] https://petsastherapy.org/

memories to some of those who had had dogs and now missed patting and stroking their pet. Now they could pat and stroke Ellie. She was especially good with dementia patients. I could never have walked into the situation of a care home alone. I would have felt too self-conscious, just as at other social gatherings, but Ellie helped me as all attention was on her, not me. She was the ice breaker. We ended up going to various meetings, where I would give a talk and demo about PAT dog work. Without her I could not have entered a room full of people.

It was this social thing. I was okay teaching swimming because I was 'in charge' If it was something done as an individual, I was okay. It all went back to being an only child, locked away for hours on end, not knowing how to interact with other kids at school. If I could shine in a subject and no one else came close to my achievement, I was happy.

Keep out. Keep off. I'm different.

Would I ever shake it off? Ballrooms, parties, dances, fake festivities, I hated the lot. Echoes of the past. Yet, I was completely at ease amongst the so-called dregs of society, the homeless that couldn't help being like that. I could be talking to them or, rather, *with* them, where most folk would step away in disgust.

Ellie and I had regular slots at different care homes and at a hospital. Even the schools wanted us! We would travel by bus, Ellie curled up obediently in a ball on a carry-mat beside my backpack. Passengers would ooh and aah at Ellie. We even went on the train; she was better behaved than most of the children travelling, who would be shrieking and running up and down the carriage.

We got well looked after whenever Ellie was wearing her uniform. One day I was wearing dark glasses as well and a child was heard to say, "Oh look, there's a blind dog!"

What they meant was a guide dog for the blind. I had to smile to myself. I had got my stick with me as well and probably looked like the old crock that I was!

Ellie was a marvellous go-between, helping the homeless by going to a job interview with them, taking them to church when they didn't want to go alone. One freezing cold night we were down by the river. A lone streetlight shone down on a hunched-up bundle of a figure sitting on a bench, a huge backpack by his side. Breath hung on the cold air. Frost was thick as icing on a cake. Night birds called across the mudflats as the tide began racing in and the pinpricks of light from headlamps of traffic reflected in the water as it flowed under the Taw bridge. The figure was shivering and coughing. Ellie, in her warm coat, wanted to go to this poor soul. She did. A grimy hand in fingerless gloves reached out.

"Evenin' missus. That's a nice dog you've got there."

More shivering.

"I was deciding which was coldest," he said, "another night on the train station or a jump into the river. It's not safe at the station; there are muggers despite the security cameras. Daren't go to sleep…"

With my backpack and carrying half of his, plus leading Ellie, I invited him back to my place for the night. But first we had a long trek to get there.

The full moon shone on the crisp, frosty grass as we crossed Castle Green, our shadows cast before us. The moon was so bright I could see our footprints and doggy paw prints etched into the white field. Mr 'Bundle' was getting weaker as we climbed the hill, his breath rasping and rattling with a bad cough.

He was hungry. I had hardly anything to eat in the place. He ate two bananas in the time it took the kettle to boil. I seldom turned the hot water on as it was too expensive, but I gave him towels for a wash. He kipped down on my living room floor on a makeshift collection of cardboard and sheepskin rugs. Cushions were his pillows as I had no spares. He coughed all night. I wedged a chair under my bedroom door handle. In the morning he had a shower. I seldom used it because of the expense. I could hear gallons of hot water flowing away. I gave him porridge and toast and pints of tea.

We went to town, where I took him to the free breakfast place, and got him registered at a doctor's. I went home and prepared my studio shed for him to sleep in at night. I put a fan heater in there. I gave him a kettle to use, water, radio, torch. I told him not to turn the main light on at night because I would be in trouble if anyone found out, from the housing association. I made sure that he understood to leave and return under cover of darkness.

All went okay for a week, until I had a visit from a nosey neighbour who said they had seen a crack of light at night coming from my studio shed. I often painted until late so they couldn't be sure, but somehow it got reported and I had a visit from the housing people. Final warning. Next time, end of tenancy.

My poor Mr 'Bundle' was so sorry and upset because he hadn't meant to stay so long but the doctor had advised him to find somewhere to spend time indoors as his cough was so bad. The council couldn't help but the volunteers gave him a tent and bedding and he joined tent city on the cold, damp riverbank by the recycling centre.

At that time, you had to prove that you were homeless for fifty-two consecutive days before you even got on the housing register, so some volunteers would go round at 7am each morning to check everyone. It was a moving population because there were so many dangers. People would even set fire to the tents, regardless of whether someone was still inside.

I witnessed several deaths; the lifestyle took its toll. Mid-forties seemed to be the limit. Just as some had reached their goal of being housed, after waiting for years, they died. It was tragic and so upsetting personally: these were my friends. There were some other shocking things that happened that I cannot bring myself write about.

Amongst all this was the calming presence of Ellie. She was loved and adored by all the homeless, at whatever stage or situation they were in. Admittedly some were on the cider, or drugs, or smoked weird stuff; but outside people assumed they were *all* like it and tarred them with the same brush.

The biggest problem was that you couldn't get a job without an address and you couldn't get a place without a job. There were a lot of decent people amongst them. I was always made to feel welcome and we would spend ages sitting on a wall by the river, chatting. I felt more comfortable with these people than with most of society. They knew never to ask me for money or offer me a drink. Some even offered to help *me* when I said that my garden was getting too much for me, with so much hedge to cut, and even offered to do some decorating. I declined because of tenancy troubles in the making.

Walking up the high street one day, backpack on, Ellie by my side and lots of shoppers around, I felt a tug on my back, turned around and saw two blokes being tackled to the ground by two of my homeless friends, who had shot out of a doorway when they saw that my backpack was about to be 'picked'. They were angry about it and dealt with the situation in their own way. I won't say what they did except that I recognised some rather dirty moves that one of the ex-Commando homeless showed me one day. Many suffered from PTSD and couldn't live indoors, some never took their boots off at night and didn't sleep inside a sleeping bag, only under it, for a quick getaway, in their minds. I saw and heard tragic consequences from ex-military homeless. Suicides.

I fell ill and ended up in hospital with a dreadful cough and chest infection. My Winden friends looked after Ellie. We were missed. A week later I arrived home to find a huge handmade card, made from odd bits of scrap, with around forty signatures on it and get well messages from all those down-and-out, roughcast, homeless, so-called dregs of society; they had cared about me and wondered where Ellie was. I cried my eyes out because it touched me so much.

After a month I was back again, but lots of changes were taking place as the volunteers and meals were shunted from one premises to another. The homeless were not wanted anywhere for long. Pushed, shoved, blots on the civic landscape and yet they did no harm. They had lost their only anchor and daily bolthole, a place to get a hot meal and a sympathetic ear, or some much-needed advice, before setting off into a dark cold night. It was like a rug pulled from under their feet.

I fell ill again. Pneumonia. Really ill this time. Repeat performance. Hospital. My Winden friends to the rescue, looked after Ellie.

"Your family and next of kin need to be informed," I was told.

"What for? I'm not going to die!"

Besides, there was no family of consequence left to inform. "Children last seen 1996, whereabouts unknown," I said.

Gosh, my Winden friends were my family now. They actually cared about me, visited me each day and took me into their home to recover. I was left with scarring on my lung, which was still there six weeks later when I saw the specialist. Despite having the pneumonia jab I still caught it.

"It says on your notes that you have been working amongst the homeless," the specialist said. "Also, your x-rays confirm that as well as scarring to your lung, you have a leaky heart valve. I advise you to stop mixing with the homeless people. You might not be so lucky next time."

Back home in the bungalow I still felt weak. I was warned it would take six weeks to two months to fully recover. Ellie helped me. I had to go out to walk her, but the traffic fumes were getting to me and I had to use an inhaler. I also suffered from dry eyes and had to use drops. Away for a day in Ilfracombe or by the sea and I was fine, my eyes no longer felt red and gritty. I felt like a traitor not mixing so much with the homeless. I still took the *Big Issue* man's dog for an occasional toilet break round Castle Green.

My neighbours either side of me were seldom seen. They all kept themselves locked away in their own little burrows. Others were too old and decrepit to go outside. Some died off. There was no sense of humour to be had anywhere. This was another of God's waiting rooms but this time it was sheltered bungalows on an estate and not a block of flats. Sheltered it was not, as it was high up and the wind whistled in my front door keyhole when blowing from the east. The warden no longer lived on site. If we wanted help then it cost a lot per week to be reconnected to an alarm system way up country, just to get help locally after the equipment you spoke into whistled and farted and the person the other end spoke in a patronising voice as if one was ga-ga with one foot in the grave.

My lovely garden, which I had built over the years, was now becoming a burden more than a pleasure. The hedges running all round it had become invaded with brambles. I had difficulty in cutting them and fell off the ladder on the steep slope, trying to get them down. I never sat in the garden as I didn't have time because I was forever trying to keep up with it and still doing artwork to sell, plus tending stuff in the greenhouse, and cutting my neighbours' hedges too. John was no longer there to appreciate it. I had done it for him, for the pride and pleasure it gave him. When the ambulance crews wheeled him in and out, they would admire it all and he would say, "That's my wife's work."

My life had run its course here. I redecorated the place, but it made no difference to how I felt. I never wanted to come here in the first place. I was sliding towards depression. I stood in the room where John died. I looked at the same ceiling that his dying eyes looked at, the windows that he had last seen the outside world from and the bird feeder. I could be doing this every day for years to come, while the garden would change into a jungle and the countryside edged further away to disappear under the planned housing estates. Soon, I would be trapped in yet more concrete, the traffic bound to increase and the noise with it. From the top of my path I could still see the far-off estuary and Braunton Burrows and the Chivenor runway lights at night. Oh, how I longed to go there, along the road to Crow Point, but it might as well be on the moon, not ten miles down the road. Besides, I no longer had my motorbike. My independence was gone. The trap was closing in. Then 2018 arrived. By the end of the year I would have moved home three times.

For the umpteenth time I trod the familiar path around the fields of the local beauty spot called Mannings Pit. Thousands before me had made the groove around the field I was walking on. Thousands of memories impacted into the soil. The bare January trees hardly concealed the yellow diggers gouging out the earth to create another estate of houses that no local person could afford. Pretend it's not happening there, in the next field. The summer foliage will conceal it later but for now I cannot ignore the whining of the yellow monster eating up the earth. The landowner had reconstructed the hedges and field edges and in the spring they were bare, save now for nettles and thistle, where once serried ranks of purple foxgloves grew. Even the dog willow trees by the squidgy boggy bit were gone. The long-tailed tits had thrived in those branches, flitting from one to another in happy parties to then spend the night huddled together in the ball of last year's nest. Where were they now? I missed them. At the first sign of a cold snap they would appear, cheerful and ever on the move. I would lean up against the old oak tree, its fissured bark a city for minute insects, then later I collected acorns and made acorn coffee, a laborious fiddly task. I would forage ash keys, too, and pickle them. Even the buzzards had disappeared this year. Above the woods they had soared by the thermals, so effortless, mewing and mocked by the crows.

For a brief couple of weeks a miracle would appear on the opposite hillside. As the spring sun popped out between the showers, the fragrance of violets drifted on the air. This large patch of miracles-in-mauve occupied a sheltered, steep slope and people I mentioned it to had never noticed it. How could one even miss it? And the river, where the cattle stood in it on a hot day beneath the shade of the trees, tails swishing the flies away from their bodies; cool water refreshing, dogs swimming, children playing, rope swings from branches, camp fires and sausages, all of these things were under threat as yet another green space lay in danger under the relentless march of the concrete jungle.

So loved was this place that many signed a petition and marched and saved money to buy it at auction. At the time of writing this, I still don't know the outcome. I won't be there to witness it. I won't be there to lose it, but I had been there to love it. I'd trod its circuit many hundreds of times in the eleven years I lived nearby, walking my dogs.

I'd got itchy feet. I went back to West Somerset for a short break to see if I could cure it. I spent a day up on the moor, turning things over and over in my mind. I was in a quandary. If I stayed in the bungalow I was secure for life, but what life? I wasn't ready to slip into old age and oblivion just yet. Then an offer came my way.

One of the volunteers I'd known had some news for me. They knew that I wanted to move, preferably to Ilfracombe, and told me of a flat that was being renovated. It seemed ideal, on the ground floor and joined to the main Victorian building. The flat had a private yard, a flat roof and a gate to a lane and garden: ideal for Ellie. It would be ready in a fortnight. It appeared to be quiet when I looked at it and I sat in the garden across the lane to get the feel of the place. I could see the sea. There was no traffic noise, just the ever-screeching gulls wheeling overhead. Yes or no? Should I? Swayed by the urgency to leave the bungalow and lured by lots of promises, I said yes.

Chapter 13 : Home

It was now summertime and very hot. I had two weeks to get organised. First, I had to give a month's notice to the housing people. They looked aghast at me when I went to their office.

"Are you sure that you know what you are doing, moving to *there*? You are giving up your security and you're not young anymore."

"Precisely!"

They seemed angry, insulted almost. It was as if I had thrown the bungalow at them.

"Go away and reconsider," they asked.

"No, my mind is made up!"

Then a letter came from them. I would have to get rid of my studio shed and greenhouse and fill in the ponds, cut that dratted hedge, get rid of all garden ornaments, bird baths, anything superfluous: pots, urns, benches, gazebo, seats, fountains. My Winden friends were a bit taken aback but they spent the hottest days of the year dismantling the shed and greenhouse to be re-erected at a future date into their own garden. My art gear and paintings presented the biggest problem. The bungalow had masses of built-in cupboards, wardrobes, and storage space. There were none in the flat, except for a dark spider cupboard under some stairs. I gave away plants. As soon as news got around that I was moving, people in the road that had not spoken to me in years swarmed like locusts to see if anything was going for free. It was a long, hard slog and sweat ran in rivulets down my body. On the day of the move the volunteers' van turned up over an hour late. It was all too casual. I could sense my Winden friends getting irritated at the non-movement of the move. Where were the supposed helpers? Meanwhile, someone was cutting the hedges for me, another person was helping me pack all of my art and framing gear. The day was not going smoothly. My eyes were red and streaming and my vertigo decided to attack out of nowhere. The van moved off with the first load. It wasn't a removal van but a large, ordinary white van. Everything became a blur. I sat outside my new flat with Ellie, whilst stuff was being shifted in. I felt quite ill. Someone made some tea and a sandwich. I was almost in a faint mode with tinnitus and hunger and worry because suddenly I was told that there would be no more moving today, the other half would have to be done some other time! This was Saturday, I had to hand the bungalow keys in on Monday. I was abandoned by the man with the van and the rest of my things took all of the next day to move, by two ladies with a mini and a scooter.

I went to bed minus curtains and awoke to a new dawn streaming in the bedroom window and, as I sat up in bed, I could see the light glinting on the sea. Then the seagulls performed a war dance on the flat roof.

Despite this, at 6am I was striding down to the harbour. This was the life, this is what I moved here for: the clean air, the sea. As we walked up Hillsborough, Ellie had a wonderful time chasing rabbits. I reached the swimming pool, where I had worked many years ago, and thought about the times I spent in the 'sweat box' longing to be free to do what I was doing now. I had arrived.

It was all quiet when I returned to the flat. How peaceful it was here. I took my breakfast across the lane and sat in the garden, gazing across the Channel. Not a soul around. I noticed all the curtains in the large Victorian building behind me were still closed. There were multiple flats.

At 11am they awoke. The windows went up and the fags leant out. Then the demolition music started, thump, thump, thump and the fag ends rained down into my yard. Next it was a used condom. Another lot of so-called music started up in another flat. From the very top floor, the hypodermic needles were thrown out, seemingly aimed at Ellie. A half-naked man on the ground floor climbed out of his window into my yard and went through it to the garden to get a signal on his mobile phone. I asked him not to go through my space and he threatened to kill me! I later learnt that he went to prison for attempted murder.

A poor thin cat kept trying to come in. It was starving and sick and may have been used to coming into my place. It had fleas and sores and runny eyes. I didn't want Ellie to catch anything. A mattress, and other rubbish, was dumped outside my gate. (It was still there a year later.) This was a Sunday morning; maybe everyone was at work during the week and it would be quiet. Not so! Armed police arrived during that coming week as a woman stabbed her partner in front of the kids. An ambulance came. Next, I was getting excrement up my front door every morning.

A black crow visited me and ate out of my hand. Was this a bad sign of worse to come? Oh yes! The gas boiler was rusted out: no hot water. The taps wouldn't work on the bath. Then the electric was cut off! Non-payment by the previous tenant. The catalogue of disasters continued. What seemed, on the surface, a quiet place to live was in fact a hell of a noisy place as people got up late. There was a weird smell creeping into my flat that I couldn't get rid of. My friend said it was 'wacky baccy'. Next night, there was a party on my flat roof as people climbed out of their windows straight onto it.

What had I come to?

"I would advise you to get out as soon as possible," said a kind lady that lived along the lane. "The person in your flat before you was a drug dealer."

So that explained the threats at night, the banging on my bedroom window and people trying my front door handle. I was truly frightened for Ellie, not for myself. I only had me to blame. *"Are you sure you know what you are doing, moving to there?"* Now I knew what the housing people meant by that cryptic remark. If only I had known then what I knew now! Why didn't someone tell me?

Out of Another Frying Pan and Into Another Fire

After going to the council and explaining my situation they said they couldn't help, except to put my name on the housing list. They didn't consider that I was in any danger, they'd 'heard it all before'. Some of them were very kind though and sympathetic and one member of staff tried really hard to help me.

What I didn't realise was that my old bungalow was still empty and not spoken for. I could have gone back to it. No, I couldn't – not after all that I had built had been torn apart. Go back with my tail between my legs and admit defeat? No way! I would survive, with Ellie by my side. Calming, sweet Ellie, not once questioning the situations we found ourselves in. She was my constant; trusting and loyal, still 'sticking like glue' but instead of Blu-tack strength it was more like super glue!

There were two vacant flats in the council block where my friend lived and yet I was not offered one, even as an emergency. They remained that way for ages. I would walk by, looking longingly as some overlooked the beach and seafront. Dogs were allowed in those flats. My friend also had a black greyhound, which was very fond of Ellie, and they would have a forty-mile-an-hour chase on the harbour beach. A man in the pub garden who had had a lot to drink said that he had better stop as he was seeing double!

Eventually a new flat was offered. As I sat in the letting agency, signing a six-month contract, little did I know that that was the worst thing I could have done. Everyone was nice towards me but at a cost, as I was to find out later. It was a difficult move, up thirty-five steps and a winding stairway into the first floor Victorian flat. The rooms had very high ceilings and the curtains, if I had any, would have to be ridiculously long! It was two rooms, basically. The bedroom looked out onto the Catholic church and presbytery and I hoped that the priest wouldn't die of shock if he saw me starkers, minus curtains! The church cross cast a shadow on my pale wall at night with the lights shining behind it, and I hoped that I had been absolved of my recent mistakes. I sure needed some help for the mess I was about to find myself in. There was to be a brief lull before that particular storm.

The new flat had a nice bath and a shower that worked; what a bonus! The two rooms had no storage space and the kitchen area was sort of crammed up into one corner. A lot of my things had gone missing in the first move. I had no fridge or freezer, oven, or cutlery. It was clean but the window frames were rotting away, and I couldn't open the window. It was so, so hot. I had boxes of stuff and nowhere to put it. I even gave away a lot of my best paintings to the charity shop round the corner. There was no refuse bin for the flat and the only way to dispose of rubbish was to put it in various public waste bins around town.

I really was in a pickle. It was so hot. My Winden friends came and helped rig up a net curtain in the front room but the light still streamed in at night. It wasn't a big room and I only just got my bedroom furniture in there as the rotting bay window took up space. That window was also stuck.

Trying to make the best of it, Ellie and I had some nice walks, and the air was good. There was lots of company to be had from holiday makers sitting on walls and benches with their dogs and enjoying ice creams and wanting to stroke Ellie. This was so much better than the solitary existence in the bungalow. The weather was good: so good that I had to find some shade and ended up in the cool church, where Ellie and I used to visit when I had some time off. It had a convenient squashy sofa at the rear, and I would eat my sandwiches, say a prayer and Ellie would kip down for a bit after her dinner. No one seemed to mind and I'm sure that the saints were smiling at me. Sometimes I was offered a cup of tea when a helper came in and my rough appearance plus dog and backpack fazed them not one iota.

Back at the flat, my Winden friends brought me a cool mini cupboard for things like marge and milk. It was quiet in this flat. One of the great joys, in between trying to sort things out, was to sit in the other bay window, which looked out onto a hotel entrance, to observe the people passing by, and a strange resident opposite and below me.

The hotel would have regular coach parties on budget holidays. The budget apparently didn't stretch to adequate food! It was quite a comical sight to see the unfortunate guests make a quick escape after breakfast to sit outside on the steps and frantically draw on a cigarette before waddling across the road to purchase more food from a café.

I met some of my homeless pals, who had migrated from Barnstaple to Ilfracombe for the summer months. Soon, I was to be glad of their protection and help. Little did I know that my new-found bubble was about to burst.

People moved into the flat above me. It was a living nightmare. They had no consideration for anyone living beneath them. They would come in at midnight, slam the main door, clomp up the stairs, then start frying onions. I could hear and smell it all as it drifted into my flat. When I opened my front door the whole stairwell was a blue stinking haze. I wondered why the smoke alarm never went off: they had removed the battery.

They often didn't go to bed until about 4am, in the meantime they would be walking noisily to and fro with plenty of other noise after that too. As the noise and occupants increased my nerves became more frayed. It all came to a head one morning when they lifted their sash window and retched out of it. This became a daily habit. I complained to the letting agency, but nothing was done. I knocked on their door, but they never answered. Soon, children arrived at weekends and I could hear them jumping around, as if launching themselves off furniture, causing my lights to rock in the ceiling. There were more than the permitted two residents in the flat above me, of that I was certain.

Soon the flat below me would be occupied and I would become the filling in a sandwich. As the piles of letters grew in the communal entrance, I saw that many residents in my flat had gone before me. I wondered who they were and what had become of them. But nothing remained in my flat of a past resident, not even a Victorian whisper from what was once grand house, no sentiment, no feeling, nothing. I would only be passing through, just like everyone else down the ages.

I was at breaking point as night after sleepless night had me screaming in my head with all the noise. One day I met them on the stairs and was shocked when they recoiled in horror at seeing Ellie. The man made a gesture of slitting his throat, then pointed at Ellie. He added, "And next time, *you!*"

I was sure he meant for real. I met my homeless friends most days and recounted that latest episode. It took all my persuasion to stop them 'dealing' with my neighbours.

I couldn't go home. I spent a few nights sheltering in the bandstand in the nearby park. My homeless friends warned me it was dangerous to try to kip down in there, so I spent the next few nights high up on the beach by the wall, sandwiched between the very people that I had helped in the past. They were very protective of me and Ellie, who suddenly had a sleeping bag all to herself. She was warm and cosy and as dawn broke over the sea we rubbed the sand from our eyes to see the guys were cooking sausages over a driftwood fire.

"No, no, you've no need to do anything," they said. "Just stay there all comfy, leave it to us."

And they respectfully disappeared behind a rock. I couldn't help laughing to myself as I didn't know which was loudest, the seawater trickling down the rocks or their competitive spirit to increase its flow! At least they washed their hands in a rock pool.

'J' was a wizened old man of forty-three. His old wool beanie hat was a permanent fixture and so was his drooping mouth. The furrowed lines on his weathered face seemed so wide that you could almost imagine a tractor had made them and that his blackheads were crows. Even his eyes were mere slits through years of squinting at the weather. He wore one plimsoll and one boot. His home-made rollie, alight or not, would stick to his lips then roll into his beard to join the previous one that had expired. But when he smiled he was beautiful. His whole face lit up and despite his missing teeth he exuded warmth and jollity.

"Do you knows wot's 'appened to me teef, missus?"

"No."

"Well I puts 'em in me back pocket one day and they bit me when I sat down!"

"Ha ha!"

"Thought I'd 'ave to 'ave a rabies injection!"

Everyone laughed as the sausages sizzled and Ellie's nose twitched at the smell. Some grimy bread appeared, and sausages were slapped in between, but they opened a fresh loaf just for me, "because she's a lady." They wouldn't take any money off me. I could trust these people more than many in so-called society that lived in nice houses. We had a lovely brew of tea, but I had to remember from my camping days that enamel mugs get mighty hot on one's lips!

As 'J' stood up, he hitched his old trousers up under his armpits and said he was off.

"Yes, thought I could smell something," joked someone.

'J' went on his way and the last I heard of him was his click-flop, click-flop as he went along the pavement with his one boot and one plimsoll shuffling forward to meet whatever the day held for him.

On the nights when it rained we had a little bivouac erected in a shelter on the seaward side of the big hill. Soon the others joined me as they didn't want me to be alone. When the wind shifted to the east and drove the rain away the sun would rise over the sea like a brass ball. Climbing up to the summit of Capstone Hill, the distant Welsh mountains looked so clear that you knew that the day would end up with worse weather. Walking round to the pier, the Oldenburg, passenger ship to Lundy, was still asleep, rocking lightly at her moorings. Memories fleeted through my thoughts. With an increasing easterly wind, above force seven, it wouldn't be sailing later today. There would probably be a three-metre swell in Landing Bay on Lundy, making disembarking too hazardous.

My homeless friends directed me to where I could get a free midday meal. I was thankful of this and their company, but I had to sort out what I was going to do about my flat. It was worse than ever that night: I just couldn't sleep. Yet I had no difficulty sleeping between those men on the beach, under the stars with the sound of the sea and Ellie snuggled between us. I couldn't tell my Winden friends what I had been doing. I was almost too ashamed but mainly I thought that they would feel obliged to help me. Then they would be right in thinking that I had got myself into this situation. I needn't have given up the bungalow. What a mess I was in. What was I to do? What happened next was to put me in dire straits for a long time to come.

I returned to the letting agency, through the same doors that I had walked with such hope not so long ago. They weren't quite so kind this time, as I said I wanted to quit my tenancy.

"You can't; you can vacate the property, but you have to fulfil the six-month tenancy agreement."

This was worse than I feared.

"And you are liable for the standing charge for the electricity and the council tax and there is a charge to have a professional cleaner in to do the carpets to get rid of fleas because you have a dog!"

That was the biggest insult, the non-existent fleas on an already protected dog. Besides, the carpet was new. Having to pay nearly six months' worth of council tax and rent, was there no way out? First I had to forfeit my deposit to pay for the first month's rent. Wherever I was moving to, I would have to keep some money back for the next deposit plus more removal expenses. I was in a shocking jam of a situation.

I returned to the flat, which had trapped the heat of the scorching day. As I watched the world go on as normal from that big bay window I laughed my head off at the stupid situation I had got myself in. I only had myself to blame and I couldn't expect anyone else to bail me out. But help was to come from an unexpected quarter. Kindness, sympathy, and a calming presence came from an ex-social worker from amongst the volunteers of the past. This person knew all the ins and outs and where I stood legally. Until a new tenant was found for the flat I was liable for the rent, but the letting agency must do all they can to re-let it, not let it just sit there. Phew! It was not over yet by a long way, despite the support of a doctor's letter, worried about what would happen to my mental health.

A Lucky Encounter

Trudging along Ilfracombe high street, feeling sad at the loss of the wonderful vision of a brand-new life in beautiful Ilfracombe, I was shaken out of my thoughts by a familiar voice.

"Anne? Is that really you? What's happened? You look dreadful!"

An old friend from the dog show days, when life was normal, had spotted me. I relayed my story. She, in her no-nonsense manner, said, "Right, we're getting on the bus now and going to Hele where I know of a nice little flat being renovated. You'd better have a look, quick, before anyone else gets it." My friend lived in Hele Bay, just a few minutes' bus ride away.

The landlord was indeed renovating the flat. New everything, as the previous tenant had trashed the place. I immediately liked what I saw and could visualise the finished project. It had a good feel about it, but would Ellie be welcome? My friend vouched for me, having known me for some years, and Ellie delicately picked her way across the half-finished floor to go and melt the landlord's heart!

I could tell that he was interested in me as a future tenant, but the rent was way out of my league. It was then lowered slightly, and I stood there sealing my fate of having to find £30 a week as the housing benefit did not cover it all. He didn't want to lose me!

The flat wouldn't be ready for three weeks. I was about to discover the generosity of the residents of Hele and what a wonderful community I was going to move into. A holiday cottage was placed at my immediate disposal for the three ensuing weeks, no charge! When I returned to the cottage later that day, the fridge had been filled and groceries were on the kitchen table. Again, no charge. My friend did some little jobs at the adjoining tea room on a voluntary basis and when I asked these kind people if there was anything I could do, seeing as they had helped me out, they said I could sweep up anytime but I didn't have to do anything, only if I wanted to!

What a relief it was to be away from that noisy flat in Ilfracombe! Here, in the little cottage all hung about with flowers beside the flowing stream, I felt calm and peace and I was able to see the daily progress on my new flat just across the way. I was only too happy to sign a contract on this place, but still had to find a month's deposit, then a removal van. But that was solved for me as the landlord and his family rallied round and did it! They moved me!

Word got around that I was missing a lot of gear. People donated things. A sofa, chairs, mats, curtains, cups, all sorts of things, towels; my friends gave me new 'moving in presents' of a bathroom set, a slow cooker. Even the landlord gave me a plant! Everyone was wishing me well.

I loved my flat with its floor-to-ceiling sliding glass doors leading to a balcony. The landlord even asked me what colour I would like the walls painted. It had lovely wooden floors and the luxury of a new bathroom. I was able to set up my art and craft gear in a separate room. I had the best of both worlds here, a washing line undercover but outside, a place to have pot plants and vegetable troughs and although it was on the first floor it was accessed by external steps and I created a place outside at ground level to grow more potted plants on some little tables. No more huge bungalow garden.

In 500 paces I am on the beach. How wonderful! Or up into the woods to the top of Hillsborough. On another day I might a walk in the sheltered valley to pick watercress and make a fine soup. I am so lucky to be here with so many birds visiting my balcony feeders and bring their babies to show me. My life is overflowing with kindness as I return from yet another beach walk to find more bags of food on my doorstep.

I have made dog-walking friends here and as we put the world to rights or laugh at our dogs mooching around just like us humans do, on the beach, I am grateful. Grateful to the Ilfracombe writing group that I joined in my darkest, blackest days. The subjects we were given to write about kept me focussed as I grappled with creating a new story to be read out the following month. It's how this story, of my life, came to be written. I was encouraged to put it down on paper and in so doing it has been a cathartic journey into my eightieth year.

I am happy again. I have found my home. I am enjoying being *me*.

I will put my pen down for a short while as Ellie and I stroll to the beach to catch the last rays of the setting sun behind the rock arch.

Footnote:

I would like to thank the Hele community for welcoming me and for all the donations of household things and food. Also to Ilfracombe foodbank and the weekly lunch. And to Belle's Place in the early days, for food and a meal. Encounter Church for spiritual uplift and food.

Dreams are renewable
No matter how old we are
Or what our condition

There are still unwrapped
Possibilities within us
And new beauty waiting to be discovered

Photograph of Anne painting on Exmoor

This is the painting she was doing at the time the photograph was taken.

About Blue Poppy Publishing

Blue Poppy Publishing was formed in 2016 by Oliver Tooley with the aim of giving his self-published novel a degree of respectability. It soon became apparent that other self-publishing authors would also like some help with bringing their books to market and since then Blue Poppy has published over a dozen authors and more than twice as many books.

If you enjoyed this book

We would really appreciate it if you could spread the word by any means that suits you. Reviews on our website, or Goodreads, or on your own blog are all appreciated, but we are just as happy for you to tell your friends or rave about it at the local library. In short, the more you talk about it, the happier we are.

You may also enjoy *A Breath of Moonscent* by Allan Boxall

A Breath of Moonscent by Allan Boxall

A Breath of Moonscent is the true story of a London child growing up in the wilds of Devon in WWII. A lyrical memoir of wartime and post-war rural Devon seen through the questing eyes of a young boy. 'A Breath of Moonscent' brings to life a time and place which is within living memory for many, yet now becoming increasingly distant and alien for most. A voice of lives now fading whispers and rhapsodic dreams.

Foreword by Liz Shakespeare

Liz is one of the foremost and best-loved authors in Devon.

"There have been few authors who have known North Devon well enough to write about it convincingly; Henry Williamson, Ronald Duncan and Ted Hughes are among the exceptions. I was, therefore, delighted when A Breath of Moonscent was sent to me. Allan Boxall has a deep understanding of North Devon that can be gained only through long acquaintance."